THE VIRTUE OF CIVILITY

THE VIRTUE OF CIVILITY

THE VIRTUES: MULTIDISCIPLINARY PERSPECTIVES

Series Editor

Nancy E. Snow
Professor of Philosophy, University of Kansas

Justice
Edited by Mark LeBar

Humility
Edited by Jennifer Cole Wright

Integrity, Honesty, and Truth-Seeking
Edited by Christian B. Miller and Ryan West

The Virtue of Sustainability
Edited by Jason Kawall

The Virtue of Harmony
Edited by Chenyang Li and Dascha Düring

The Virtue of Solidarity
Edited by Andrea Sangiovanni and Juri Viehoff

The Virtue of Hope
Nancy E. Snow

The Virtues of Endurance
Nathan L. King

The Virtue of Open-Mindedness and Perspective
Wayne D. Riggs

The Virtue of Courage
Edited by Blaine J. Fowers

The Virtue of Civility
Edited by Andrew Peterson

THE VIRTUE OF CIVILITY

Edited by Andrew Peterson

OXFORD
UNIVERSITY PRESS

Oxford University Press is a department of the University of Oxford.
It furthers the University's objective of excellence in research, scholarship,
and education by publishing worldwide. Oxford is a registered trade mark of
Oxford University Press in the UK and in certain other countries.

Published in the United States of America by Oxford University Press
198 Madison Avenue, New York, NY 10016, United States of America.

Library of Congress Cataloging-in-Publication Data
Names: Peterson, Andrew, 1976– editor
Title: The virtue of civility / edited by Andrew Peterson.
Description: New York, NY, United States of America : Oxford University Press, [2026] |
Includes bibliographical references and index.
Identifiers: LCCN 2025050809 (print) | LCCN 2025050810 (ebook) |
ISBN 9780197653807 paperback | ISBN 9780197653791 hardback |
ISBN 9780197653838 | ISBN 9780197653821 epub
Subjects: LCSH: Courtesy
Classification: LCC BJ1533.C9 V57 2026 (print) | LCC BJ1533.C9 (ebook)
LC record available at https://lccn.loc.gov/2025050809
LC ebook record available at https://lccn.loc.gov/2025050810

DOI: 10.1093/9780197653791.001.0001

Paperback printed by Integrated Books International, United States of America
Hardback printed by Lightning Source, Inc., United States of America

The manufacturer's authorized representative in the EU for product safety is
Oxford University Press España S.A. of Parque Empresarial San Fernando de Henares,
Avenida de Castilla, 2 – 28830 Madrid (www.oup.es/en or product.safety@oup.com).
OUP España S.A. also acts as importer into Spain of products made by the manufacturer.

CONTENTS

CONTENTS

Typically, having a virtue means being disposed to having certain kinds of perceptions, thoughts, motives, emotions, and ways one is inclined to act. The end of the twentieth and the beginning of the twenty-first century have seen an upsurge of interest in the topic of virtue. This is true not only in philosophy but also in a variety of other disciplines, such as theology, law, economics, psychology, and anthropology, to name a few. The study of virtue within disciplines is vitally important, yet the premise of this series is that the study of virtue in general, as well as of specific virtues, can be enhanced if scholars take into account work being done in disciplines other than their own.

Cross-disciplinary work can be challenging. Scholars trained in one field with its unique vocabulary and methods do not always move seamlessly into another discipline and often feel unqualified to undertake the task of serious cross-disciplinary engagement. The upshot can be that practitioners of disciplines can become "siloed"—trapped within their own disciplines and hesitant to engage seriously with others, even on important topics of mutual interest.

This series seeks to break the silos, with fifteen volumes on specific virtues or clusters of virtues. For each book, an introduction by the editor highlights the unity of writings by identifying common themes, threads, and ideas. In each volume, the editor seeks to include a chapter from a "wild card" discipline, a field one would not expect to see included in a collection of essays on a particular virtue. We do this both to highlight the diversity of fields in the study of specific virtues and to surprise and challenge readers to broaden their horizons in thinking about virtue.

The audience for this series is practitioners of different disciplines who seek to expand their thinking about virtue. Each volume contains chapters that are accessible and of interest to scholars from many disciplines. Though the volumes are not comprehensive overviews of the work on virtue that is occurring in any given field, they provide a useful introduction meant to pique the curiosity of readers and spur further engagement with other disciplines.

Nancy E. Snow,
Professor of Philosophy, University of Kansas

CONTRIBUTORS

Aurélia Bardon is a junior professor in political theory at the University of Konstanz. Her research focuses on public justification, religion, liberal neutrality, cultural appropriation, and civility. Her work has been published in the *American Journal of Political Science*, among others, and she has co-edited the volume on *Religion in Liberal Political Philosophy* (Oxford University Press, 2017).

Matteo Bonotti is an associate professor of politics and international relations at Monash University in Melbourne. His research interests include democratic theory, political liberalism and public reason, linguistic justice, free speech and civility, and food justice. His work has appeared in journals such as the *American Political Science Review*, the *Journal of Politics*, the *British Journal of Political Science*, and *Political Studies*. He is the author of *Partisanship and Political Liberalism in Diverse Societies* (Oxford University Press, 2017) and the co-author of *Healthy Eating Policy and Political Philosophy: A Public Reason Approach* (Oxford University Press, 2022) and *Money, Parties, and Democracy: Political Finance Between Fat Cats and Big Government* (Oxford University Press, 2025).

Rachel Buchanan is an associate professor in education in the College of Human and Social Futures at the University of Newcastle, Australia. Her research interest centers on social justice and equity in education, leading to her research in educational technologies, educational policy, digital identity, and the equity implications of the increased use of digital technologies. Her latest book, *Online Research Methods* (Bloomsbury, 2024), provides an overview of research methods for online social science research. https://www.newcastle.edu.au/profile/rachel-buchanan.

Frank Deer is a professor in the Faculty of Education of the University of Manitoba. Frank is Kanienkeha'ka from Kahnawake, a community that lies just south of Tiotia'ke in the eastern region of the Rotinonshonni Confederacy. Frank studies Indigenous language education and Indigenous religious and spiritual orientations in schools. Frank has previously served as a classroom teacher in northern Manitoba and in the inner city of Winnipeg.

Laura D'Olimpio is associate professor of philosophy of education at the University of Birmingham, U.K., and co-founding editor of the *Journal of Philosophy in Schools*. Her books include *Media and Moral Education: A Philosophy of Critical Engagement* (Routledge, 2018), *Educating Character Through the Arts* (Routledge, 2023), *Short Cuts: Philosophy* (Icon Books, 2023), *The Necessity of Aesthetic Education: The Place of the Arts on the Curriculum* (Bloomsbury, 2024), and *Philosophy of Education* (Palgrave Macmillan, 2025).

Katherine Fierlbeck is McCulloch Research Chair in Political Science at Dalhousie University and fellow-in-residence at the C. D. Howe Institute in Toronto. She received her PhD from Cambridge University, followed by a Killam postdoctoral fellowship at the University of Alberta. Her area of research is democratic accountability and governance, both within the field of political theory and, with a more applied focus, within the field of health policy.

Valentina Gentile is associate professor in political philosophy at Luiss G. Carli University of Rome. She is the editor of *FQP-Philosophy and Public Issues Journal.* She specializes in normative political philosophy, liberal theory, and, especially, the work of John Rawls. Her research focuses on moral stability, pluralism, the principles of reciprocity, toleration, and civility, and transitional justice. Her work has appeared in several peer-reviewed journals, including *International Theory, Journal of Social Philosophy, Critical Review of International Social and Political Philosophy,* and *Philosophia.* She is the author of *From Identity Conflicts to Civil Society* (Luiss University Press, 2013) and co-editor of *Rawls and Religion* (Columbia University Press, 2015) and *Spaces of Tolerance* (Routledge, 2020). She is currently finalizing a monograph, "Freedom with Religions."

Rebeca Heringer is an assistant professor in the Department of Child and Youth Study at Mount Saint Vincent University. Originally from Brazil, Rebeca has lived for many years in Manitoba, where she pursued her graduate studies. Her main teaching and research expertise revolves around (forced) migrations and subsequent exclusions, oppressions, and inequities in education; antiracism education; and research ethics/anti-oppressive research methodologies.

Paul W. Ludwig teaches liberal arts at St. John's College, Annapolis. He is the author of *Rediscovering Political Friendship: Aristotle's Theory and Modern Identity, Community, and Equality* (Cambridge University Press, 2020) and *Eros and Polis: Desire and Community in Greek Political Theory* (Cambridge University Press, 2002), as well as numerous articles on ancient political thought.

Amy McPherson is a senior lecturer in the School of Education and a research affiliate of the Teachers and Teaching Research Centre at the University of Newcastle, Australia. Amy's research examines education and its relationship to social change, drawing on philosophical inquiry and empirical research methods.

Andrew Peterson is professor of character and citizenship education in the Jubilee Centre for Character and Virtues, University of Birmingham, U.K. Andrew's research focuses on conceptual and operationalized understandings of core concepts central to moral and civic education. He has published many articles and books on such themes, including *Civility and Democratic Education* (Springer).

Tristan J. Rogers teaches logic and Latin at Donum Dei Classical Academy in San Francisco. He has also taught philosophy at Santa Clara University, the University of Colorado–Boulder, and the University of California–Davis. He is the author of *Conservatism, Past and Present: A Philosophical Introduction* (Routledge, 2025) and *The Authority of Virtue: Institutions and Character in the Good Society* (Routledge, 2020).

Suzanne Whitten is a senior lecturer in political theory and philosophy in the School of History, Anthropology, Philosophy and Politics at Queen's University Belfast. Her work focuses on issues relating to freedom of speech, neo-republican political theory, civility, academic freedom, and theories of recognition. Her last book, *A Republican Theory of Free Speech: Critical Civility*, was published by Palgrave Macmillan in 2022.

Steven T. Zech is a senior lecturer in politics and international relations at Monash University. His general research interests include political violence, human security, militias, contentious politics, civility, and countering threats to liberal democracy. His work has appeared in journals such as *International Studies Review,* the *British Journal of Political Science,* the *Journal of European Public Policy, Conflict Management and Peace Science, Political Studies,* and *Terrorism and Political Violence.* He is the co-author of *Recovering Civility During COVID-19* (Palgrave Macmillan, 2021).

Introduction

The "Virtue" of Civility

ANDREW PETERSON

Eagle-eyed readers will have spotted that the title of this introductory chapter is "The 'Virtue' of Civility" and not, as might have been chosen "The Virtue of Civility." The use of the speech marks is intentional and highlights—perhaps unlike the book itself—that it should not be assumed that civility is, indeed, a virtue. It would be illogical to include a book on civility in a series titled "The Virtues" (edited by Nancy E. Snow) if I, as the book's editor, did not take the view that civility *can be* a virtue. That said, my purpose in this introduction is to not only set out the general focus of the collection and to say something about each of the contributions contained within but also to make some attempt to explain why civility is a virtue, albeit a contested one.

In 2019 a short book I composed titled *Civility and Democratic Education* was published. As many others have done, including some of the contributors in this collection, I sought to distinguish between civility as a form of social politeness and civility as a vital, though challenging, moral and political virtue necessary for the healthy

Andrew Peterson, *Introduction* In: *The Virtue of Civility*. Edited by: Andrew Peterson, Oxford University Press. © Oxford University Press 2026. DOI: 10.1093/9780197653791.003.0001 functioning of democratic communities. In that book I invoked the distinction between *everyday civility* and *political civility*. In simple terms, *everyday* civility represents its lay usage and refers to general politeness, manners, and courteousness. Everyday civility is found in relations between people as they go about their lives and are typically determined by social norms and customs (whether and when to say please and thank you, expected norms when driving, basic interactions with neighbors, to give just a few examples). Civility in this everyday sense is concerned largely with social niceties. The key point so far as this introduction is concerned is that while not unimportant, everyday civility could hardly be characterized as a virtue if we understand a virtue to be a positive, stable, morally worthwhile, and intrinsically valuable disposition of human character.

Political civility, on the other hand, moves us closer to virtue given its fundamental concern with how citizens encounter and engage with each other in the public sphere of political communities. In a democracy, political civility requires much more of citizens than everyday civility due to the general expectation of remaining engaged with other citizens with whom one disagrees and, perhaps, when faced with incivility. Yet, beyond this general account of civility there are scholars who value civility as a democratic necessity but remain skeptical of the claim that civility is, indeed, a virtue. The roots of such skepticism are varied. Some, of which Rawls or work in the liberal republican tradition are perhaps the leading examples, view civility not as a virtue in the deep, Aristotelian sense but rather as a duty of citizens. Others raise concerns about the misuse of civility, suggesting that "civility" is used as a tool by those with power to limit and suppress those with whom they disagree. Still others contend that civility is not a virtue *per se* given that the concept is reducible to, and is potentially a synonym for, other concepts (for instance, tolerance, agreeableness, or respect). Cheshire Calhoun (2000, 259), for instance, posits that lists of political and polite civil behavior do not appear to depend on a prior understanding of civility as a distinct virtue. Instead, they appear to be entirely derived from a prior understanding of tolerance, considerateness, mutual respect, and a sense of justice. The question, "What should a civil person do?" appears to be interchangeable with the questions "How should mutually respectful citizens treat each other?" or "How should considerate social participants treat each other?" or "What does being tolerant of others' differences involve?"

In countering such concerns, and in seeking to make the case for civility as a distinct virtue, a further consideration (this time within political civility) is instructive in thinking through whether and in what way(s) civility might be a virtue. This distinction, which I have drawn upon previously (Peterson 2019; see also Edyvane 2017), conceives political civility as comprising two distinct but related components: (1) civil conduct and (2) mutual fellow feeling. This distinction suggests that political civility is concerned with how citizens interact with fellow citizens (including their motivations, actions, emotions, and so on) and also with the bonds and relationships that exist between citizens. Civil conduct and mutual feeling are mutually reinforcing and/or mutually weakening, and both occur within social and political contexts of human interactions. As Boyd (2006, 865) suggests, "a sense that we are all part of one moral collectivity or public can only exist when we are in the habit of treating one another in ways that observe the formal conditions of civility." In addition, the existence and operation of civil conduct and mutual fellow-feeling must be cultivated and nurtured within a democratic society.

Indeed, it is often the absence or diminution of civility in public life that sparks a focus on civility (Mount 1973). While concerns about civility were apparent within political science and in public life more widely across a range of contexts over the previous century, it is the case that such concerns have manifested deeply and more extensively over the past decade or so. Such concern, which some refer to as a *crisis* of civility (see, for instance, (Carter 1998; Bejan 2017; Boatright et al. 2019), has become inextricably tied to more general trends toward political polarization that have characterized many Western democracies in recent years. This polarization has been, and continues to be, intimately tied to other discontents that have plagued Western liberal democracies in that time, including populism, fake news, echo chambers, ongoing injustices, and increasing inequalities. In essence, civility allows us to disagree with others, but to do so in ways that sustain rather than damage democratic life. Put simply, when flourishing, civility enables citizens to encounter others, to share interests, to build and sustain bonds of mutual well-being, and to exchange ideas in the public sphere—all of which have been under increased pressure and threat in recent times.

There also exist some pressing and urgent critical questions that accounts of civility must respond to—and two of these stand out in the context of this edited collection. The first set of questions concerns the way that civility can be used, and has been used, by those with power to "exclude(s) or dilute(s) those voices already most likely to be lost in the conversation" (Boyd 2006, 873; see also Elias 2000). Historical and contemporary misuses of "civility" pose serious questions about the viability of civility as a virtue. These include (1) whether non-dominating and equitable forms of civility are possible in heterogeneous societies increasingly characterized by social, economic, and political divisions and (2) what the boundaries of civility are and whether (and if so what) forms of incivility can be justified in liberal democracies. A second set of questions concerns whether, and if so how, civility as a virtue is supported and/or suppressed in online forms of political engagement and communication. Empirical research on online communication has suggested that civility often begets further civility and facilitates the sharing of new information and perspectives (Galarza Molina and Jennings 2018; Han et al. 2018). Others have argued that continued aggressive behaviors in an online context can lead to these being viewed as acceptable, particularly when actors are able to hide behind anonymous profiles (Hmielowski et al. 2014). Empirical studies such as these raise important philosophical questions about how "online" civility is theorized and conceptualized.

It was with these questions and this general context in mind that the contributors of this book were tasked to respond. The scope of the book, and the definition of civility as a virtue, was left intentionally wide for contributors to take their own stance and to make their own cases—including, where they wished to, offering some critique of the very idea of civility as a virtue.

The collection comprises nine chapters. In Chapter 1, "Civility as a 'Political' Virtue: Exploring Civility's Social and Moral Features," Valentina Gentile offers an account of civility as a political virtue. Cognizant of the ways that civility as a political virtue has been read as a demand for social conformity, Gentile seeks to bring together certain social, moral, and political features of civility as a political virtue. Central to the argument is a distinction made and explored between civility as a pro-social disposition of citizen engagement over disagreement and three other conceptions of civility: "mere civility," "moral civility," and "public political civility." On the foundation of this exploration Gentile proposes a "friendly" amendment of public political civility which takes seriously the social and moral features that reinforce citizens' allegiance to civility norms in contemporary liberal democracies. Central to this latter contention, Gentile argues that the idea of a culture of civility can serve to complement civility as a fundamentally political virtue and in doing so can provide citizens of contemporary diverse democracies with the proper social and moral context for deliberation.

In Chapter 2, "Can't We Be Friends? Civic Friendship in an Age of Incivility," Tristan J. Rogers grapples with the civility crisis in American public discourse, using as a frame and stimulus the January 6, 2021, Capitol riot. Central to Rogers's thesis is that the crisis in civility results from a deterioration of civic friendship, which Rogers casts as "a bond among citizens characterized by mutual respect and shared commitment to a common political life." A central interest of the chapter is the partisanship that serves to undermine civility and which, in turn, generates incivility in public discourse. Rogers offers insights into the relationship between civility and shared values, positioning civic friendship as a daily and ongoing commitment of citizens to coexist under and in recognition of a shared political community. Here, Rogers centers the virtues of love and justice as essential for the formation and sustenance of the degree of civic friendship necessary for navigating political disagreements.

In Chapter 3, "Critical Civility: A Critical Republican Approach to Harmful Speech," Suzanne Whitten brings a critical republican approach to bear on the perennial issue of free speech and, more specifically, on the concept of harmful speech. In doing so, Whitten concentrates the analysis on how citizens express themselves toward one another in their political interactions and discourse. Whitten's core argument is that a critical republican conception of civility provides a meaningful and substantive understanding of how citizen–citizen exchanges can contribute to the undominated status of citizens. In the chapter Whitten pays direct attention to how civility looks in theoretical and practical terms when understood as involving formal institutions and social norms combining together to secure freedom in this critical republican sense. Moreover, the argument offers a way to address harmful speech while maintaining the protection of free speech.

In Chapter 4, "Online (In)Civility," Laura D'Olimpio, Amy McPherson, and Rachel Buchanan tackle the challenging matter of online civility, focusing their attention on the various ways through which technologically mediated engagement places real pressure on social norms and practices. Indeed, these authors contend that online technologies actually serve to encourage epistemic vices and foster incivility, political polarization, and hostile disagreement. The chapter is particularly interested in how online environments shape and effect the experiences of children and young people, including their educational experiences. In response to these conditions, the authors focus on those epistemic virtues that work to support civil online engagement, identifying a key educative role for pedagogies of Socratic dialogue, questioning, and student-centered deliberation that are constative of a community of inquiry.

In Chapter 5, "Civility Across Nations: Challenges and Opportunities for Constructive Dialogue Between Indigenous and Non-Indigenous Peoples in Canada," Frank Deer and Rebeca Heringer offer a valuable account of the idea of civility across nations with a focus on constructive dialogue between Indigenous and non-Indigenous peoples in Canada. Highly attuned to the challenges and opportunities involved, Deer and Heringer pay close attention to historical and ongoing injustices and, in doing so, draw on the inspiration of the ninety-four calls-to-action of the Truth and Reconciliation Commission of Canada (2015) to examine the five distinct areas of reconciliatory concern—land, public sector work, justice, health, and education—to provide a vivid picture of reconciliatory concern and of how civility may be understood and problematized by participants in reconciliatory dialogue. Central to the chapter is the view that traditional interpretations of civility can act to perpetuate colonial structures and to silence Indigenous voices. The chapter offers telling insights into Indigenous perspectives that prioritize holistic balance, respect, and genuine relationships. Moreover, Deer and Heringer reflect that a key challenge on the reconciliatory journey is to cultivate relationships of respect and understanding across cultures, arguing that while on this journey civility might form part of the process, but the importance of respect and truth should not be neglected.

In Chapter 6, "The Hidden Source of Civility," Paul W. Ludwig is interested in the motivations of civility. In the chapter, Ludwig takes issue with the idea that civility's motivation lies in morality or self-interest, arguing instead that the motivation required for civility lies in civic friendship. In his Aristotelian account, Ludwig sets out ways of cultivating civic friendship that can act to revitalize civility in turn. Though suggesting that as a virtue civility "is pedestrian," "is not exciting," and is not "glamorous," Ludwig offers love and friendship as the drivers of civility and presents the hopeful view that if the current anger in public life is a sign of disappointed friendship, then greater civility can result from a reparation and healing of that disappointment.

In Chapter 7, "Is Civility Always a Virtue? On the Toppling of Edward Colston's Statue," Matteo Bonotti, Aurélia Bardon, and Steven T. Zech take as their focus the concept of civility in the context of contentious politics and, more precisely, the contentious politics surrounding controversial monuments. Using the example of Edward Colston's statue in Bristol, England, during the Black Lives Matter protests on June 7, 2020, the chapter considers arguments against the toppling of the statue and brings these into direct conversation with conceptualizations of civility. The authors are particularly concerned with the forms of civility at play in each of the three arguments identified. Attentive to the complexity of civility, including civility as a virtue, the authors ultimately contend that violations of norms of civility can be justified in pursuit of moral civility.

In my own offering, Chapter 8, "Civility, Listening, and the Cultivation of Sustained Attentiveness," I seek to give a more detailed account of listening as a civic act, one crucial to and for civility. While listening has received some attention in literature on civility and on civic participation more generally, the chapter argues that civility as a virtue requires a particular form of listening—namely, sustained attentiveness. The chapter advances a brief account of a crisis of listening in civic discourse today, before arguing that sustained attentiveness is not just needed for civility but is an important and necessary component of civility as a virtue. In addition to offering some thoughts about educating sustained attentiveness in high schools, I argue that through practicing sustained attentiveness citizens are better able to examine and answer important questions about civic life and the purposes of civic life, questions that could not be answered by citizens alone nor by citizens conversing only with those with views similar to their own.

In Chapter 9, "Civility, Power, and the Fragility of Democracy," Katherine Fierlbeck takes as one of the starting points for the analysis the idea that incivility operates not only as a threat to democracy but as an extension of democracy. In making this point, Fierlbeck pays particular attention to the inter-relationship between civility and human rights, arguing that over time democratic thought and democracies themselves embraced human rights and, in doing so, began to privilege first-order principles (values or beliefs) over second-order principles (processes and protocols). The chapter moves to contend that the strong rights-based political context today prohibits the facilitation of a "civil" and stable political environment. Fierlbeck concludes pointedly, "The task of protecting democracy is at least partly the task of bringing civility back to the forefront of public discourse."

Before this introduction closes, it is important that certain acknowledgments are offered. This book has been long in the making—too long. I will be eternally grateful for the continued and gracious patience and support of the series editor, Nancy Snow, as well as for Nancy's insightful and thoughtful comments. I am similarly grateful to Lucy Randall and Chelsea Hogue at OUP and to Kayalvizhi Ganesan at NewGen for their patience, support, and commitment to the book. I also owe a debt of gratitude to each of the contributors to this collection, not only for their considered and astute scholarship but again for their patience. I asked too much, but each of you was considerate and supportive and I appreciate your kindness and generosity.

REFERENCES

Bejan, T. M. 2017. *Mere Civility: Disagreement and the Limits of Toleration*. Harvard University Press.

Boatright, R. G., T. J. Shaffer, S. Sobieraj, and D. Goldthwaite Young. 2019. *A Crisis of Civility? Political Discourse and Its Discontents*. Routledge.

Boyd, R. 2006. "The Value of Civility." *Urban Studies* 43 (5–6): 863–878.

Calhoun, C. 2000. "The Virtue of Civility." *Philosophy & Public Affairs* 29 (3): 251–275.

Carter, S. L. 1998. *Civility: Manners, Morals and the Etiquette of Democracy*. Basic Books.

Edyvane, D. 2017. "The Passion for Civility." *Political Studies Review* 15 (3): 344–354.

Elias, N. 2000. *The Civilizing Process: Sociogenetic and Psychogenetic Investigations*. Blackwell.

Galarza Molina, R., and F. J. Jennings. 2018. "The Role of Civility and Metacommunication in Facebook Discussions." *Communication Studies* 69 (1): 42–66.

Han, S.-H., L. M. Brazeal, and N. Pennington. 2018. "Is Civility Contagious? Examining the Impact of Modelling in Online Political Discussions." *Social Media + Society* 4 (3): 1–12.

Hmielowski, J. D., M. J. Hutchens, and V. J. Cicchirillo. 2014. "Living in an Age of Online Incivility: Examining the Conditional Indirect Effects of Online Discussion on Political Flaming." *Information, Communication & Society* 17 (10): 1196–1211.

Mount, F. 1973. "The Recovery of Civility." *Encounter* XLI: 31–43.

Peterson, A. 2019. *Civility and Democratic Education*. Springer.

Civility as a "Political" Virtue

Exploring Civility's Social and Moral Features

VALENTINA GENTILE

INTRODUCTION

"Empowered by faith, consistently, prayerfully, we need to find our way back to civility," said Barack Obama in 2010. More than ten years later, liberal democracies seem to be as divided as ever. Various forms of incivility (e.g., instances of hate speech, insults, lies) as well as extreme forms of political partisanship characterize daily social and political interactions in most modern democracies. Advocates of "civility" suggest that we need to (re-)learn how to communicate our disagreement without being disagreeable and (re-)envision "civility" as a fundamental virtue of democratic citizenship (e.g., Meyer 2000; Boyd 2006). The very idea of "civility," however, is also fiercely contested by some who take it as a demand of social conformity that delegitimizes dissent and marginalizes the least powerful (Zerilli 2014). What, then, is the role of the virtue of civility in contemporary liberal democracies?

Valentina Gentile, *Civility as a "Political" Virtue* In: *The Virtue of Civility*. Edited by: Andrew Peterson, Oxford University Press. © Oxford University Press 2026. DOI: 10.1093/9780197653791.003.0002

This chapter contributes to the discussion by seeking to reconcile the social, moral, and political features of the virtue of civility. In *Political Liberalism*, Rawls presented an influential "political" understanding of this virtue associated with liberal democratic citizenship.[1] It holds that free and equal citizens in liberal democracies must honor their "duty of civility," a moral duty to appeal to the political values of public reason when deliberating on fundamental matters of justice and constitutional essentials (Rawls 2005; see also Watson and Hartley 2018, 63ff.). This duty establishes a connection between citizens' public deliberations and the normative stability and legitimacy of diverse modern liberal democracies. Given the pluralism of religious and moral doctrines, citizens are morally—albeit not legally—bound to uphold this "duty of civility." Rawls takes the view that political power always implies some form of coercion. In a democratic polity, however, such a coercive power must be justifiable to all citizens. An extension of this view is that when citizens wield political power over fellow citizens, for example by voting in elections when constitutional essentials and/or issues of basic justice are at stake, citizens act coercively toward each other—hence the requirement to honor their duty of civility(Rawls 2005, 215–217).[2] Similarly, governmental officials and judges are to observe this duty when they support laws and decisions about fundamental political questions.

Rawls's view has recently faced a number of important criticisms. Understood as a principle of restraint in public deliberation, this view of civility is charged with silencing precisely those people who experience forms of injustice in the less formal social sphere (Zerilli 2014; Edyvane 2020). Not only might the Rawlsian account of civility blind ordinary citizens to these injustices (on this see also Griffin 1997, 118), but it might also dismiss the role of citizens' moralities and religious doctrines in enhancing justice. In addition, the very ideal of public political civility appears to disconnect the social and the moral from the political dimension of civility.[3]

In this chapter, I reconceptualize the virtue of civility in a way that is both consistent with Rawls's political view and yet takes seriously the various social and moral features that drive the appeal to civility in contemporary diverse democracies. Building on my earlier works (see especially Gentile 2018), I elaborate on the idea of a "culture of civility." Such a culture is distinct from both the "background culture" of civil society and the more robust "public political culture" on which the ideal of political liberal civility rests. A "culture of civility," informed by a set of widely shared social and cultural norms and practices, provides citizens with the proper (social and cultural) context for everyday deliberation.

In the following sections, I unpack the concept of civility, understood as a pro-social disposition of citizens to engage with one another in circumstances of deep disagreement. I then identify three distinct conceptions of civility, which I label "mere civility," "moral civility," and "public political civility." These conceptions introduce different ways in which the ideal of civility has been constructed and defended as a "virtue" in contemporary normative political theory, namely civility as a minor virtue, civility as a *thick* moral virtue, and civility as a political virtue. In this chapter, I propose a friendly amendment to Rawls's public political civility. I suggest that while remaining committed to an account of "civility as a political virtue" it is necessary to take seriously all those social and moral features that reinforce citizens' allegiance to civility norms.

ONE CONCEPT AND COMPETING CONCEPTIONS OF CIVILITY

In recent times, a growing literature has emerged around the concept of civility. In this literature, civility has both a descriptive and a normative component. Descriptively, "civility" represents a mode of social interaction, an attitude or behavior that conforms to a given system of social norms. In this sense, acting with civility stands for different forms of compliance with such norms. This component says nothing about the morality or desirability of acting with civility, or indeed whether civility should or could be considered a virtue. That is the normative component of civility, which is under scrutiny in this chapter.

From a normative perspective, the problem is to understand whether being "civil," and thus being compliant with certain norms, can be conceived as a "virtue," one that ought to characterize social and political interactions not just between individuals but between political agents in a shared liberal democratic horizon. Philosophers disagree about both the nature and proper role of civility. For some, civility is a virtue as far as it forms the basis for respect in democratic societies (e.g., Meyer 2000; Boyd 2006). Others warn that civility as a pattern of social or political conformity might suppress radical disagreement and resistance to injustices (e.g., Zerilli 2014). In this second sense, civility may be seen as a minor virtue at best (Bejan 2017). Thus, while under the latter understanding civility retains a merely *functional* role in easing social tensions for facilitating interactions, under the former view the role of civility is a *substantive* one, as it expresses a sense of equality of membership typical of a liberal democracy (on this distinction, see also Boyd 2006 and Laegaard 2010).

Furthermore, even those endorsing the substantive, inherently moral character of civility disagree about both its justification and its scope. Some works provide justifications of civility grounded in robust conceptions of the good life (e.g., a duty to obey, the harm principle) and suggest that this virtue should extend to all social and personal interactions (e.g., Calhoun 2000; Edmundson 2002; Sinopoli 1995; Rawls 1999). Others defend a strictly political conception of civility, which ought to regulate the deliberation of citizens in liberal democracies.[4]

By adapting the familiar distinction between concept and conception,[5] it is possible to single out one concept of civility, understood as a pro-social disposition of citizens to engage with one another in circumstances of deep disagreement, and competing conceptions that clarify the scope, nature, and principles that apply to this concept. The concept of civility, in turn, includes two enabling conditions: generally accepted social norms (Calhoun 2000, 260) and a certain other-regarding disposition. So understood, civility is a regulative ideal governing interpersonal relationships.

When someone acts with civility, she is not merely complying with a generally accepted system of norms butis also actively expressing *consideration* for others in doing so (Calhoun 2000, 260). Both components are essential to civility. It is not enough to show consideration by, for example, being kind or generous, as civility names a distinctive act or behavior that conforms with a reasonable social expectation. A person who donates the bulk of her income to charity may be extraordinarily generous, and yet this does not in itself constitute civility. Similarly, conforming to socially accepted norms without any other-regarding attitude also does not count as civility. Consider the case of an employer who complies with gender-based affirmative action regulations but then tells newly hired women: "You got this job just because you are women!" Though complying with the ideal of non-discrimination implicit in such regulations, the employer cannot be said to show consideration to the new employees, and therefore cannot be seen as acting with civility.[6] Furthermore, different cultural and social settings might give rise to different norms of civility, so it is not clear what should count as civility in circumstances of deep diversity and disagreement such as those that characterize contemporary societies.

In sum, the concept of civility entails two components: compliance with a given system of norms and other-regarding concern, as an expressive effort of consideration toward others. Whereas the former requires some degree of social attachment to the system of norms in question, the latter introduces the fundamental relational dimension of civility. Finally, since systems of norms can be plural and culture-specific, different views of civility belonging to different cultural and social settings might emerge, so a conception of civility should tell us which account should take priority in deeply plural societies.[7]

Competing conceptions of civility therefore provide different theoretical responses to the following questions: (1) how the very idea of social attachment to a given system of norms has to be interpreted and justified and, in particular, what the link is, if there is one, between civility and justice; (2) how interpersonal relationships should be structured under the ideal of civility; and, finally, (3) which conception of civility should prevail when divergent social and cultural norms yield incompatible demands. In this chapter, I outline three distinct normative conceptions, namely "mere civility," "moral civility," and "political liberal civility."[8] In the following sections, I consider these three conceptions in turn. I will defend an expanded version of the last conception, one which takes seriously the various social and moral factors that drive the appeal to civility in contemporary diverse democracies.

CIVILITY AS A MINOR VIRTUE

One version of the first conception, named "mere civility," is defended by Teresa Bejan (2017) in her historical reconstruction of three early modern theorizations of civility, those offered by Roger Williams, Thomas Hobbes, and John Locke. Only Williams's ideal of "mere civility," she argues, offers a promising solution to the standard liberal concern about reconciling "difference" and "disagreement" in pluralistic societies. "Mere civility" entails abandoning the hopeless aspiration, shared by several liberal theorists in recent times, of "civilizing the disagreement without dissolving it altogether," either via consensus or via social conformity (13). Rather, it only requires "minimal conformity to norms of respectful behaviour or decorum expected of all members" (9). For Bejan, such minimalism is the best we can hope for in circumstances of radical disagreement such as those characterizing both early modern post-Reformation Europe and contemporary pluralistic democratic societies. Mere civility does not require adherence to robust moral or political principles, such as respect and mutual recognition, nor does it demand conforming to a particular moral doctrine. It is a standard that governs deeply conflicting relationships, such as those between ex-spouses and hostile neighbors (14). Thus, it cannot be invoked to reconcile diverse societies, nor to sustain a moralized ideal of social interactions at the cost of excluding those who are either at odds with or uninterested in endorsing such an ideal.

A slightly different version of this conception is articulated by Derek Edyvane (2017a, 2017b, 2020). According to him, civility introduces an ideal of accommodation that neither suppresses nor affirms differences; rather, it entails a form of coexistence that "sets differences aside" (2017b, 466–467). Civility thus promotes a politically shared horizon where forms of solidarity might emerge irrespective of different values, cultures, and religions (469). The normative stability of such a shared horizon, however, is not what matters, since "moral agreement and shared justification of the shared experience of subjection to moral authority" lose their significance under a scheme of civility (459). This view is minimal insofar as it rejects a robust link between institutional justice and its related ideal of shared justification for compliance (2020, 106) and sympathetically looks at some forms of uncivil disobedience. Following Shklar, Edyvane suggests that the traditional liberal focus on realizing highly idealized institutional justice is likely to conceal, or even intensify, informal instances of injustice (105). Under these circumstances, acts of "*incivility*," which are sharply distinguished from "anti-social" behaviors (97), might be seen as "intelligible" modes of expressing democratic dissent (94) and therefore as a legitimate democratic practice. Edyvane, however, warns that perpetrators of "*in*civility-as-dissent" should be able to "violate the prevailing civility code without displaying contempt for that underlying commitment" (106).

Although differently articulated, these conceptions of civility share important similarities. First, civility is understood as an alternative way of conceptualizing coexistence in modern diverse societies, as opposed to competing and more robust theorizations of toleration. In both schemes, the appeal to civility is said to contrast a tendency in contemporary liberal theory to treat diversity and disagreement in abstract and idealized terms, in contexts where "the kind of problems civility is needed to address do not even arise" (Bejan 2017, 161). Second, the kind of solidaristic bonds emerging under a framework of mere civility cannot be grounded in thick moral justifications; thus a system of civility does not regulate robust relationships, like those of camaraderie or fraternity (Edyvane 2017b). More modestly, civility is meant to regulate a different kind of relationship, ranging from those among friends who share no more than "the common fear of meaninglessness" (461) to overtly conflicted relationships (Bejan 2017, 14). Some degree of instability in such relationships is unavoidable under the circumstances of deep diversity such as those that mere civility attends to. Finally, forms of "*in*civility" might well emerge as legitimate forms of resistance to social conformity and injustice.

One major problem with this conception of civility arises from its intrinsic instability. As I showed above, this view does not rely on a shared form of political morality, nor does it presuppose a somehow "unrealistic" removal of all differences among citizens. The fact that very modest norms of civility might characterize the relations among citizens in diverse societies is what counts, and we should abandon the hope of thinking of these relationships as stable over time. Some degree of instability is unavoidable if we are to endorse a model of coexistence compatible with the form of radical disagreement that characterizes our democracies. We must accept that existing forms of "minimal conformity" might vanish very easily in contexts where extreme forms of partisanship are also present. Furthermore, within this scheme, it is difficult—if not impossible—to distinguish between the sphere of legitimate "civil" political interactions and the informal sphere of "*in*civil" and yet legitimate forms of resistance to social conformity. Yet, if civility cannot perform any normative work to help draw this distinction, it loses most of its theoretical appeal and becomes merely a descriptive tool that defines a set of practices that may or may not be desirable in a liberal democratic society.

CIVILITY AS A MORAL VIRTUE

On the opposite side of the spectrum lies the second conception, which I call "moral civility." An example of "moral civility" is provided by John Rawls in his first book, *A Theory of Justice* (hereafter, *TJ*), where he refers to a "duty of civility" as "due acceptance" and compliance with those laws citizens perceive as unjust, provided that no severe violations of justice are at stake (1999, 308–312). Furthermore, Rawls explains that invoking the faults of social arrangements as an excuse for noncompliance is a form of incivility (312). Surprisingly, this formulation of the "duty of civility" (hereafter *DoC*-1) has not received much attention in the literature (though some references can be found in Calhoun 2000; Edmundson 2002; Garcia 2022; and, more extensively, in Weithman 2016, 107ff. and Kaufman 2021). *DoC*-1 requires not merely that citizens participating in a fair scheme of social cooperation comply with just laws but that they refrain from undermining that scheme of cooperation for its accidental imperfections. Hence, civility ensures that autonomous agents stay committed to such a scheme even when they disagree with laws or statutes enacted by a nearly just state and, by doing so, they recognize the equal dignity and autonomy of others. To put this in Rawls's words, "this conclusion is not much stronger than that asserting our duty to comply with just laws" (1999, 312).

Rawls, therefore, links *DoC*-1 to both the legitimacy and the normative stability of a system of social cooperation governed by his two principles of justice.[9] As Kaufman (2021, 83) rightly observed, "unless citizens have a duty to obey the moderately unjust legislation of a normally just regime . . . the stable maintenance of a just constitution may not be feasible. Rather, if institutions and laws could have been generated through a just process and do not invade fundamental liberty interests, they satisfy the minimum criterion of legitimacy." Accordingly, as long as it is tied to the preservation of a nearly just state, the duty of civility as obedience to moderately unjust laws should be seen as a key element of normative stability of a "well-ordered society" (Rawls 1999, 397ff.).

For Rawls, the stability of a "well-ordered society" encourages its members to act in accordance with its governing moral principles. The problem of the stability of justice therefore primarily concerns how to connect the first-person perspective, i.e., how I relate to the principles of justice, and the third-person perspective, namely how each person relates to the same principles. As Weale (2020, 304) has rightly observed, the very idea of stability in Rawls's *TJ* is important as far as it responds to "the problem of how to avoid individual alienation from a normative order of associates." Rawls believed that representatives in the original position would want their favored moral principles to endure over time (see also Klosko 1994, 1883 and 1885). However, their stability requires people acquiring certain moral psychological predispositions, or in Rawls's words, a "sense of justice" (1999, 397), which guarantee the internalization of the principles of justice and enduring compliance with a scheme of cooperation regulated by them. Indeed, Rawls thought, a system governed by utilitarian principles would not generate stability on its own, while a system governed by "justice as fairness" would generate a sense of justice strong enough to minimize "impulses and temptations to act unjustly" and to naturally resist disruptive forces (398). Notably, in *TJ*, the account of the development of a sense of justice is supplemented by the argument for congruence between the *good* and the *right* (see, especially, Rawls 1999, 499–505). These two ideas together show that, in a well-ordered society governed by the two principles, individuals will be internally motivated to support its stability over time.

Yet, Rawls also acknowledged that exogenous forces might weaken the confidence of individuals in a just constitutional order, thus undermining its stability. In this context, the problem of ensuring the legitimacy of laws and policies enacted by a nearly just institutional system becomes crucial. For Rawls (1999, 311), a just constitution necessarily entails imperfections, since "there is no feasible political process which guarantees that the laws enacted in accordance with it will be just." Accordingly, a robust commitment to compliance with moderately unjust laws, imposed via *DoC*-1, is meant to affirm citizens' commitment to a just constitution and the legitimacy of its laws and policies. This duty further specifies the scope and the limits of citizens' commitment to the maintenance of a nearly just scheme of cooperation, which is effectively regulated by the two principles of justice.[10]

A similar understanding of moral civility is provided by Cheshire Calhoun (2000, 2015). Yet, whereas Rawls's *DoC*-1 refers to the ideal level of a fair system of cooperation regulated by his two principles, civility on Calhoun's account operates at the non-ideal level of existing social schemes of cooperation. For Calhoun, moral civility combines socially rooted norms and universal morality in a particular way.

The distinctive moral quality of civility lies precisely in the possibility of distinguishing compliance with *socially* established moral rules of respect and consideration from that of obeying norms derived from a socially critical ideal of a just society. On her account, the respect required by civility norms might differ from the robust moral ideal of respect articulated within the Rawlsian model or within a Kantian or Millian liberal critical framework.

Calhoun's moral civility sheds light on the fundamental nexus between morality and a contingent social consensus. In contrast with socially critical viewpoints that understand civility as analogous to integrity, she defends an ideal that is tied to civil obedience (2000, 272), in a way that importantly departs from Rawls's view. Civility, for Calohun, requires more than mere compliance with social moral norms, which might nonetheless be objectionable from a universalist moral perspective. Given its dependance on actual "socially shared moral understandings" (263), there might not be guarantees that what civility demands corresponds to what an ideal of justice, guided by a socially critical morality, would require. Civility is therefore a moral virtue that regulates interactions between autonomous agents who, albeit endorsing different critical moralities, still show willingness to endorse *socially* shared norms and thereby treat others with respect.[11]

Whereas Calhoun insists on the relevance of socially shared moral understandings in guiding agents' moral interactions, Edmundson (2002) invokes a different and more radical understanding of civility, understood as a way to resist forms of social moral pressures. Edmundson's argument is largely based on Mill's harm principle. He argues that social pressure is an intrusive force that too often interferes with individual choices, more so than even legal enforcement (2002, 228). Thus, an ideal of civility is invoked especially in the social sphere to protect freedom of choice. Following Mill, however, Edmundson suggests that civility as a virtue has a more important social than public dimension. At the public level, he believes, critical moral disagreement should be voiced rather than suppressed, for example "a right to lifer . . . has a right to make a case for legislation banning abortion . . . but does not have a right to make that case 'in the face' of pregnant women at the doorway of the abortion clinic" (229).

In a similar vein, Sinopoli (1995) criticizes Kantian status-based conceptions and defends what he calls a Millian interest-based view of civility. For Sinopoli, Mill's harm principle was meant to balance two allegedly opposing goals: the good of protecting individuals' sphere of choice from conformist social pressure vis-à-vis the utilitarian ideal of promoting the good of our fellows. Mill's "thick-skinned" liberal civility thus requires us to suppress the inclination to stigmatize "unconventional conduct" while still being committed to criticizing the ways of life we find humiliating (1995, 614–615): "Mill's notion might lead to a less "polite" society than he lived in and for us a society that is unpolite in different ways" (614–615).

In sum, the second conception focuses on the moral character of civility. Scholars advocating this view offer different grounds for justifying this ideal and articulate different arguments for defending the distinctive moral character of civility. As I have shown, for Rawls and Calhoun, acting with civility arises from a moral duty to comply with norms that regulate shared schemes of social cooperation, as a standard of respect we owe to each other. Yet, while fulfilling the "duty of civility" on Rawls's view amounts to realizing the ideal of respect by nearly just institutions regulated by "justice as fairness," on Calhoun's view there might be—and often there is—a discrepancy between the respect expressed by civility norms and the abstract universalist moral ideal of respect. In both cases, however, the morality of civility lies in individual agents' willingness to endorse a shared scheme of cooperation. Edmundson and Sinopoli, instead, provide a different understanding of civility grounded in Mill's harm principle, one that aims at protecting individuals' autonomy from conformist social pressure but also allows forms of paternalistic interference with the life plans of others.

Although different, these two views of "moral civility" share important similarities. Both connect the ideal of civility to the realization of individual autonomy. Yet, whereas on the first view agents' autonomy is realized by their complying with norms that regulate a shared cooperation scheme, on the second it is associated with the ability of individuals to develop and pursue their own "authentic" identity. Thus, in the first case, the distinctive moral function of civility is that of reinforcing agents' commitment to a "shared system of moral understandings"—to use Calhoun's expression—whereas, in the second case, the virtue of civility is meant to protect the ability of individuals to give authentic meaning to their life. In both cases, civility is construed as a decidedly moral feature, one that rational and free individuals are expected to endorse. Also, these accounts of moral civility face the same type of weakness: in both versions the justification of "moral civility" disregards the degree and depth of moral disagreement that characterizes contemporary democracies. Yet, it is precisely this form of disagreement that the ideal of civility is expected to regulate.

By providing a robust moral justification, these theories fail to offer a convincing rationale for cultivating civility in deeply diverse democracies. On both Rawls's *DoC*-1 and Millian views, the ideal of civility is overtly tied to morality, since it is—at least partially—congruent with a robust conception of the good life. The link between morality and civility is different on Calhoun's conception: she insists on the relevance of a contingent consensus on actual social moral practices. One might object that Calhoun's reference to actual "*socially* shared moral understandings" makes her proposal less idealized and thereby more consistent with moral and religious diversity. My impression, however, is that this version of "moral civility" appears to displace the problem of moral disagreement from the level of socially critical moralities to that of socially embedded forms of morality. If the focus is moral civility, be it a universalist or a contingently situated view of morality, this conception is confronted with the same kind of weakness. Moral disagreement does affect not only the level of universalist moral viewpoints—something that Calhoun recognizes—but also the one of socially shared practices and norms. Contemporary liberal theories converge upon resisting a socially unified ideal of morality as it conflicts with the ideal of autonomy that Calhoun's theory is meant to defend. The social sphere is in fact where our moral disagreement is often more acute and where our everyday interactions with others are profoundly influenced by our robust conceptions of the good life. This is the realm of the associations, sources of normative authority for their members: different ideals of social relationships and norms apply to different associations. By placing such robust expectations on a socially embedded moral consensus, Calhoun's account of civility therefore appears to disregard a fundamental commitment to the inclusion of those who are marginalized, powerless (e.g., cultural or religious minorities), or simply those who do not endorse that same moralized ideal of social relationships.

CIVILITY AS A POLITICAL VIRTUE

Interestingly, in *Political Liberalism* (hereafter *PL*), Rawls reintroduces the "duty of civility" (hereafter, *DoC*-2), this time associated with the practice of public justification (2005, 217ff.). He argues that this is one of the "central innovations" linked to the idea of public reason (257; also quoted in Boettcher 2014, 229). Indeed, the scope of this duty importantly differs from *DoC*-1 discussed in the previous section, although it seemingly remains connected to both liberal legitimacy and normative stability of a well-ordered society.[12]

But Rawls now rejects one part of his earlier formulation of stability, one which entailed a partial "congruence" between the "*right*" and the "*good*" (2005, xvi; on this point, see also Gauss 2014, 236ff.; Weithman 2016, 98ff; Reidy 2017, 368–369). He comes to realize that a main source of instability of a fair system of social cooperation stems from the fact that citizens of well-ordered societies have different and sometimes conflicting ethical, philosophical, and religious normative commitments. Although some of these conflicts might be mitigated via citizens' adherence to a shared political liberal conception of authority, this form of disagreement cannot and should not be suppressed altogether. Rawls now affirms that liberal institutions should promote a reasonable pluralism of ethical and religious doctrines.

Both the principle of liberal legitimacy and the argument for a stability "for the right reasons" of a well-ordered society are restated in light of this important fact, or as he calls it, "the fact of reasonable pluralism." Rawls's theory, i.e., justice as fairness, is now presented as a reasonable political conception of authority that regulates the special "political" relationship of free and equal citizens in circumstances of diversity of reasonable religious and philosophical doctrines (Rawls 2005, 217). The problem of stability, in turn, is dual: one part is still related to how citizens might develop a sense of justice strong enough to comply with just institutions; the second part, however, reflects this chiefly "intersubjective" (Gentile and Foster 2022, 514) and relational understanding of political justice and is connected to the new ideas of "overlapping consensus" and "public reason" (Rawls 2005, 141). The recasting of the argument for stability requires a parallel revision of the view of civility associated with it.

This new "duty of civility" echoes such a relational understanding of political justice in an important sense. It still requires citizens to be committed to "maintaining" a well-ordered society by appealing to a shared framework of public reasons when exercising coercive political power over one another, by voting or by supporting laws or statutes, in circumstances of deep and yet reasonable disagreement about different conceptions of the good life. *DoC*-2 is, once again, a "moral duty," which now applies to chiefly "political agents," namely citizens and governmental officials, in deliberations occurring in the public forum when issues of basic justice and constitutional essentials are at stake (Rawls 2005, 217). It not only entails a form of public restraint, asking citizens to be committed to public reason when advocating particular principles or policies, but also, and perhaps most important, introduces an other-regarding disposition, requiring "willingness to listen to others and a fairmindedness in deciding when accommodations to their views should be reasonably made" (217).

In this sense, *DoC*-2 is connected to Rawls's broader concern related to a "political turn" for his liberalism. The acknowledgment of the fact of "reasonable pluralism" leads him to sharply distinguish between moral and political philosophy. Rawls now believes that it is the task of political philosophy to present a unified and yet substantive conception of political authority regulating a well-ordered society that, if not entirely congruent, is at least compatible with competing and yet reasonable conceptions of the good life. As a political liberal virtue, civility requires political agents to recognize that laws and policies enacted by a just constitutional order might not just be imperfect from an abstract viewpoint. Being aware of their moral diversity, they should now be ready to acknowledge that laws might vary in their impact on citizens who endorse different conceptions of the good life. Thus, in contemporary plural democracies the lawmaking activity is legitimate if it is firmly anchored in a framework of publicly shared reasons. This ideal of legitimacy helps to ensure stability "for the right reasons" by encouraging citizens of a well-ordered society to establish overall compatibility between their conceptions of the good life and the just constitutional order even if specific laws or policies are incompatible with their beliefs.[13] Thus,

DoC-2 requires citizens and public officials to be committed to the justificatory framework of (public) reasons supporting the unified view of political authority when exercising coercive power over one another.

Construed as a virtue that pertains to "the political," civility therefore plays a key role in ensuring that a fair system of social cooperation of free and equal citizens, who reasonably disagree about the good, is stable over time. Over the past decades, this sophisticated view has deeply influenced the scholarly debate on civility. Yet, as I have shown in the previous sections, important criticisms have been raised against it. Critics warn that the appeal to civility in public deliberation might silence vulnerable, powerless, and marginalized people (Zerilli 2014) or those who experience forms of injustice in less formal social or domestic spheres (Edyvane 2020). Not only might the appeal to civility blind ordinary citizens to these injustices (on this, see also Griffin 1997, 118), but it is also unduly dismissive of the role of citizens' moralities and religious doctrines in enhancing justice. For example, some critics claim that it was in fact religious insight (see Sandel 1995 on this point) that guided the abolitionists and the civil rights movement in the United States. Thus, Rawls's requirement of civility does not adequately take these cases into consideration. Other critics draw attention to the difficulty of applying such an idealized and abstract conception to real-world circumstances of radical diversity. Finally, some argue that by confining the appeal to civility to the sphere of the political, this view disregards the social relevance of civility norms in guiding people's everyday interactions in less formal social spheres (Calhoun 2000; Edmundson 2002). In sum, while disagreeing about their conclusions on civility, these critics largely agree that Rawls's view arguably disconnects the political and the contingent social and moral dimensions of civility. In the next section, I propose reconsidering Rawls's late view on civility in connection to what I call a "culture of civility." The idea of a culture of civility is meant to complement rather than substitute Rawls's *DoC*-2. Hence, what I suggest in the following section does not deny that the deliberation of political agents in the public political forum should be guided by a robust view of public political civility.

COMPLEMENTING PUBLIC POLITICAL CIVILITY: THE IDEA OF A CULTURE OF CIVILITY

Important objections are raised to public political civility. Rawls's *DoC*-2 is often said to be excessively exclusionary and unduly hostile to religious and moral diversity. Most important, critics argue, *DoC*-2 problematically disconnects a highly moralized political ideal of civility from real-world social contexts. In dealing with these objections, one should emphasize that *DoC*-2 is presented as a moral and not a legally enforceable duty (Rawls 2005, 217). Furthermore, the appeal to public political civility has a narrow scope, in two important ways. First, it arises when especially important matters, i.e., constitutional essentials and issues of basic justice are at stake (Rawls 2005, 214).[14] Second, only political agents—including judges, government officials, political candidates, and to a certain extent citizens—are expected to honor *DoC*-2 when deliberating in the public political forum (215). In the broader sphere of civil society, which is governed by the "background culture" and where comprehensive doctrines play a vital role, people's deliberations should not be restricted in the same manner (see Rawls 2005, 215, 220, 463n51). Furthermore, important elements in Rawls's treatment of public reason suggest that the conditions for the fulfillment of *DoC*-2 are more nuanced and context-sensitive than critics have suggested. When considering the cases of abolitionism and Martin Luther King Jr., Rawls explicitly argues that the appeal to comprehensive doctrines in supporting their struggle against racial segregation in the United States did not amount to a violation of *DoC*-2 (249–251). In his later writings, Rawls appears to concede even more to comprehensive doctrines in presenting what he calls the "wide view of public political culture" (462–464). *DoC*-2 is said to be generally fulfilled even if non-public, religious, and moral reasons are introduced in the public discussion, provided that in "due course" sufficient public reasons are also given when deliberators are asked to do so (462).

Yet, how shall we distinguish between cases in which the inclusion of comprehensive doctrines does not amount to a violation of civility owed to free and equal citizens from those in which it clearly does? Rawls is (unsurprisingly) silent about this issue. Indeed, he initially endorsed a strict version of *DoC*-2, which he called the "exclusive" interpretation of public reason (Rawls 2005, 247). Over time, however, he recognized that the appeal to comprehensive doctrines does not always contrast with civility, as in some circumstances it might foster mutual trust and public confidence, and thus the stable endorsement of shared political values (249). What, then, is the right interpretation of "political liberal civility"? Rawls's readers are divided about this issue as well. For some, prohibiting the appeal to one's comprehensive doctrine where public reason applies is essential to the civility owed to free and equal citizens in circumstances of reasonable pluralism (Watson and Hartley 2018, 63). Others criticize Rawls from the opposite side. Reidy (2000, 52), for example, has argued that Rawls's view is "not wide enough," given that a number of political issues on the agendas of contemporary liberal democracies arguably cannot be settled without invoking comprehensive views. I deem that the wide view presents the most plausible interpretation of *DoC*-2, yet I recognize the difficulty of evaluating when exactly the appeal to comprehensive views in public deliberation possesses a degree of liberal legitimacy. Boettcher has attempted to provide a solution to this conundrum by distinguishing between a strong version of public justification, one committed to a strict interpretation of *DoC*-2, from "weak public justification." Whereas the former represents "an aspirational ideal" (Boettcher 2015, 198), the latter is more appropriate to less idealized real-world situations. On this weak interpretation, political liberal civility might be accomplished when "reasonably acceptable and widely accepted" (198) procedures are followed. On Boettcher's account, a "reasonably acceptable procedure is one that is fully consistent with a reasonable political conception of justice and facilitates ongoing democratic deliberation about matters of law and policy. Reasonable acceptability is thus primarily a normative notion." The idea of "wide acceptance," on the other hand, is a contextual element which is "sustained by ongoing successful practices and historical experience" (199).

Following Boettcher, I believe that a plausible interpretation of public political civility in real-world modern democracies cannot be isolated from existing, historically rooted practices that are "widely accepted" at the societal level. It is in fact precisely in this context that shared experiences and shared practices of mutual recognition and civility might emerge, which I have called a culture of civility (Gentile 2018). Furthermore, I believe that the very idea of civility should not be confined to debates about the standards that should guide deliberation in the narrow public political forum. Although largely inspired by political liberal civility, the idea of a culture of civility suggests rethinking the role of civility in everyday interactions among ordinary citizens within the various associational spheres of contemporary democracies.

In real-world liberal democracies, a culture of civility is what provides a set of prima facie shareable (but not necessarily public) reasons that inform a pre-political,[15] social consensus and thereby reinforce the long-term stability of a liberal democracy. This culture is distinct from both the background culture of civil society and the more robust public political culture. Several passages in *PL* emphasize the continuity between these two camps (see especially Rawls

2005, 382–383, 443n13, 463). Yet, they are generally considered separate domains (462). A government official who is exercising her legislative power in a legislative chamber is expected to comply with *DoC*-2, and yet the same requirement does not extend to that official when she is at home with her family or performing religious rites at a place of worship. The idea of a culture of civility does not add anything to this distinction. Yet, it suggests that there is an unavoidable overlap between the background culture and the public political culture in our societies, which gives rise to social norms of civility that are relatively unrelated to institutional roles and associational boundaries. Failing to comply with such norms might erode reciprocity and undermine social cooperation. Imagine that, in Italy, a public official—say, a judge of the highest constitutional court—is involved in a religious-based pro-life campaign. The official participates in media talks and writes newspaper articles and blog opinions defending the *sanctity of unborn life*, thereby likely influencing a non-public and yet broad sphere.[16] The restrictions associated with *DoC*-2 do not apply to this case, as the public official is expressing her view outside the narrow public political forum. Yet, by expressing a potentially divisive view to a wide audience, the official seems to be expected to honor some degree of civility. It is precisely in these cases that the culture of civility is of help in appreciating the norms that should regulate everyday deliberation in contemporary democratic societies.

This "culture," informed by a set of widely shared social and cultural norms and practices, provides citizens with the proper social context for deliberation. The appeal to a culture of civility suggests that a *thinner* requirement than Rawls's *DoC*-2 might be at work in everyday deliberations occurring in the associational sphere of contemporary democracies. Here, compliance with norms derived from a shared culture of civility anticipates and provides the proper context for the more robust requirements imposed upon citizens and public officials in the public political forum. This culture is nurtured in the associational sphere of civil society and might not exclude, at least prima facie, certain reasons that, albeit non-public in the Rawlsian sense, might still be widely accepted forms of respectful interaction rooted in "reasonably acceptable" values. Consider, for example, societal norms of hospitality or inclusion. Norms of this kind might range from minimal procedural civility, such as making agreements in good faith and prohibiting violence in public spaces, to thick forms of civility in which common substantive values are accepted, such as respect for differences, condemnation of misogynist and racist rules, and so on (see Gentile 2018). Yet, in a way, it is *thicker* than Rawls's political view as it expresses certain ways of engaging civilly in the social sphere, which is generally left unconstrained by political liberal civility. Although linked to the social, the culture of civility is also important for shaping political liberal civility, which should regulate the deliberation of political agents in the public political forum.

A culture of civility should not be understood as derived entirely from liberal institutional norms and values; rather, it is a culture informed by both bottom-up social forces and top-down political values. In this sense, it might well inform subsequent institutional changes by calling attention to progressive social forces. Consider, for example, struggles to advance diversity and inclusion norms in the workplace. This might include programs aimed at hiring and accommodating the needs of a diverse set of employees, to introduce strict policies against acts of discrimination and harassment, to improve workplace accessibility, or to provide training programs so as to promote relevant social norms.[17] Bottom-up social norms and values, including religious values, can play a vital role in fostering social awareness about inclusion in these contexts.[18]

This culture might also help in reinforcing compliance with existing schemes of cooperation by drawing upon practices and values widely endorsed at the social level, such as inter-group dialogue and cooperative behavior, rooted in common historical traditions as well as shared experiences of respectful relations. Another example could be taking part in governing a not-for-profit faith-based organization. Despite the shared religious identity, the organization members might still disagree strongly about a number of matters, e.g., mission priorities, everyday operations, organization structure, etc. These disagreements must be handled through the standard organizational channels, such as regular board meetings guided by the organization's rules. The form of cooperation taking place here might be entirely based on "civic" standards or rules—e.g., an orderly discussion, voting, adherence to procedure and protocol, expressive restraint[19]—but it might also draw on shared religious values and behaviors, e.g., by appealing to religious values that emphasize their shared sense of purpose and connectedness to solve disputes. In both cases, participating in this organization helps to solidify those schemes of cooperation highly relevant to our democratic societies.[20]

This ideal of civility is neither a minimal view of civility, as suggested by mere civility, nor a highly moralized view of "good relationships," as envisaged by "moral civility." It is also distinct from the substantive institutional ideal expressed by *DoC-2*—as envisaged in Rawls's ideal case of a well-ordered society. This account suggests that a commitment to civility in real-world democracies should take seriously the fact that normative and empirical elements are necessarily intertwined. As in Calhoun's view, it takes the form of a socially contingent consensus, which takes place primarily in the social sphere and yet anticipates the political values expressed by the political conception of justice. However, since it is normatively constrained by the "reasonable acceptability" of its underlying values, this contingent consensus reflects a shared pre-political social ethos, one that might contribute to making the political struggles of traditionally silenced people "normatively empowering" (Richards 1994, 834).

In line with the "weak interpretation of public justification," a culture of civility requires that two conditions are met: the first, eminently empirical, asks that the invoked norm is effectively and widely accepted; the second, explicitly normative, entails that the value expressed in the norm is reasonably acceptable, that is, that it does not contradict fundamental values and ideas supporting a reasonable political conception of justice. As Boettcher (2015, 197) stresses, these ideas include that "persons are free and equal citizens with an interest in exercising their basic moral powers . . . [that] society is a fair system of cooperation under conditions of ongoing reasonable pluralism and the burdens of judgment." On my view, this requirement can be *in-practice* verified if the values expressed in the civility norm in question are consistent with the overall understanding of political justice as expressed by its constitutional essentials. "Reasonable acceptability" implies only a weak form of shareability of the values underpinning these norms, which may nonetheless suffice to ground their legitimacy. Yet, where wide acceptance of a norm and reasonable acceptability of its underpinning values are both present, these values might be considered available to all citizens.

Returning to the case of the pro-life campaign, let's assume that the public official openly defends the *sanctity of unborn life* on the basis of an argument encompassing the following: (1) respect for God's creation and (2) fetuses are persons. The question is whether the official is required to meet minimal restrictions associated with civility. The idea of the "culture of civility" suggests that the issue largely depends on the two above-mentioned features: whether defending the *sanctity of unborn life* can be considered reasonably acceptable and if its religious rationale is widely accepted within, for instance, Italian culture. The *sanctity of unborn life* might be considered prima facie reasonable, as supporting it might not be in contrast with the fundamental general principle of equal treatment and concern for all. Of course, Catholicism is deeply ingrained in Italian culture.[21] Yet, in Italy the right to terminate pregnancy is guaranteed by law, and Law 194/78 retains wide support within the society.[22] Thus, while there might be wide acceptance of an idea grounded in religion that fetuses are persons, a large part of the society also appears to support the right to a safe and legal abortion within the first three months of pregnancy. We might therefore conjecture that, for many Italians, to support the former does not necessarily imply rejecting the latter. Returning to the official's arguments, if these are expressed without openly attacking the right to abortion and Law 194/78, we can conclude that a minimal degree of civility is met in this case.[23]

To conclude, I have suggested that the ideal of civility as a political virtue should be complemented by certain social and moral features that are highly contextual. This is what I call a culture of civility. This ideal is consistent with a wide interpretation of *DoC-2*, as it does not exclude certain non-public (and often religious) reasons when they are employed to justify political values that are consistent with fundamental political values. It also helps to complement *DoC-2*, and yet it does not invoke a problematic expansion of the scope of public reason.[24] It envisages certain ways of engaging with civility in the social sphere that importantly differ from the more robust *DoC-2* that applies to the public political forum. Although linked to the social, this ideal of civility is important in shaping the more institutionalized political liberal conception of civility (expressed in *DoC-2*), one which constrains our public role as free and equal citizens.

CONCLUDING REMARKS

In this chapter, I have presented an analytical distinction between one concept and competing conceptions of civility. Civility is a pro-social disposition to engage with one another in circumstances of deep disagreement. This concept includes two components: (1)

compliance with a given system of norms and (2) other-regarding concern, which entails an expressive effort of consideration toward others.

Along with the concept, three distinct normative conceptions of civility have been considered, each associated with a different understanding of civility as a virtue. First, I presented a minimal conception focusing on the relational and intersubjective dimension of civility under conditions of deep disagreement. In profoundly diverse societies, what civility requires should be kept distinct from what a robust view of justice demands. More modestly, the appeal to civility here entails a focus on those minimal conditions for coexistence among citizens who are profoundly divided across religious, moral, and political lines. While forbidding violence and forced religious conversion, this minimal understanding of civility might well be consistent with forms of zealotry and mutual contempt. On the opposite side of the spectrum lies a second conception, which I labeled "moral civility." Here civility, understood as a *thick* moral virtue, is attached to a substantive ideal of moral relationships. This view privileges the inner dimension of the justification for compliance with civility norms. It does not allow for a separation between personal and political spheres and favors, what we might call a "comprehensive" view of civility. This account entails a robust understanding of the moral norms underpinning civility, one which ought to guide everyday interactions of individual agents in liberal societies. Finally, I have considered Rawls's public political civility. This view establishes a fundamental link between this eminently political virtue and the liberal appeal to public justification. On this view, civility is meant to apply to particular "political relations" of free and equal citizens in liberal democracies.

In the concluding section, I have suggested that the idea of a culture of civility can complement an ideal of civility as a fundamentally political virtue. A culture of civility is a pre-political social ethos that should guide the everyday interactions among ordinary citizens in the social sphere. The "culture of civility," informed by a set of widely shared social norms, moralities, and cultural practices, provides citizens of contemporary diverse democracies with the proper social and moral context for deliberation. Although linked to the social and the moral, this ideal of civility is importantly connected to public political civility, which ought to regulate our political relations as free and equal citizens.

NOTES

1. On the "political" account of virtues within anti-perfectionist theories and especially in Rawls's political liberal theory, see Hartley and Watson (2014, 419ff.).

2. Rawls is explicit in suggesting that the idea of public reason and the related duty of civility apply to citizens when they vote and rejects the view that voting is a private or a personal matter (Rawls 2005, 219). On this account, when citizens vote or deliberate on fundamental issues of justice—as well as, in the case of representative democracies, when they vote for their representatives—they are in fact acting "as if they were legislators" (Rawls 2005, 444–445) and should fulfill the requirements of public reason. In a liberal democratic order, power—including that wielded by citizens—should be publicly justified, otherwise it would be arbitrary.

3. For different versions of this critique see Calhoun (2000) and Edmundson (2002).

4. Different versions of the political conception have been offered, for example, by Rawls (2005), Edyvane (2017a), and Peterson (2019).

5. Following H. L. A. Hart in *The Concept of Law*, Rawls (1999, 5) uses this distinction to stress the difference between one unified concept and competing conceptions derived from different sets of principles of justice. Other scholars have been influenced by Rawls in this respect. Particularly, in his monumental work on toleration, Rainer Forst (2013) was largely inspired by Rawls albeit with some important differences. Whereas in Rawls's understanding the unified concept of justice retains a moral connotation, in Forst's work, the concept of toleration is descriptive and value-free. Only as a conception does "toleration" acquire normative and moral significance. The distinction between one general and largely value-free concept and several normative conceptions of civility presented in this chapter is significantly indebted to Forst's use.

6. Similar examples are provided by Bardon et al. (2023) and Calhoun (2000).

7. This is why civility is often associated with other concepts aimed at dealing with diversity and disagreement, such as respect and tolerance.

8. Bardon et al. (2023, 309) have interestingly distinguished between "thin" and "thick" conceptions of civility, which they call "civility as politeness" and "civility as public-mindedness." Examples of the former include conforming to conventional, minimal rules of politeness, such as not interrupting others when they are speaking and avoiding offensive language. Examples of the latter instead require complying with robust moral and political norms associated with our role as free and equal citizens, such as exercising restraint when deliberating publicly and treating other citizens with whom we deeply disagree with concern and respect. The thickest version of civility is further disaggregated into "justificatory" and "moral" civility (312). These authors therefore show how the various dimensions and subdimensions of civility might interact with each other, giving rise to further forms of (in)civility and (im)politeness (320ff.). Whereas this effort of disaggregating civility is helpful in capturing most of the claims associated with the concept, it does not help in isolating the distinctive normative claims that support different conceptions of civility, which is what I seek to show in this chapter.

9. The "duty of civility" and its relation to both liberal legitimacy and normative stability was further developed and duly amended in Rawls's later work, as we shall see in the next section.

10. While *DoC*-1 suggests that citizens have a general duty to obey unjust laws, Rawls also considers forms of justified noncompliance entailing civil disobedience and conscientious refusal. In line with his idea of the "duty of civility," civil disobedience is for Rawls a form of a nonviolent political act of resistance to a law of the majority that somehow violates the spirit of the principles of justice. Thus, the idea of civil disobedience is also construed as a way of maintaining and avoiding the corruption of the ideal of "justice as fairness."

11. Interestingly, this ideal of civility, while highlighting the connections between this virtue and law-abidingness or civil obedience, does not entail the idea of civil disobedience.

12. In discussing the role of legitimacy in Rawls's political liberal project, Weithman (2016, 107) argues that "*Political Liberalism* does not add to *A Theory of Justice*'s treatment of the duty to obey the law." Thus, to understand what is truly innovative in *DoC*-2, we need to relate it to the new understanding of stability "for the right reasons" and the accompanying idea of liberal legitimacy.

13. On this understanding of the principle of liberal legitimacy as a standard for compatibility, see also Weithman (2016, 107).

14. Most ordinary legislation (including tax legislation, statutes protecting the environment and pollution control) is not subject to the restrictions of public reason. Indeed, while conceding that it is often valuable to invoke the values

of public reason to settle political disputes, Rawls warns that when it comes to issues of ordinary legislation, having to abide by the requirements of public reason can sometimes be undesirable (2001, 91n13).

15. I use here the term "pre-political" to suggest that the social consensus is not entirely derived from a kind of liberal public political culture, something that is implicit in Rawls's idea of overlapping consensus. The pre-political social consensus that I have in mind is still somehow constrained by the political (later, I refer to top-down political values) and yet is not entirely drawn from the public political culture.

16. Rawls's distinction between the public and non-public spheres does not overlap with Habermas's account of the "public sphere." While emphasizing this discontinuity, however, Rawls concedes that the "non-public" political culture—which is the culture of media, televisions, newspaper, etc.—somehow lies in between the background and the public political culture (2005, 443n13).

17. Several firms in the high-tech sector have made strides in promoting the inclusion of neurodiverse persons. These efforts already presuppose a set of shared underlying norms, which may include interacting with co-workers "respectfully" and "professionally," and include reshaping these norms by improving the understanding of the dynamics of interaction that relate to neurodiversity. Such experiences not only foster social awareness about the inclusion of neurodiverse persons but also help to inform changes at the institutional level. SAP, for example, pioneered the endorsement of neurodiversity when in 2013 they launched the "Autism at work program" (https://jobs.sap.com/content/Autism-at-Work/?locale=en_US, last accessed on March 24, 2024).

18. Empirical research on a group of 156 Italian firms has shown a positive correlation among personal and local (community) religiosity, gender inclusion, and Corporate Social Responsibility (Harjoto and Rossi 2019).

19. I am indebted to James Boettcher for suggesting these two examples.

20. Talisse (2019, 25) has famously argued that engaging with one another to pursue collective goals that are non-political is critically important to democratic politics. According to him, crucially important social goods, such as cultivating civic friendship, are often better achieved in social collaborative endeavors, e.g., joining a bowling team or a book club (163ff.). My thesis in this paper is that there are social norms regulating interactions among people that are not distinctively "political" and yet are very relevant for supporting civility.

21. Nearly 80% of Italians profess themselves to be Catholic.

22. According to a recent Ipsos survey, the legalization of abortion in Italy is supported by 70% of respondents (https://www.ipsos.com/sites/default/files/ct/news/documents/2023-08/Global%20Views%20on%20Abortion%202023%20Final.pdf, last accessed March 29 2024).

23. I am grateful to Aurélia Bardon for valuable discussion of this case.

24. Several public reason theorists have argued that the appeal to public political civility should be extended to all citizens' deliberation and therefore go beyond the "narrow" public political forum as the proper scope of public reason (see, especially, Quong 2011 and Vallier 2019). While I believe that the appeal to public political civility and the social norms of civility operating at the social level of real-world democracies should be mutually supportive, I do not agree with these authors that broadening the scope of public reason should be the means of achieving this. I have discussed this issue elsewhere; see Gentile (2026, 155–158).

REFERENCES

Bardon, A., M. Bonotti, S. T. Zech, and W. Ridge. 2023. "Disaggregating Civility: Politeness, Public-Mindedness and Their Connection." *British Journal of Political Science* 53 (1): 308–325.

Bejan, T. 2017. *Mere Civility: Disagreement and the Limits of Toleration.* Harvard University Press.

Boettcher, J. 2014. "Duty of Civility." In *The Cambridge Rawls Lexicon*, edited by J. Mandle and D. A. Reidy. Cambridge University Press.

Boettcher, J. 2015. "Against the Asymmetric Convergence Model of Public Justification." *Ethical Theory and Moral Practice* 18: 191–208.

Boyd, R. 2006. "The Value of Civility?" *Urban Studies* 43 (5–6): 863–878.

Calhoun, C. 2000. "The Virtue of Civility." *Philosophy and Public Affairs* 29 (3): 251–275.

Calhoun, C. 2015. *Moral Aims: Essays on the Importance of Getting It Right and Practicing Morality with Others.* Oxford University Press.

Edmundson, W. A. 2002. "Civility as Political Constraint." *Res Publica* 8: 217–229.

Edyvane, D. 2017a. "The Passion for Civility." *Political Studies Review* 15 (3): 344–354.

Edyvane, D. 2017b. "Toleration and Civility." *Social Theory and Practice* 43 (3): 449–471.

Edyvane, D. 2020. "Incivility as Dissent." *Political Studies* 68 (1): 93–109.

Forst, R. 2013. *Toleration in Conflict: Past and Present.* Cambridge University Press.

Garcia, E. V. 2022. "Rethinking Acts of Conscience: Personal Integrity, Civility, and the Common Good." *Philosophy* 97 (4): 461–483.

Gauss, G. 2014. "The Turn to a Political Liberalism." In *A Companion to Rawls*, edited by J. Mandle and D. A. Reidy. Blackwell.

Gentile, V. 2018. "From a Culture of Civility to Deliberative Reconciliation in Divided Societies." *Journal of Social Philosophy* 49 (2): 229–251.

Gentile, V. 2026. *Freedom with Religions: Rethinking Civility through Political Inclusivism in Liberal Democracies.* Routledge.

Gentile, V., and M. Foster. 2022. "Towards a Minimal Conception of Transitional Justice." *International Theory* 14 (3): 503–525.

Griffin, L. 1997. "Good Catholics Should Be Rawlsian Liberals." *Southern California Interdisciplinary Law Journal* 5: 297–373.

Harjoto, M. A., & F. Rossi. 2019. "Religiosity, Female Directors, and Corporate Social Responsibility for Italian Listed Companies." *Journal of Business Research* 95: 338–346.

Hart, H. L. A. 1994. *The Concept of Law*. Oxford University Press.

Hartley, C., and L. Watson. 2014. "Virtue in Political Thought: On Civic Virtue in Political Liberalism." In *Virtues and Their Vices*, edited by K. Timpe and C. A. Boyd. Oxford University Press.

Kaufman, A. 2021. "Liberalism: John Rawls and Ronald Dworkin." In *The Cambridge Companion to Civil Disobedience*, edited by W. E. Scheuerman. Cambridge Companions to Philosophy. Cambridge University Press.

Klosko, G. 1994. "Rawls's Argument from Political Stability." *Columbia Law Review* 94: 1882.

Lægaard, S. 2010. "A Multicultural Social Ethos: Tolerance, Respect or Civility?" In *Diversity in Europe: Dilemmas of Differential Treatment in Theory and Practice*, edited by G. Calder and E. Ceva. Routledge.

Meyer, M. J. 2000. "Liberal Civility and the Civility of Etiquette: Public Ideals and Personal Lives." *Social Theory and Practice* 26 (1): 69–84.

Peterson, A. 2019. *Civility and Democratic Education*. Springer.

Quong, Jonathan. 2011. *Liberalism Without Perfection*. Oxford University Press.

Rawls, J. 1999. *A Theory of Justice*. Rev. ed. Harvard University Press.

Rawls, J. 2001. *Justice as Fairness. A Restatement*. Edited by Erin Kelly. Belknap Press of Harvard University Press.

Rawls, J. 2005. *Political Liberalism*. Rev. and exp. ed. Columbia University Press.

Reidy, D. A. 2000. "Rawls's Wide View of Public Reason: Not Wide Enough." *Res Publica* 6: 49–72.

Reidy, D. A. 2017. "Moral Psychology, Stability and the Law of Peoples." *Canadian Journal of Law & Jurisprudence* 30: 363–398.

Richards, D. A. J. 1994. "Public Reason and Abolitionist Dissent." *Chicago-Kent Law Review* 69: 787–842.

Sandel, M. J. 1995. "Political Liberalism." *Harvard Law Review* 107: 1765–1794.

Sinopoli, R. C. 1995. "Thick-Skinned Liberalism: Redefining Civility." *American Political Science Review* 89 (3): 612–620.

Talisse, R. 2019. *Overdoing Democracy: Why We Must Put Politics in Its Place*. Oxford University Press.

Vallier, K. 2019. "Political Liberalism and the Radical Consequences of Justice Pluralism." *Journal of Social Philosophy* 50 (2): 212–231.

Watson, L., and C. Hartley. 2018. *Equal Citizenship and Public Reason: A Feminist Political Liberalism.* Oxford University Press.

Weale, A. 2020. *Modern Social Contract Theory.* Oxford University Press.

Weithman, P. 2016. *Rawls, Political Liberalism and Reasonable Faith.* Cambridge University Press.

Zerilli, L. M. G. 2014. "Against Civility: A Feminist Perspective." In *Civility, Legality, and Justice in America,* edited by A. Sarat. Cambridge University Press.

Can't We Be Friends?

Civic Friendship in an Age of Incivility

TRISTAN J. ROGERS

INTRODUCTION

For many decades, political commentators have bemoaned the lack of civility in our public discourse. This "civility crisis" renders public discourse toxic and threatens the very stability of liberal democratic society. On January 6, 2021, the civility crisis reached its nadir when an angry mob of Trump supporters stormed the U.S. Capitol building in Washington, D.C.[1] No longer a mere "uncivil war," the civility crisis is now metastasizing into an epidemic of political violence.[2]

Although comparisons between the plight of the United States and the end of the Roman Republic are commonplace, the historical parallel remains useful, if not as a simple one-to-one analysis (e.g., America *is* Rome), then as a reservoir of neglected yet newly relevant political concepts. Civic friendship is among these neglected concepts.[3] Civic friendship consists in the friendly bond shared by fellow citizens. It is perhaps best illustrated by attacks upon it. For instance, here is Appian of Alexander's description of the blow to

Tristan J. Rogers, *Can't We Be Friends?* In: *The Virtue of Civility.* Edited by: Andrew Peterson, Oxford University Press. © Oxford University Press 2026. DOI: 10.1093/9780197653791.003.0003 civic friendship generally agreed upon to have been the beginning of the end of the Roman Republic:

> No sword was ever brought into the assembly, and no Roman was ever killed by a Roman, until Tiberius Gracchus, while holding the office of tribune and in the act of proposing legislation, became the first man to die in civil unrest, and along with him a great number of people who had crowded together on the Capitol and were killed around the temple. (1996, 1)

Even though Tiberius's cause of redistributing state-owned land to the disenfranchised soldier and lower classes was arguably just, the boldness of his actions in pursuit of this cause bitterly divided the Romans. Cicero (2012, 88), for instance, chastises Tiberius's friend Gaius Blossius for admitting to a willingness to set fire to the Capitol on behalf of Tiberius's cause. For Cicero, this was among the worst breaches of friendship. Our first duties must be to one another as civic friends.

Civic friendship usefully explains the collective moral harm of political violence. An unlawful attack on a symbolic public building (e.g., the U.S. Capitol), in addition to any loss of life and property damage, harms the political community itself because it damages the fragile bond that unites citizens in one political body. Such attacks, while unthinkable in times of stability and concord, are not only tolerated but encouraged in times of civil strife because their perpetrators receive partisan honors and praise for their misdeeds, a situation that has only intensified in the age of social media.[4] Consequently, as Cicero observes, in the wake of political violence, "[m]ore men will learn how to cause this kind of trouble than how to resist it" (Cicero 2012, 88). How, then, should we resist this kind of trouble? How should we understand and respond to civil disturbances, so that the cycle of political violence ceases?

I will argue that the only exit from escalating political violence and enmity is for fellow citizens to reaffirm their commitment to civic friendship. While sometimes conceived as a moral ideal of mutual respect based in shared values, civic friendship is better understood *descriptively* as the daily resolution to live together within a shared constitution and territory. In its absence, mounting incivility will continue to degenerate into outright hostility and violence. But if we reawaken to the importance of civic friendship, fellow citizens may reunite and be civil in their disagreements, yet resolute in their over-arching commitment to the civitas as the source of their friendship.

I begin with an analysis of the civility crisis, focusing on political polarization. Because of the tendency of political polarization to incentivize acts of incivility, I argue that the virtue of civility becomes irrelevant and inert. So long as there is relative peace and order, citizens may hold out the possibility of reaffirming their commitment to one another as civic friends through the shared activities of common life. The virtues of civic friends—love and justice—indicate what we should expect of virtuous citizens in our efforts to mend the frayed bonds of civic friendship.

THE CIVILITY CRISIS

Political opinion has become much more polarized in the United States. For instance, according to Pew Research published in 2014—a comparatively calm year by today's standards—not only has the center of the political divide hollowed out, but the portion of each party with a "highly negative view" of the other party has doubled since 1994. More troubling, extreme partisans believe that the policies of the rival party "are so misguided that they threaten the nation's well-being" (Pew Research Center 2014). From this belief it is a short step to thinking that one's ideological opponents are not simply making errors in moral judgment; they are morally deficient *persons*.

Unsurprisingly, this high degree of polarization is ripe for incivility. Civility is usually characterized by norms of respect, including listening, speaking calmly, and refraining from making personal attacks. "Civility" derives from the Latin *civilis*, an adjective relating to citizens, and so apart from the usual connotations of politeness or giving courtesy, civility also means to behave in a manner that befits a citizen. Civility is the treatment owed *to* a fellow citizen on account of this distinct role relationship. But if some believe that their fellow citizens are morally deficient because of their political opinions, we can see how some may begin to support the view that some citizens do not deserve civility. What ought to be the default expectation of goodwill and trust gives way to distrust, suspicion, and, inevitably, mistreatment or violence.

The civility crisis should be viewed in the context of political disagreements within liberal democratic societies. Following Aristotle (1998, 1252b30, 1260b25, 1278b24), let's first assume that the purpose of a political community is the well-being or happiness of its members (however specified). This much we can agree on: a good society is one in which its individual members flourish together. But exactly what does it mean to "flourish," and how might we jointly achieve flourishing? For some believe that flourishing is a life of pleasure or social status, others communion with God, and some reject an overarching human telos altogether. Besides, even if we agreed about such an end, there are at least as many disagreements about the best means to achieve such an end.

While disagreement about the good epitomizes the human condition, in the conditions of a liberal democracy we have what John Rawls calls "the fact of reasonable pluralism": "the fact that a plurality of conflicting reasonable comprehensive doctrines, religious, philosophical, and moral, is the normal result of its culture of free institutions" (1999a, 765–766). Rawls's insight consolidated around his attempt to elucidate and defend a theory of justice. According to Rawls, a just society is one in which basic liberties and fair opportunities are secured, while ensuring that any economic inequalities raise the prospects of the least advantaged members of society ([1971] 1999, 52–56). But given the comprehensive moral theory required to support this view, Rawls eventually conceded that even the view defended in *A Theory of Justice* unjustifiably invokes a "comprehensive doctrine," leaving justice as fairness as one among a family of liberal views.[5] Rawls later set out to develop a strictly political (or non-sectarian) theory of justice that could reconcile in an overlapping consensus the set of conflicting comprehensive doctrines in a democratic society.

Rawls's theoretical focus, however, conceals our real divisions. The philosophically reasonable-sounding "comprehensive doctrines" rationalizes our differences into rival bodies of *thought*, negotiated by norms of public *reasoning*, whereas a major source of our differences seems to occur pre-rationally, at the level of moral perception or *narrative*, which is impervious to reason because reason ultimately rests on top of this deeper psychological foundation. A moral narrative tells a story about the essential goodness of who we are, what we believe, and where we are going. Jonathan Haidt (2012, 330), drawing on the work of sociologist Christian Smith, calls these "grand narratives," which "identify and reinforce the sacred core of each [moral] matrix," where a moral matrix is a concatenation of moral beliefs and emotions. The "liberal progress narrative," for instance, emphasizes the emancipation of persons from systems of oppression: authority, hierarchy, power, etc. Meanwhile, the rival conservative narrative stresses the defense of authority, national loyalty, and what is held sacred (e.g., the flag, life, God) against the forces of egalitarian leveling and liberation (see 330–335).

Since people adopt narratives for their meaning and not necessarily for their correspondence to factual reality, it would be a mistake to view grand narratives as "conflicting," as if one were, in fact, true, the other false. Rather, grand narratives are rival visions, each plainly capturing certain moral truths about life in political society, yet neither capturing the whole truth on its own. This is why, as John Stuart Mill observes, "it is almost a commonplace, that a party of order or stability, and a party of progress or reform, are both necessary elements of a healthy state of political life" (2015, 47). We don't need a true narrative; we need a *complete* narrative.

"Conflict" is the appropriate term, however, when we begin to piece together *what ought to be done* politically from what is implied by rival grand narratives. Take immigration, for example. The conservative narrative telegraphs a policy of securing national borders and admitting newcomers only on the bases of having demonstrated loyalty and a positive benefit to the nation. But according to the liberal narrative, because borders are morally arbitrary, and since would-be immigrants often suffer misfortune and oppression in their home countries, it would be morally wrong to neglect our obligation to welcome them as fellow citizens. Indeed, for the liberal, immigrants are a way of further enriching an already rich society.

In a healthy democracy, these conflicting narratives get worked out in public discourse and, eventually, adjudicated through the political process. The issue of immigration is particularly instructive because of how poorly it is often discussed and the fact that legislative bodies and law enforcement agencies, especially in the United States, have so thoroughly neglected their responsibilities. In overly simplistic terms, conservatives are ready to accuse liberals of destroying the rule of law by welcoming as new citizens those who have violated the law, while liberals are ready to accuse conservatives of being xenophobic for daring to distinguish citizen and non-citizen, legal and non-legal immigrant. Similarly, legislative proposals range from blanket amnesty to total deportations, neither of which is a feasible (much less desirable) political response to what remains a serious public policy problem. Voters witnessing this dysfunctional state of affairs should perhaps be excused if they decide to simply pick a team and root for victory.

Nevertheless, in a democracy, public discourse must be regulated by norms of civility, which allow us to engage in political debate about the best way to live together without recourse to acrimony or violence. Unless the ancient critique is true, viz. democracy is undermined by the ignorance of the average voter, we must have some faith that democracy will reliably generate good outcomes.[6] Civility encourages open and reasonable debate by serving as a set of regulative norms that moderate disagreements over what should be done. Civility norms are among the "rules of the game," purportedly neutral principles—adhered to by both sides—that preserve the integrity of the playing field among rival parties. If we cannot agree to *what* should be done, then at least if there are functioning civility norms, we can agree about *how* to discuss what should be done.

But in times of civil strife, when polarization drives us further apart, respect for civility norms will too often be cast aside for the sake of narrative supremacy or wielded cynically to enforce one-sided compliance. Because we engage in motivated reasoning—especially when the stakes are high—it will seem to many that it is morally incumbent to disregard civility for the sake of the highest value of one's grand narrative (e.g., "social justice" or "national greatness"). In other words, the perceived sacredness of our values gives cover to excuse ourselves from the rules of the game, if only temporarily, so that we might achieve a short-term victory, at the expense of the long-term stability of the game itself.

In this way, one side may temporarily defeat its ideological enemies. But so long as the defeated side lives to fight another day, the same dynamic eventually plays out in the other direction. Some liberals, for example, may argue that civility norms merely prop up what is an unjust status quo. On this view, civility is "a tool of the oppressor" that serves only to entrench existing injustices, disadvantaging those who fight for social justice. Therefore, for the sake of liberation from oppression, it is argued that we should sometimes opt out of treating our opponents civilly when important matters of social justice are at stake. Conservatives, on the other hand, because they reject the liberal vision of social justice, may reluctantly tolerate incivility as a defensive stance against *any* advance of the liberal cause, since if they do not, they face the strategic disadvantage of playing by rules that the other team is willing to break with impunity. While liberals view conservatives as apologists for injustice, conservatives view liberals as usurpers in service of the mirage of social justice.[7]

With this entrenched tit-for-tat strategy, the civility crisis advances apace. But we still must confront the pressing question of how to live together in a society divided by warring narratives. For these narratives issue in conflicting public policy proposals, which ordinarily may be resolved through healthy public debate and the political process. But, as I have argued, motivated reasoning and the high stakes of vindicating one's narrative encourage the violation of civility norms in such a way that to renounce incivility *as a tactic* would be tantamount to surrender. The predictable result: incivility and political violence. Returning to another classical source, Thucydides's commentary on the civil war in Corcyra is a striking and compelling parallel of where we find ourselves:

> Love of power, operating through greed and through personal ambition, was the cause of all these evils. To this must be added the violent fanaticism which came into play once the struggle had broken out. Leaders of parties in the cities had programmes which appeared admirable—on one side political equality for the masses, on the other the safe and sound government of the

aristocracy—but in professing to serve the public interest they were seeking to win the prizes for themselves. In their struggles for ascendancy nothing was barred; terrible indeed were the actions to which they committed themselves, and in taking revenge they went farther still. . . . As for the citizens who held moderate views, they were destroyed by both the extreme parties, either for not taking part in the struggle or in envy at the possibility that they might survive. (1972, 243–244)

CIVILITY AS A VIRTUE

In states of civil conflict like the one Thucydides so vividly describes, given the glaring absence of moral character, what could be more obvious than the need for citizens to exercise the *virtue* of civility? Andrew Peterson defines the virtue of civility as consisting in (a) civil conduct toward and (b) fellow-feeling with one's fellow citizens (2019, 8). A civil person will abide by the rules of the game for its own sake, even if others are not complying, and will assiduously avoid translating differences of political opinion into ill-tempered feelings toward fellow citizens. Peterson's account is endorsed by Nancy Snow (2020, 7), who writes that "political civility, understood as an approach to political relations in the absence of a commitment to shared values, is precisely what we need in today's fractured world."

What should we make of this appeal to the virtue of civility? While we plainly lack the moral character that would forestall the spiraling effect of uncivil interactions between citizens—because even the virtue of civility depends to some extent on shared values and mutual expectations—I will argue that, perhaps paradoxically, the virtue of civility is the wrong response to the civility crisis. I will focus on the first element of Peterson's account, civil conduct, and show how violations of civil conduct reliably undermine the second element of his account, that is, fellow-feeling among citizens.

Cheshire Calhoun writes, "[B]ecause communicating our moral attitudes is central to civility, being genuinely civil ... requires that we follow *whatever the socially established norms are* for showing people considerateness, tolerance, or respect" (2000, 260, emphasis added). If Calhoun is right, the content of Peterson's "civil conduct" is given, not by an independent consideration of what a virtuous person would characteristically do in the circumstances, but by the existing social norms that specify what it means to act civilly in a particular society. In this sense, as Calhoun observes, the requirements of civility are similar to those of civil obedience, which sometimes may require compliance with morally suboptimal (or even substandard) rules (272).

Calhoun's analysis indicates that we should distinguish two points of view when thinking about the virtue of civility.[8] The first is the point of view of an existing social practice, consisting of a set of social norms (or rules) that specify what it means to act with civility in a given society. Refraining from making personal attacks, for instance, is one such norm familiar in liberal democratic societies. To exercise the virtue of civility from this perspective just is to behave in the manner that communicates considerateness, respect, or tolerance in the customary ways. The second perspective is what Calhoun calls the "socially critical moral point of view," where we apply some substantive moral view (e.g., utilitarianism) to externally critique or revise what counts as *genuine* respect in a way that goes beyond mere civility (2000, 263). Until very recently, for example, simply using the pronouns that correspond to someone's apparent gender identity would not be considered a potential sign of disrespect or act of incivility. But from a socially critical moral point of view, some have called this default social norm into question, arguing that genuine respect requires us to conform our language to reflect accurately someone's professed gender identity.

Since one of the functions of civility norms is to regulate moral discourse about the content of social critical morality, it is easy to see how moral disagreements about controversial subject matter (e.g., gender identity) can go off the rails so quickly. For, as the previous example shows, the very terms of what it means to act with civility are often called into question by the substance of the issue under discussion. We cannot civilly discuss gender identity, for example, if adherence to either viewpoint is seen as prejudicing the question of what counts as civil treatment in the context of the discussion itself. More generally, as I've argued, when the stakes are high, the perceived importance of one's adopted social critical morality—that it prevails above all—will often sanction the abandonment of civility norms, rendering healthy public discourse nearly impossible.

If this analysis is right, then calls for citizens to exercise the virtue of civility are likely to fail in all the situations in which civility is most needed. After all, we develop the virtues, as Aristotle reminds us, by developing good habits (2000, II.2). But if the incentives of the game—as it is currently being played—encourage us to win at all costs, it is no surprise that many players are ready to violate the rules of the game. Good habits are crowded out and civility recedes from political discourse. Instead, we should expect players to carefully avoid getting caught violating the rules, to protest when others break the rules, and to view fellow citizens as enemies to be defeated rather than citizens to be reasoned with. Therefore, without a minimal assurance of civil conduct, fellow-feeling is impossible, and without fellow-feeling, there is little reason to expect civility, which, as I will argue later, depends on amity. The vicious cycle continues, as we appear to be locked in a classic prisoner's dilemma, as shown in Table 2.1.

Table 2.1 CIVIL DEBATE PRISONER'S DILEMMA.

	Ted is civil	*Ted is uncivil*
Fred is civil	Civil debate	Ted defeats Fred
Fred is uncivil	Fred defeats Ted	War

Suppose Fred and Ted, who disagree politically, are engaged in public discourse over a controversial moral issue. Fred reasons that since he cannot trust Ted to treat him civilly, he better not treat Ted civilly either, otherwise Ted is sure to "win" the debate by casting Fred's views (and perhaps Fred himself) as morally repugnant or beyond the pale. Ted reasons similarly. Consequently, Fred and Ted remain in a stable state of "war," and neither are able to make a persuasive case for their moral point of view, although they manage to save face by "returning fire" on each other. Of course, this result is suboptimal as both would prefer—if it could be assured—a civil debate, where both sides get a fair hearing, the better or at least more persuasive argument wins the day, and both sides continue on friendly terms.

The stalemate between Fred and Ted raises an important question: On what basis do we owe others respect? Who deserves protection from the rules of the game, so that political disputes can be resolved peacefully and amicably? Given the current state of play, partisans are likely to reply, "Those who are *genuinely* moral persons deserve genuine respect." Paraphrasing Aristotle, equals should be treated equally (1998, III.9). Unsurprisingly, the content of what qualifies one as a genuinely moral person often coincides entirely with adherence to a socially critical moral point of view, the very subject of our deepest disagreements. The inevitable conclusion: those who disagree with us do not deserve our respect. So we need not treat them with civility. We have unwittingly endorsed the ancient dictum that justice requires us to benefit our friends and harm our enemies, and we have utterly abandoned Christ's injunction to "love our enemies."[9] It is no wonder, then, that the spiral of incivility continues.

CIVIC FRIENDSHIP

But there is an obvious and compelling answer to the question "On what basis do we owe others respect?": if not the mere fact that they are fellow human beings, then the fact that they are our fellow citizens. Although relations between citizens may be viewed through a purely legal lens, citizens also typically share a friendly bond that supports their moral obligations to one another. Given equal human dignity, while a fellow citizen's life is not worth more than a stranger's, it is not unreasonable to recognize that citizenship occasions a stronger sense of obligation.[10] Just as the bond between family members necessitates respect and heightened moral obligations, so too the relationship between citizens occasions heightened norms of respect, fellow-feeling, and moral obligation. This is why the nationality of the victims of a natural disaster or terrorist attack are always reported in the news—and why it interests us—as if we were waiting to hear whether a loved one had perished. While the degree and intimacy of this feeling differs, both are plausibly forms of friendship, what the ancient Greeks called *philia*.

What is civic friendship? Snow defines "robust civic friendship" as the "relatively robust relationship among citizens that is characterized by a commitment to shared values," where "these values provide a normative basis for standards of social and political interaction" (2020, 3). As Snow acknowledges, understood in this way, it can be difficult to see how civic friendship could be applicable to our own societies, since it is precisely this commitment to shared values that we seem to lack. Civic friendship, then, appears to be just another moral ideal among many, a matter of dispute for the very reason we cannot treat each other civilly: our lack of shared values.

But there is another way to think about civic friendship that more plausibly captures our situation. Instead of understanding civic friendship as a moral ideal, I propose we follow Paul Ludwig (2020), who thinks of civic friendship differently. According to Ludwig, "civic friendship is a *descriptive* feature of liberalism," in the sense that citizens of a liberal democracy really do share friendly relations, even if they go unnoticed because liberalism itself seems to lack a theoretical framework to conceptualize this relationship (6, emphasis added). "Like health," Ludwig observes, "civic friendship is a good that is often achieved in the real world" (13). Otherwise we would not be living in a functioning society at all. Thus, so long as the bond of civic friendship is not irreparably broken, we might hold out hope of repairing it. Our situation is that of a friendship on the rocks, not the absence of friendly relations altogether, since that is precisely the condition that describes outright civil conflict. Instead of seeking Snow's moral ideal of civic friendship, then, we could simply repair the existing bonds of friendship that have exposed holes in our leaky ship of state.

Building on Ludwig's conception, I propose that civic friendship is the daily resolution to live well together within the bounds of a shared constitution and territory. Much like personal relationships, civic friendship is something that must be positively affirmed as a good, otherwise it will be taken for granted and eventually deteriorate or collapse altogether. But unlike the moral ideal of civic friendship, descriptive civic friendship does *not* presuppose that we share the same values. Instead, it points to a shared common life, characterized by joint activity under a constitution (or rule of law) that governs the territory of a nation-state. Much like the relationship between neighbors, a shared life mutes the effects of differences in values and allows us to trust one another because we recognize our joint membership in a political community as that without which we could not live well together.

Many societies have formed around religious, ethnic, or national identities. But these seem no longer feasible or even desirable in multiethnic, multifaith, and pluralistic modern states. The United States is often thought to have broken the mold with its commitment to a common *creed* that transcends our differences: *e pluribus unum*. But this too has come under question as the old loyalties of race, tribe, and religion—under the guise of so-called identity politics—reassert themselves amid the uncertain expectations formed by our complex social, political, and economic circumstances. More fundamentally, there are questions about what our common creed actually is, and what it means given the political, social, and moral changes that have taken place since the American Founding.

To better understand the source of unity in a political community, we need to first define what a political community is. According to Aristotle, a political community is not simply occupying the same territory under a set of laws that prevent unjust actions and enable economic exchange. Rather, while a political community needs these things, it also must consist in shared activities for the sake of living well (Aristotle 1998, III.9). "For things of this sort," Aristotle points out, "are the result of friendship, since the deliberative choice of living together constitutes friendship" (1280b35). Like friendship, then, membership in a political community is a constitutive not an instrumental good. We recognize it as a good in itself—apart from its external benefits—and we care about the moral character and well-being of our fellow citizens, quite apart from what they can do to benefit us instrumentally.

Aristotle concludes that because the political community exists for the sake of living well, not life merely, a distributive principle follows: "those who contribute the most to *this* sort of community have a larger share in the city-state" (1998, 1281a, emphasis original). And for Aristotle, since virtuous activity is the purpose of the city-state, virtuous persons ought to have a larger share in the city-state's distribution of power and benefits. In this sense, Aristotle's ideal constitution is aristocratic. But since we are in non-ideal conditions and vastly different historical circumstances, we may instead opt for the basic liberal democratic idea that the benefits and burdens of membership in a political community ought to be distributed on the basis of equality of citizenship.

What, then, are the minimum shared premises of a liberal democracy? Among political theorists these are usually understood to be liberty and equality, themselves of course matters of deep dispute among both theorists and the general population. But I believe even liberty and equality can be specified clearly enough to form the basic agreement of membership in a liberal democracy out of which civic friendship and its accompanying virtues may flourish.

First, liberty must be understood not as the negative freedom to be free from interference (per libertarianism), nor the positive freedom to be free to do what one authentically desires (per left-liberalism), but liberty under law. Berlin's "two concepts" of liberty do not properly distinguish liberty from license, thus ignoring the important connection between liberty, law, and the virtues required for participation in democratic life. This is why Aristotle, arguing against the extreme democrats of his day, writes, "[L]iving in a way that suits the constitution should be considered not slavery, but salvation" (1998, 1310a35). Life as a liberal democratic citizen, then, means much more than doing what one desires within the constraints of formal law in a way that doesn't interfere with others' liberty. It must also mean living in ways that complement and contribute to our shared political life.[11] Arguments about freedom of speech, for instance, often focus on governmental activities that violate forms of expression. But, as John Stuart Mill was well aware, we can silence one another in ways that render government censorship unnecessary. For this "social tyranny," as Mill puts it, can be "more formidable than many kinds of political oppression, since . . . it leaves fewer means of escape, penetrating much more deeply into the details of life, and enslaving the soul itself" (2015, 8).

Equality should be similarly qualified to mean equality under the law. While the extent to which equality under the law ought to give rise to relative degrees of economic equality is a matter of debate within a liberal democratic order, the means through which that end is sought cannot undermine equality under the law itself. To take an extreme case, the confiscation and redistribution of private property to achieve equal outcomes would seem to violate equality under the law, whereas using tax revenue to collectively provide some form of economic benefits does not. The former treats people equally but not equally under the law, whereas the latter does not treat people equally, but at least does so in a lawful manner. As in the case of liberty, then, equality is not to be specified in such a way as to settle important debates about public policy within a liberal democracy. Instead, equality describes the equal status of citizens, who enjoy equal rights of political participation and equal protection under the laws.

If the foregoing sounds controversial, this is proof of how far we have strayed from the most basic premises of constitutional government. We may still ask, however, what follows from this specification of liberty and equality under the law. Are we not still stuck with our fundamental disagreements over the good life and the just society? And if that is the case, won't these disagreements resurface when we begin to debate what *genuine* liberty and equality substantively require for questions of public policy? In other words, the minimal terms of civic friendship appear tenuous so long as they reveal so little about our shared values.

Rosalind Hursthouse claims that, even among rights-based political theories, "the question 'What rights must be secured by a society if its members are to be enabled to achieve *eudaimonia*' is covertly guiding the discussion" (1991, 244). Hursthouse's observation implies that our disagreements about public policy actually operate at the level of disagreement about the good life (*eudaimonia*), not as some political philosophers would have us believe, at the level of rival theories of justice (see, e.g., Sen 2009, 13–14). If that is so, then we might make progress in our moral divisions by a mutual acknowledgment of our pursuit of the same goal, namely, living well together. *What* this turns out to be matters less than the fact that we jointly accept that this is, in fact, what we are trying to achieve *together*. It is a genuinely joint activity.

This matters a lot for our understanding of civic friendship. For the requirement of shared values is appropriately weakened once we understand that, in a descriptive sense, civic friendship simply means the shared understanding that (a) we desire to live well as members of the same community and (b) we agree to resolve disagreements about what this means lawfully and amicably. Civic friendship is the resolve to carry on the conversation about the best life in spite of disagreement, while honoring acts of friendship above a personal desire to win. We escape the prisoner's dilemma of incivility by valuing the fact that we are cooperating *together*, that is, by valuing civic friendship itself. Those who care about cooperation with a civic friend for its own sake will not defect and resort to incivility to win an argument (or an election).

THE VIRTUES OF CIVIC FRIENDSHIP: LOVE AND JUSTICE

Even if reaffirming civic friendship would allow us to escape the civility crisis, the depth of the crisis itself gives us reason to believe that civic friendship is on its last legs. What's more, a mere acknowledgment of civic friendship is not sufficient, as friendships cannot be sustained, much less salvaged, without shared activity and virtuous actions. So, to buttress the descriptive sense of civic friendship, we must also describe its characteristic virtues.

Put another way, our problem is how to moderate our disagreements about what we earlier, following Calhoun, called "socially critical moral points of view." Civic friends must accept that they are left with the difficult task of determining how to live well together, given the fact of reasonable pluralism. We can imagine, for instance, debates about what justice requires among liberal, socialist, conservative, and libertarian points of view. While the democratic process may determine which view wins at the ballot box, in order for this process to be seen as legitimate and beneficial we still need healthy debate about which view *deserves* to win. The legitimacy of democracy rests on the belief that, in some sense, the majority view deserves to win, or else public debate and the democratic process will be seen as a sham by those who hold views perpetually in the minority.

Public policy debates are usually about the justice of institutions or social practices. For example, would a just society provide a system of public healthcare to its citizens? Or does a just society require institutional support for traditional family structures? While our desire to remain civic friends cannot itself resolve these difficult questions about the justice of our institutions, pursuing these questions in a spirit of friendship can incentivize virtuous actions that make them more tractable and resolvable.

What would it look like for civic friends to debate and enact public policy well? I propose we focus on the character (i.e., not institutional) virtue of justice. According to David O'Connor (1998), the character virtue of justice has a corrective and an expressive sense. The corrective sense is the disposition to act in accordance with the existing social and legal norms of one's political community, where deviations from justice consist in instances of norm breaking (hence *corrective*).[12] This would correspond to and include, for instance, abiding by existing norms of civil conduct, thus exhibiting the virtue of civility in Calhoun's sense. But justice, according to O'Connor, also has an expressive sense: "justice is the virtue of a human being who is a good partner in the pursuit of some worthwhile goal, especially the goal of virtuous action within the context of a political community" (1998, 425–426). This expressive sense of justice corresponds to the affective (or friendly) aspect of our relationship to fellow citizens.

A good civic friend, then, is characterized by the virtue of justice, understood as (a) abiding by existing social and legal norms and (b) fellow-feeling toward other citizens. The former requirement rules out incivility or lawbreaking for the sake of one's ideal of (institutional) justice. The latter requirement prevents a good civic friend from holding ill will toward those who do not share her ideal of justice. Taken together, a good civic friend has respect for the existing social order, even if it is deficient in some (or many) respects, and has enough fellow-feeling with those who disagree that proposals for reform can be evaluated for their contribution to the common good, which, minimally speaking, ought to preserve the tie of civic friendship.[13]

This view is strengthened by analogy to personal friendship. We cannot trust our friends if they display a willingness to violate the basic norms of friendship, such as honesty, refraining from gossip or slander, or harming our personal interests or economic prospects. Likewise few true friendships can sustain serious lawbreaking or other forms of illegal activity. But mere adherence to the basic norms of friendship is not enough to make someone a good friend. Good friendships are also characterized by a kind of love, that is, a willingness to put the interests of another before oneself. In this sense, "love," as Cicero writes, "means nothing other than to cherish the one you love without pursuing your needs or your advantage" (2012, 106).

And since plausibly friendship is among the best goods, we ought to prioritize the good of friendship above partisan political concerns.

Further support for our view is found in the oft-neglected political thought of G. W. Leibniz, whose view of justice is contained in the dictum "Justice is the charity of the wise."[14] Wisdom, which, for Leibniz, is "knowledge of our own good," minimally requires lawfulness, i.e., abiding by existing legal and social norms, or what he calls *ius strictum* (strict justice), with a view to maintaining the social order (1998, 57). But mere adherence to the law—refraining from invading another's rights—is insufficient as an account of justice because the just person also has concern for the positive good of others.[15] Hence, for Leibniz, justice in the full sense includes charity within the limits of wisdom. For this reason, Leibniz argues that "it is not permitted to deprive the rich of their goods to accommodate the poor," not because it wouldn't be charitable but "because the disorder which would be born of it would cause more general evil and inconvenience, than this particular inconvenience" (64). The just person, then, abides by the laws and exhibits charity (or love) to the extent wisdom counsels.

Leibniz's view of justice as a character virtue is an excellent model for thinking about our disputes over institutional justice. For even when institutional reform is necessary, a just person will accept and defer to existing social and legal norms, including norms of civility, in regulating both the discussion and content of proposed institutional changes. Similarly, because the just person is also motivated by charity (or love), i.e., the true good of another, she will resist the temptation to cast one's ideological opponents as enemies and instead, in the spirit of civic friendship, treat them with due respect and fellow-feeling.

How do the virtues of love and justice illuminate our case for civic friendship? Snow claims that "[t]hough political civility falls short of robust civic friendship as I've understood that relationship, *the former can be an important pathway toward the latter*" (2020, 7, emphasis added). What I have argued is that Snow's diagnosis gets things backward: civic friendship must be (re)affirmed prior to the practice of political civility. In other words, political civility cannot take root without the mutual recognition that we are civic friends first.[16] In this respect, civility is like good sportsmanship: civility presumes a love for the game, mutual commitment to the game's rules, and some degree of fellow-feeling with one's competitors. In terms of the virtues, civility requires that we are prepared to act justly by (a) following the existing rules and (b) having fellow-feeling for those who must cooperate with us to shape the rules for our mutual benefit.

What might this look like in practice? Again, take a difficult issue like healthcare.[17] How might two virtuous civic friends, who are on opposite sides, navigate this issue? Fred, who opposes a public healthcare system, might first acknowledge that Ted, who favors a public system, is correct that the current system is not functioning well to achieve their mutually endorsed goal of living well together, which they both acknowledge requires a healthy population. Ted, on the other hand, could acknowledge that there are serious practical obstacles to implementing a public healthcare system in the United States and that doing so might come at the cost of personal liberty, two issues Fred cares deeply about. Finally, both can acknowledge that any changes should occur within existing institutional mechanisms, with fair and open debate, and that compromises on both sides might be necessary to achieve the common good such that friendly relations among citizens continue. Seen in this light, civic friendship is the resolve to carry on public debate about difficult issues while placing the good of one's fellow citizens (and one's relationship to them) above one's own ideal of what justice requires. In this way, we agree to sacrifice some part of our ideal for the greater good of civic friendship and the common good.

CONCLUSION

What are the prospects for a revival of civic friendship in our time? As Robert Talisse (2021) has noticed, friendship is not the kind of good that we can secure by aiming at it directly. Instead, we make and maintain friendships by jointly pursuing things other than friendship, and by doing so, friendship emerges. This is part of the reason why I have emphasized the central place of virtuous activity in the recovery of civic friendship. "Can't we be friends?," after all, is not much different from Rodney King's plaintive "Can we all get along?" So too in the wake of the storming of the Capitol, many undoubtedly have had similar thoughts of hopeless optimism. After all, civic friendship in the United States has suffered a serious attack and it is not at all clear how we might come back from it, especially as one side looked for collective responsibility, and the other wished to forget it ever happened.

If we are to find unity among our divisions, it may be found in what we can unify *against*. There is unity in standing against the extremes on both the left and the right. There is unity in denouncing destructive, violent, and unlawful actions. There is unity in choosing to maintain friendships outside one's circle of political allies and refusing to grandstand on social media for "clicks," "follows," and "likes." With some of this ground cleared, it may become possible to reaffirm some of the things we share in the spirit of friendship: institutions, history, language, culture, community, faith, and so on. For this is the fertile ground of virtue out of which the bonds of civic friendship might begin to regrow. May we possess Cicero's fondness for friendship and Leibniz's wise love to make it so.

NOTES

1. For what it's worth, this essay was composed in the days following this event.
2. Far from the first event of its kind, the storming of the U.S. Capitol followed previous incidents of political violence in recent years, significant among them: various rallies and counter-protests surrounding the election of President Donald Trump in 2016, the attempted murder of Rep. Steve Scalise and his Republican colleagues in June 2017, the Charlottesville vehicle attack in August 2018, the August 2019 El Paso mass shooting, and the violence in Minneapolis, Kenosha, and other major American cities that accompanied protests against racial injustice in the summer of 2020. I leave it to the reader to conjur the most recent and egregious examples of political violence on both sides of the political divide.
3. Interest in civic friendship appears to have been partially rekindled in the last decade. See, e.g., Healy (2011); Brudney (2013); Woods (2013); Leontsini (2013); Georgieva (2013); Bentley (2013).
4. For a thorough analysis of this phenomenon, see Tosi and Warmke (2020).
5. See the introduction to Rawls (1993, xiii–xxxiv).
6. For a recent defense of the ancient critique, see Brennan (2016).
7. The expression "mirage of social justice" is borrowed from Hayek (1973).
8. This distinction roughly parallels that made by John Rawls in "Two Concepts of Rules" (1999b, 20–46), viz. that we should distinguish how to act *within* the rules governing an existing practice from whether we ought to adopt or accept a practice itself.
9. This ancient view of justice is defended by Polemarchus in Plato's *Republic*, 331d–336a. For a recent defense of the latter Christian view of justice, see Brooks (2019).
10. Even a cosmopolitan like Adam Smith has occasion to remark, "the care of the universal happiness of all rational and sensible beings, is the business of God and not of man. To man is allotted a much humbler department, but one much more suitable to the weakness of his powers, and to the narrowness of his comprehension; the care of his own happiness, of that of his family, his friends, his country: that he is occupied in contemplating the more sublime, can never be an excuse for his neglecting the more humble department" (1982, part VI, sec. II, ch. 3).
11. This is, after all, the aim of a *liberal* education.
12. I defend a similar view of the virtue of justice in Rogers (2018).
13. I defend this view in Rogers (2020, ch. 5).
14. See, e.g., "Meditation on the Common Concept of Justice" and "*Codex Iuris Gentium*" in Leibniz (1988, 45–64, 165–176). See also Riley (1996, ch. 4).
15. Leibniz argues for this claim by denying the substance of the distinction between refraining from harm and failing to do good: "whether one does evil

or refuses to do good is a matter of degree, but that does not chance the species and the nature of the thing [i.e., both are acts of injustice]" (1998, 55).

16. Relatedly, in a broken marriage, it's hard to see what civility earns the two parties without the presence of love.

17. Note that if we track the latest rise in incivility back to the early 2010s, along with the rise of smartphones and social media, one thing it seems to track is the passage of the Affordable Care Act in 2010.

REFERENCES

Appian. 1996. *The Civil Wars*. Translated by John Carter. Penguin Classics.

Aristotle. 1998. *Politics*. Translated by C. D. C. Reeve. Hackett.

Aristotle. 2000. *Nicomachean Ethics*. Translated by Roger Crisp. Cambridge University Press.

Bentley, R. K. 2013. "Civic Friendship and Thin Citizenship." *Res Publica* 19: 5–19.

Brennan, Jason. 2016. *Against Democracy*. Princeton University Press.

Brooks, Arthur C. 2019. *Love Your Enemies: How Decent People Can Save American from the Culture of Contempt*. Broadside Books.

Brudney, Daniel. 2013. "Two Types of Civic Friendship." *Ethical Theory and Moral Practice* 16 (4): 732–743.

Calhoun, Cheshire. 2000. "The Virtue of Civility." *Philosophy & Public Affairs* 29 (3): 251–275.

Cicero. 2012. "On Friendship." In *On Living and Dying Well*, translated by Thomas Habinek. Penguin Classics.

Georgieva, Mihaela. 2013. "The Forgotten Ideal of Friendship in Modern Political Theory." *Res Publica* 19: 95–102.

Haidt, Jonathan. 2012. *The Righteous Mind: Why Good People Are Divided by Politics and Religion*. Vintage Books.

Hayek, F. A. 1973. *Law, Legislation, and Liberty*. Vol. 2. University of Chicago Press.

Healy, Mary. 2011. "Civic Friendship." *Studies in Philosophy and Education* 30 (3): 229–240.

Hursthouse, Rosalind. 1991. "After Hume's Justice." *Proceedings of the Aristotelian Society* 91: 229–245.

Leibniz, G. W. 1988. *Political Writings*. Edited by Patrick Riley. Cambridge University Press.

Leontsini, Eleni. 2013. "The Motive of Society: Aristotle on Civic Friendship, Justice, and Concord." *Res Publica* 19: 21–35.

Ludwig, Paul W. 2020. *Rediscovering Political Friendship: Aristotle's Theory and Modern Identity, Community, and Equality*. Cambridge University Press.

Mill, John Stuart. 2015. "On Liberty." In *On Liberty, Utilitarianism and Other Essays*, edited by Mark Phelp and Frederick Rosen. Oxford World Classics.

O'Connor, David. 1998. "Aristotelian Justice as a Personal Virtue." *Midwestern Studies in Philosophy* 13: 417–427.

Peterson, Andrew. 2019. *Civility and Democratic Education*. Springer.

Pew Research Center. 2014. "Political Polarization in the American Public." June. https://www.pewresearch.org/politics/2014/06/12/political-polarization-in-the-american-public/

Rawls, John. (1971) 1999. *A Theory of Justice*. Rev. ed. Harvard University Press.

Rawls, John. 1993. *Political Liberalism*. Exp. ed. Columbia University Press.

Rawls, John. 1999a. "The Idea of Public Reason Revisited." In *Collected Papers*, edited by Samuel Freeman. Harvard University Press.

Rawls, John. 1999b. "Two Concepts of Rules." In *Collected Papers*, edited by Samuel Freeman. Harvard University Press.

Riley, Patrick. 1996. *Leibniz' Universal Jurisprudence*. Harvard University Press.

Rogers, Tristan J. 2018. "Justice as Lawfulness." *Journal of the American Philosophical Association* 4 (2): 262–278.

Rogers, Tristan J. 2020. *The Authority of Virtue: Institutions and Character in the Good Society*. Routledge.

Sen, Amartya. 2009. *The Idea of Justice*. Harvard University Press.

Smith, Adam. 1982. *The Theory of Moral Sentiments*. Liberty Fund.

Snow, Nancy. 2020. "Citizens' Relationships, Political Civility, and the Civic Virtue of Listening." Jubilee Centre for Character and Virtues Insight Series, Jubilee Centre for Character and Virtues, University of Birmingham.

Talisse, Robert. 2021. "The Paradox of Unity." *Arc-Digital*, January 26. https://med ium.com/arc-digital/the-paradox-of-unity-feb6b093a827.

Thucydides. 1972. *History of the Peloponnesian War*. Translated by Rex Warner. Penguin Classics.

Tosi, Justin, and Brandon Warmke. 2020. *Grandstanding*. Oxford University Press.

Woods, Kerri. 2013. "Civic and Cosmopolitan Friendship." *Res Publica* 19: 81–94.

Critical Civility

A Critical Republican Approach to Harmful Speech

SUZANNE WHITTEN

INTRODUCTION

The widespread use of "uncivil" speech against members of oppressed minority groups raises difficult questions about how we might tackle the resulting harms without sacrificing freedom of speech. One proposed solution, according to theorists, is to look to citizens themselves to counteract oppressive expression, such as through counterspeech, protest, or "calling out" wrongdoers on social media. Skeptics of this position, however, warn that such "bottom-up" measures potentially pose just as much of a threat as state-led measures, pointing to practices of "canceling" or "public shaming" as examples of the ways in which bystander intervention can actually *reduce* the amount of freedom of speech enjoyed by citizens.

In response to these concerns, and by focusing on the specific issue of public expression which undermines the equal standing of oppressed groups, this chapter constructs and recommends a *critical republican* account of civility. On the "critical" account of civility

Suzanne Whitten, *Critical Civility* In: *The Virtue of Civility*. Edited by: Andrew Peterson, Oxford University Press. © Oxford University Press 2026. DOI: 10.1093/9780197653791.003.0004 that I defend, individual citizens, in their capacity as direct or indirect "bystanders," have a basic civil duty to intervene in harmful speech, understood as speech which contributes to dominating social hierarchies. In contrast to competing versions of civility, the civility I put forward is not aimed toward maintaining social peace (though this may be a long-term side-effect) but toward securing the freedom as non-domination of all citizens. In that sense, critical civility requires that individual citizens respond to forms of public speech that threaten the equal *freedom* of target groups by ranking targets according to unjust status hierarchies, such as those based on race, gender, ethnicity, and so on. *Critical* civility, I suggest, illuminates the necessary role that the exercise of such positive citizen duties of civility plays in dismantling harmful social hierarchies and can help us construct norms of civil conduct that allow citizens to express respect for one another without falling prey to the historically oppressive features of "top-down" calls for a more "civil" public sphere. While the version of civility I put forward recognizes the importance of shared norms of mutual expressive respect among citizens, it also provides a guide for determining the grounds upon which, in order to express respect appropriately, citizens must "step in" in their role as bystanders to protect the non-dominated status of others. Further, critical civility also tells us when institutional or social constraints placed on individuals in the name of "civility" are, in fact, aimed at securing freedom or instead attempt to suppress the kind of dissent on which freedom depends.

My argument will proceed as follows. I outline what I take to be a key dividing issue in specifying the responsibilities of civility: public speech that harms individuals by enacting and enforcing the norms that underpin unjust hierarchies of status. Here, I explore and critique recent attempts made by "counterspeech" theorists to describe the role individual citizens might play in counteracting harmful speech. While the body of work that has emerged on counterspeech is rigorous in its analytical acuity, the field so far has struggled to conceptualize the specific responsibilities that might be attached to counterspeech practices, particularly as they pertain to the relationships between members of a shared political community. By adapting and amending neo-republican claims regarding the joint formal and informal conditions of freedom, I argue that a critical republican account of civility provides a clear and substantive basis upon which we might ground citizen responsibilities to respond to harmful speech in a way that avoids both the repressive conformism and the formal apathy for which previous versions of civility have been criticized. I outline and respond to two criticisms of critical civility: the first concerns the potential demandingness of my account, and the second concerns the threat of repressiveness.

CIVILITY AND ITS CRITICS

Civility, broadly understood as a set of norms or rules that guide public interactions among individuals in their roles as citizens, has a somewhat checkered reputation in liberal political thought. In the long and varied debate about civility, two broad competing visions have emerged. Advocates of civility argue that it plays an important role in maintaining good social relations among those of us who potentially share nothing more in common but social (or virtual) space (Calhoun 2000, 257; Laegaard 2011). On this view, abiding by civility norms does more than simply announce one's adeptness at upholding local customs and mores (Daly 2015). Rather, civility norms serve an indispensable *pragmatic* purpose in the form of signaling one's commitment to a shared, harmonious social project and a fundamental *moral* purpose in expressing mutual respect and reciprocity toward one's fellow citizens (Edyvane 2020; Buss 1999; Boyd 2006). In more recent years, the increasing interest in civility talk has accompanied a perceived fracture in democratic discourse and an explosion in the amount of racist, misogynist, and anti-LGBTQ+ speech that circulates throughout society, leading many to advocate for a civility that requires that citizens take a more proactive approach to counteracting prejudice (Bonotti and Zech 2021, 48). Similarly, others argue that the technological advancement and growth of social media of the past couple of decades, in contributing to a fraught public sphere, means that we need a renewed civility that proves capable of guiding the unique and constantly shifting norms of online interaction (Antoci et al. 2016; Aly and Simpson 2019, 131). For civility's defenders, this (notable) shift in acceptable norms of public discourse toward previously unheard-of forms of incivility only reinforces the notion that civility is indeed an essential value for liberal democracies to function effectively and to secure the equal standing of all individuals.

But not all are fans of civility. An alternative story about the concept points to its oppressive, dominating history as a "disciplinary apparatus" (Cloud 2015). For as long as civility has featured as a value of liberal societies, so critics argue, it has been used to impose restrictive and repressive norms and practices upon members of minority groups, to silence diversity and dissent, and, ultimately, to retain and reinforce unjust structures of power (Zerilli 2014; Celikates 2020). The case of Steven Salaita, the Palestinian American professor whose job offer was rescinded because of "uncivil" tweets, is one widely known example in which civility norms are thought to have been weaponized in such a way. In 2014, Salaita was offered a (tenured) position in the University of Illinois at Urbana–Champaign American Indian Studies Program. In the six months between his acceptance of the position and his agreed start date, Salaita posted a series of tweets commenting on the unfolding conflict in the Gaza war. The tweets, which were highly critical of Israel, were perceived by many to be anti-Semitic,[1] leading to a mass online public shaming campaign against Salaita. Facing mounting pressure from the media, pro-Israel organizations, and the general public, and following a threat of withdrawal of funds from wealthy donors, University Chancellor Phyllis Wise decided to rescind Salaita's appointment. The judgment was heavily criticized for undermining freedom of speech and academic freedom in the name of "civility."[2] Speaking in an interview after the event, Salaita notes how civility, particularly in the way in which it is practiced in the academy, is not a method of ensuring mutual respect but is a "mechanism of plutocratic common sense" which "forces us to identify with the logic of colonialism" (Espiritu et al. 2015, 70). Any critique or calling into question of such a mechanism, in Salaita's view, "automatically assumes the burden of intemperance or disrespect" (70), which must itself be repressed. A call for civility, in his view, thus does not foster but "actively forestalls honest communication" (70).[3] Just as recent defenders of civility have urged a renewed commitment to its use in public life in response to the political and social turmoil of today, so civility skeptics have expressed concern that "civility talk" is nothing more than an attempt at re-asserting norms of dominance upon the oppressed classes and to squash dissent when it emerges.[4]

When it comes to civility's role in mediating social relations and securing a society of equals, then, a concern for the standing of oppressed groups appears to pull us in two different directions. On the one hand, the capacity for society's members to interact and deliberate on an equal footing seems to rely in large part on the existence of common civil norms, norms which specify the shared "social script" required for properly responding to injustice and for navigating the everyday tasks of democratic life. On the other hand, however, we see within civility discourse an oppressive historical precedent which, rather than serving the interests of social justice, actually further reinforces the wrongful constraints placed upon some of society's members.[5]

In the following section I explore one of the areas in which this tension is most keenly felt: cases where citizens are confronted with hateful or oppressive speech. A closer look at these cases reveals important insights about the range of duties involved for bystanders who encounter such speech, and thereby helps us refine our understanding of civility as a duty of individual citizens.

HARMFUL SPEECH AND THE DUTIES OF BYSTANDERS

It is now widely accepted that speech can harm, and that it gives rise to a particularly injurious harm for members of already marginalized and oppressed groups (Delgado and Yun 1994; Maitra and McGowan 2012). Newspaper headlines warning readers about "invasions" of asylum seekers, misogynistic verbal abuse on public transport, social media posts which spread false and hate-filled rumors about Muslims, and racist graffiti on the front wall of a Black family's home are all examples of speech that harm in incredibly damaging ways. Such speech is thought to contribute to a broad range of negative effects, including psychological distress (Delgado and Stefancic 2019, 14), silencing (MacKinnon 1993), and the enforcement and perpetuation of norms which "rank" members according to unjust social hierarchies (McGowan 2012; Langton 2018a). According to Matteo Bonotti and Steven T. Zech (2021, 48), such speech can be understood as a form of "moral" incivility, or incivility which, while very often couched in "polite" language, undermines the equal civic standing of members of targeted groups. Crucially, moral incivility is not concerned with those rules of etiquette or manners often associated with the term, but with respecting the "free and equal" standing of others, which includes avoiding speech that violates their "fundamental rights, liberties, and equal civic standing" (48). A neo-Nazi who "politely," and without the use of slurs, shares Holocaust denial posts on their social media will thus be someone who is engaging in moral "incivility" on this account.

What should we as individual citizens do when we see such harmful speech in action? One option would be to invoke the power of the state by calling upon the authorities. Those countries that include "hate speech" laws in their statutes aim to protect people who suffer denigrating speech that harms their social standing and enjoyment of equal dignity. Here, legislators recognize the importance of the law not only for deterring would-be hate-speakers from espousing hateful views but also for giving expression to the standards of the community, thereby reminding all that the group in question deserves respectful treatment and that hateful expression has no place in a society of equals (Waldron 2012).

However, while hate speech laws receive strong support from certain quarters as necessary for protecting the equal dignity of targeted groups (Matsuda 1989; Parekh 2006), such laws are thought by many others to have only a limited effect on the amount of harmful speech that circulates in society (Strossen 1990; Hare 2009). While some of the blame can be aimed at state inefficiency and the limited resources of those investigating and punishing hate speech, perhaps the most pressing issue when it comes to tackling harmful speech comes from its sheer *ubiquitousness*. The harms of speech can be seen not just in their downstream effects but, as pointed out by Lynne Tirrell, in the way harmful speech is "woven through the whole social fabric" (2019, 2435). Harmful speech is found in online comment sections and memes posted on social media, the speeches of our political representatives, in art and music, in comments made between acquaintances and colleagues, and generally any sphere that might ordinarily be considered part of "civil society." Interactions between individuals, even on a seemingly "micro" level, can, especially when taken cumulatively, have very real effects on the perpetuation of unjust social hierarchies (McGowan 2019; Rini 2020). Even for those forms of harmful speech that are addressed non-reciprocally from an authority to the wider public (such as via the mainstream media), the reactions and potential responses of the audience, including speaking out and to one another about the speech in question, can have a highly influential effect on the "uptake" that speech will receive and, ultimately, the impact it will have for members of oppressed groups (Saul 2019). It is this "fact of ubiquity" of harmful speech, combined with the potential for individual action to influence and disrupt its eventual downstream effects, that compels much of the recent demand for greater civility in the public sphere (Bolotin 2011; Lysaker and Syse 2016). The suggestion from such quarters is that civility requires more of us than simply refraining from using harmful speech ourselves. Instead, civility requires an active citizen concern for *incivility*, or behavior and speech which undermines the standing of our fellow citizens.

What might norms of civility require us to do in such cases? While not couched in the language of civility, a recognition of the limits of legal responses to harmful speech has generated a burgeoning literature on the role that civil society might play in tackling such harms. Theorists who work on "counterspeech,"[6] understood as "communication that tries to counteract potential harm brought about by other speech, either face-to-face or remotely" (Cepollaro et al. 2023, 1), suggest that hate speech law is either insufficient or inadequate for dealing with the widespread effects of harmful speech.[7] For many defenders of counterspeech, racist, homophobic, misogynist, and anti-Semitic forms of speech are so ubiquitous and potentially damaging that state-led mitigation efforts in the form of the criminal or civil law may not be sufficient. Here, both explicit and casual expressions of bigotry often require, either instead of or in addition to state-led measures, the intervention of individual citizens who come across such expression in their day-to-day lives.[8]

In practice, counterspeech can work in a variety of different ways.[9] I might, for example, use counterspeech when I intervene and challenge a man who cat-calls a young woman in the street. I could also carry out counterspeech online by "sharing" and criticizing a harmful comment made by someone on social media.[10] I might also engage in counterspeech by holding a "counterprotest" at a far-right rally. We can think about how these cases work by drawing on the feminist tradition in speech-act theory. Using this framework, we see how counterspeech operates by harnessing linguistic features of the surrounding communicative apparatus by, for example, blocking (Langton 2018b), "bending" (Caponetto and Cepollaro 2022), preventing uptake, or inserting ambiguity into the harmful exchange. When I use such mechanisms in responding to harmful speech, I attempt to prevent the accommodation of presuppositions and assertions that generate certain "permissibility facts" about how the target group is spoken about going forward (Tirrell 2012). The ultimate aim of such interventions, then, is to prevent harmful speech from enacting and reinforcing particular *norms* regarding the target group, norms that rank, undermine, and diminish their standing within the surrounding community.

Counterspeech may be a useful and effective way of mitigating the effects of harmful speech. But do we have any *duties* to step in and engage in counterspeech when we see harmful speech being used, or is it just something that is "good" to do, a supererogatory action that we are under no moral obligation to carry out if we don't feel like it? More important for the purposes of this chapter, can we count counterspeech as part of our duties of *civility*, or does a concern for the "moral" civility described by Bonotti and Zech simply demand that we refrain from employing such harmful speech ourselves? Indeed, while some counterspeech theorists stress the importance of challenging harmful speech when we encounter it in our day-to-day lives (Howard 2021),[11] others are more cautious in recommending "more speech" as a catch-all answer to harmful expression (Lepoutre 2017; McGowan 2018). Quite apart from the difficulties faced by victims who attempt to use counterspeech, bystander attempts at using counterspeech may "misfire" due to their relative lack of discursive authority in that particular domain. Such communicative failure is more likely to occur when the harmful message of the speech in question is "hidden" and presented covertly, for example, through "dog whistles" (Saul 2019). Worryingly, bystander counterspeech also has the potential to amplify the harmful message of the original expression by making its claims more *salient* (Simpson 2013; McGowan 2019). When carried out by a collective or in online spaces, counterspeech itself can also engender great harm (Billingham and Parr 2020). As we saw in the Steven Salaita example, we should also be cautious about the possibility that counterspeech measures, especially those advanced in the name of "civil" discourse, could stifle the voices of those speaking out against injustice.

Despite these concerns, both the risks of extensive institutional intervention and the critical potential of citizen-led responses to harmful speech give us good reason to seek to refine civility in ways that avoid some of these pitfalls. While stepping in to contest injustice may indeed result in undesirable side effects, an alternative prescription of civic apathy is also ethically unappealing and pragmatically inadequate. Mindful of these difficulties in determining which kind of counterspeech will be most effective or appropriate in a given context, several counterspeech scholars have articulated a need for greater sensitivity to the individual circumstances and context of each speech situation as a necessary component of any counterspeech measure (Cepollaro et al. 2023; Fumagalli 2021). Looking ahead to how we might promote and more systematically adopt citizen-led techniques for handling harmful speech in future, such contextual approaches appear to be the most fruitful.

Building on this debate, the following section proposes that the value of civility, suitably revised along critical republican lines, can help explain why, despite issues with efficacy and salience, bystander counterspeech remains a worthy and important duty of individuals committed to securing a society free of unjust status hierarchies. Importantly, and in contrast to common forms of civility as polite restraint, the "critical" civility I propose is guided not by a concern for peace for peace's sake but by a desire for securing the social and political freedom of all, which in many cases will require typically "uncivil" forms of contestation and dissent. A civility that aims toward equal freedom will thus be incompatible with the kinds of civility that are oppressive and disciplining in nature and instead serves a key function in contesting dominant relations of power.

A CRITICAL REPUBLICAN CIVILITY

Republicanism and the Formal and Informal Conditions of Non-Domination

An increased interest in republicanism as a political theory during the past several decades has prompted a sizable shift in the discipline's understanding of freedom. Beginning with the work of J. G. A. Pocock (1975), Quentin Skinner (1998, 2008), and Philip Pettit (1997, 2012), "neo"-republicanism has blossomed a new generation of thinkers concerned with the theoretical and political limits[12] of what had become a dominant liberal conception of freedom, which is primarily concerned with interferences or obstacles.[13] Critical of a liberal picture which sees freedom rooted in the protection of a clear public/private distinction combined with the rigorous enforcement of individual rights, republicans stress the necessarily *intersubjective* nature of freedom, realized via a contestatory and deliberative style of politics where citizens[14] strive toward a common set of basic values.[15] The conceptual grounding of the revival which ties the various strands together can be found in the republican idea of freedom as non-domination, understood as an absence of arbitrary or uncontrolled interference (Pettit 2012, 82; Lovett 2018), and it is from this foundation upon which republican theorists have developed a theoretical lens and program with which to understand and respond to the political and social problems of present-day liberal democracies.

The appeal of freedom as non-domination as a conceptual lens stems from its ability to accurately capture the kinds of unfreedom which are not easily understood using previous liberal models of freedom. Pettit's early example of a wife living under the thumb of a tyrannical husband in a patriarchal society neatly illustrates those kinds of unfreedoms which emerge under structural conditions of unequal power, which cannot be understood in the language of obstacles or constraints alone (Pettit 1997, 5). In the ensuing decades since Pettit first articulated his version of republican freedom, others have effectively employed a version of non-domination to describe the unfreedoms present in the structures that make up the global order (Bachvarova 2013; Fine 2014), in the relationships between managers and workers (and between workers and the labor market more generally) (Gourevitch 2013; O'Shea 2019), between men and women (Costa 2013), within the criminal justice system (Braithwaite and Pettit 1990), and between majority and minority groups within multicultural societies (Laborde 2008). Building on the work of the early revivalists, "critical" or "radical" republicans point to the critical potential of the republican project for exposing and responding to forms of unfreedom which operate beyond the agential relationship between dominator and dominated and which instead take place at the level of deeply entrenched social structures (Laborde 2008; Gädeke 2020; Garrau and Laborde 2015). Taking inspiration from the work of critical and feminist theory, critical republicans point to the way in which power differentials contribute to norms, attitudes, and practices which work in covert ways to inhibit the equal, undominated status of oppressed groups (Laborde 2008, 10). Norms that essentialize certain groups, thereby enforcing social attitudes toward those groups, are thus the kind that dominate in a purely structural sense, even without the threat of arbitrary interference (Laborde 2013, 522). For example, women who internalize norms of inferiority in patriarchal societies will be dominated in their choices even where no formal obstacles stand in their way. Such structural constraints impact a woman's choices when it comes to things like participation in the job market, the distribution of domestic labor, and their engagement (or lack thereof) with beauty norms. Critical republicans in particular will thus be deeply concerned about the kind of norms and structures perpetuated by those morally uncivil forms of harmful speech which impact an individual's equal civic standing (Krause 2013). On a critical republican framing, then, engaging in morally uncivil speech is to contribute to the conditions under which target groups experience domination (Bonotti and Seglow 2019).

Quite apart from the usefulness of republicanism for understanding how certain kinds of speech contribute to the unfreedom of targets, the theory also offers a clear set of prescriptive resources for responding to such unfreedoms. In contrast to the liberal theoretical focus on identifying the appropriate limits of state intervention in speech, republicanism advocates a combination of both formal institutions *and* informal social norms for the maintenance of a free and equal political community. On this account, while democratically controlled laws are indeed central for the enjoyment of freedom as non-domination, their existence is in large part dependent on the existence of good, supportive social norms (Pettit 1997, 241). The rule of law and the social norms that accompany it are thus thought to be *mutually supportive* in nature. Without a good set of laws, citizens will not be motivated to behave well in their dealings with one another and will instead be driven by competition, suspicion, and distrust (Dagger 2005, 179). Absent a robust set of good norms, however, citizens will not be motivated to follow even the most well-controlled laws, nor will they feel moved to ensure that political institutions are properly responsive to their interests and that they remain free from corruption (Pettit 1997, 249). When it comes to dealing with the effects of harmful speech, then, a republican will recognize the need for both formal and informal measures. On the formal end, this may involve introducing hate speech laws which express respect toward members of target groups and deter would-be hate-speakers from engaging in harmful speech. On the informal end, a republican will advocate a shared civic ethos in which norms against the use of harmful speech are widespread and consistently enforced.

For an individual to enjoy freedom as non-domination in a republic, then, the mutually supportive network of laws, institutions, and norms that govern their social relations must be such that no one is subject to arbitrary infringement. There is an additional *psychological* element to the republican framework which must be noted. As described above, on the republican version of freedom as non-domination an individual need not actually be interfered with in order to be considered unfree. Even where a worker on a precarious contract is lucky enough to have a benevolent manager, for example, their status is such that they do not enjoy the kind of non-domination necessary in order to live a free and equal life (O'Shea 2019). Here, it is the lack of security in the worker's status, the fact that their position makes them vulnerable to interference with impunity, that is of real concern for the republican. Apart from the potential future interference that such an individual might suffer, exposure to an uncontrolled vulnerability and dependence on another contributes to their misrecognition by necessarily distorting their ability to interact with others as an equal (Hirvonen and

Breen 2020). Where dependency on another's goodwill is required in order to protect your basic interests, then you will be strategic in your dealings with them. In contrast, a republican society of equals will be one in which "free persons can walk tall ... and look others in the eye," where "they relate to one another in a shared, mutually reinforcing consciousness of enjoying this independence" (Pettit 2012, 82). Such a person will "not have to bow or scrape, toady or kowtow, fawn or flatter ... [or] live on their wits, whether out of fear or deference" (Pettit 2012, 82). In order to enjoy one's freedom as non-domination, then, not only do the laws and norms that make up society need to reflect the equal standing of all individuals, but this fact needs to be reliable, well-established, and widely known. The widespread public awareness that each individual enjoys formal and informal standing is, therefore, necessary to satisfy both the subjective and intersubjective aspects of freedom as non-domination. This psychological, intersubjective element of the conditions for a non-dominated status supports the view that civil society, and not just the state, is fundamental to protecting members of certain groups from the impact of speech that aims to undermine their civic standing. For individuals vulnerable to harmful speech, their ability to enjoy social freedom requires that they can move through society without fear of verbal attack or denigration from others. A society which lacks norms outlining the appropriate norms of civil discourse, where "civil" refers to expression that upholds the equal standing of everyone, will not be one in which the psychological component of freedom is adequately satisfied.

A (Critical) Republican Civility

By shedding light on the pervasive effects of harmful speech on the freedom of targeted groups, the neo-republican account presented thus far provides a useful addition to the existing harmful speech literature discussed earlier. Importantly, and as I show next, the theory also tells us what our *responsibilities* to combat such domination should look like.

For republicans, the "dual track" system of laws and norms, and the intersubjective sense of security it affords us, is upheld by norms of civility or "civic virtue," understood as a value, a set of role-specific norms or practices, an ethos, attitude, or disposition that citizens display toward those with whom they share a polity (Dagger 1997). Strongly aware of the necessary place social interdependence holds in human freedom (Honohan 2003), contemporary republicans have endeavored to articulate the kinds of behaviors individual citizens need to exhibit toward one another in a way that both secures equal standing while also respecting the "fact of pluralism" (Rawls 1996, 4) of present-day societies. Philip Pettit, for instance, argues for "widespread civility" to describe the basic set of norms which must be followed by citizens to protect the proper functioning of republican institutions (1997, 242). On Pettit's version of civility, civility is less about securing stable traits of character and more about the mechanisms by which citizens keep one another's behavior in check using the forces of approbation and disapprobation (241; Brennan and Pettit 2004). Emphasizing the citizen-led nature of the conditions of non-domination, the language of civility in Pettit's account is thus informed by a wider duty to exercise *vigilance*, where those who abide by civility will be moved to ensure that those in power are held to account. Accordingly, and given the key role that informal social norms play in the maintenance of a free society, citizens will also be motivated to provide a check on *one another's* behavior. Freedom, therefore, depends for republicans upon individual citizens abiding by "civil" norms of ongoing mutual respect, which includes an expressed concern for the equal standing of others and a commitment to checking and contesting exercises of arbitrary power.

In contrast to traditional republican associations of civility with perfectionistic ideals of the good life, rooted in political participation, Pettit's civility is guided by a concern for the basic conditions of freedom, namely non-domination. Such a vision also avoids some of the problems associated with competing forms of civility understood as rules of etiquette or manners, or with images of a repressive "civilizing process" (Berenstain 2020). To that end, the responsibilities of civil behavior for Pettit do not require a commitment to some conservative or homogeneous conception of the good, nor do they demand that citizens take on the burdens of a populist style of political participation. Instead, citizens who exercise the norms of civility will be moved, either by fear of sanction from others or because they have internalized the prescriptions which accompany the norms, to hold themselves, each other, and institutions to account when they fail to uphold the conditions required for the widespread enjoyment of non-domination. On a republican account, then, the freedom of all depends on individual citizens engaging with civility norms and abiding by the laws and rules of republican institutions. Crucially, when those laws and norms no longer serve the non-dominated status of others, vigilant citizens must contest and shape them in a direction that secures freedom for everyone.

When it comes to working out what citizen responsibilities in the face of harmful speech might look like, then, republican theory, particularly in its "critical" guise, looks to be especially illuminating. First, the stress on mutually supportive laws and civility norms reveals the importance of citizen-led action in the maintenance of social freedom. On a critical republican view, a society that deals with harmful speech using criminal and civil law only, without the support of shared civility norms that express the inherent equality of each citizen, would not be one in which members of targeted groups would enjoy the psychological, intersubjective security of status necessary for non-domination. A critical republican civility thus recognizes that basic civil norms are necessary as a component of a shared social life among equals, while also recognizing that such norms must be of sufficient *quality*. Civility norms that maintain social peace at the expense of equal standing, then, are not the kind that will be supported in a republican society. Second, and relatedly, the republican duty of *vigilance* tells us that freedom depends not just on individual citizens abiding by "good" norms and rules but also on their active contestation and engagement with those that are "bad" or which contribute to domination. To secure the laws and norms necessary for widespread freedom, citizens must take an active concern for the unfreedom of others. On a critical republican account of civility, then, it seems that individual citizens have a prima facie duty to secure the freedom of others by contesting and responding to harmful speech. In contrast to competing understandings of "civil" behavior which typically involve constrained non-intervention and non-participation in instances of harmful speech, critical civility demands active and positive civic engagement with such speech via, for example, forms of citizen-led "counterspeech."

TWO OBJECTIONS

In the remainder of the chapter, I unpack and respond to what I consider to be the most pressing objections to critical civility as a response to harmful speech: demandingness and repressiveness.

Demandingness

So far, I have argued that individual citizens, in their capacity as "bystanders," possess a prima facie duty to engage in counterspeech in response to harmful speech as part of their wider responsibility to abide by the value of civility. Given the "fact of ubiquity" of harmful speech, however, this duty appears to be overly demanding, and may be particularly so for those individuals who belong to groups frequently targeted by hateful or humiliating expression. Does critical civility require, for instance, that I defiantly turn up to confront the crowd in a far-right rally that is occurring in my hometown? Does it require that I spend my days on social media "calling out" those who leave misogynistic comments under posts made by women? The criticism that civility is overly demanding is common and, for many, brings to mind an image of the civil or virtuous citizen as one who dedicates their life to cultivating a disposition entirely committed to the common good (Schwarzenbach 1996). While some civility advocates do indeed argue for a civil disposition characterized by common bonds of fraternity or solidarity, the civility I present here is concerned only with the kinds of behaviors that make political and social freedom possible. Critical civility should thus be understood as a guiding value not for all of our relationships with others, but only for those related to our role as citizens (Boyd 2006, 864). As a citizen, abiding by the value of critical civility requires both that I refrain from contributing to the domination of others and that I contest those conditions of domination where they arise (865). Critical civility does indeed require mutual expressions of respect among citizens, but the content of those expressions will include, and often require, a great deal of tolerance for social disagreement and conflict. While basic expressions of respect and mutual constraint are necessary for each to enjoy freedom equally, citizen freedom also requires eternal vigilance, which is, by definition, incompatible with the sort of tight-lipped deference we might exhibit toward close friends and family.

When it comes to dealing with harmful speech, then, critical civility may involve publicly confronting a hate-speaker who targets their victim on their commute to work, or it might include joining our neighbors in a counterprotest against a far-right rally taking place in our town square. What critical civility does *not* require, however, is for citizens to always sacrifice other competing commitments attached to those roles they occupy besides that of citizen, such as those relating to their family life, friendships, career, and so on. How do we know which role-specific demands take precedence over others in a particular case? The demands of critical civility to "step in" and confront harmful speech will be more pressing in those cases where (1) the threat of domination is greater and (2) my relative proximity and potential influence over outcomes mean that I am better placed than others to contest the threat to freedom. In sum, critical civility will require citizens to take a critically reflexive and context-sensitive approach to each instance of harmful speech, reflecting on how a potential response might influence resulting relations of (un)freedom and on how the response aligns with the other role-related commitments they must uphold in other areas of their lives.

Repressiveness

How do we ensure that critical civility does not result in the kind of silencing and repressive practices very often carried out in civility's name? Further, how do we protect against potential abuses of citizen-led contestation, such as those found in the social media pile-on suffered by Steven Salaita? That critical civility is guided toward securing the conditions of non-domination, rather than social peace, demonstrates its distinctiveness from the typical view of civility as a "disciplinary apparatus." While critical civility will require that citizens refrain from employing the kind of "moral" incivilities found in hate speech, it does not require that citizens refrain from using offensive or "vulgar" expression in the appropriate context. Indeed, critical civility will require in certain circumstances that individuals deliberately employ impolite expression or behavior, where that expression is used for the purpose of securing the conditions of freedom.

Noisy and disruptive public protests against an authoritarian or unjust government are examples in which critical civility demands, rather than condemns, the use of "impolite" expression (Lai 2020). Calling out a senior colleague who makes a misogynistic joke, while typically perceived to be a betrayal of etiquette, is another kind of action which may be justified (and even encouraged) by critical civility. While the appropriateness and effectiveness of each individual response is highly context-dependent, critical civility will, in general, be strongly opposed to those forms of formal and informal constraint typically used to stifle expression for the purposes of a more "civil" public sphere.

What, then, can an account of critical civility reveal about the Steven Salaita case? We can understand both Salaita and his critics as exercising their duty to engage in the kind of social contestation that civility requires. Salaita, in calling out the Israeli government and its leaders, was directly challenging the arbitrary exercise of power over Palestinians. While his tweets were indeed offensive, they were not *morally* uncivil in that they did not aim to undermine the equal civic standing of the individuals discussed.[16] The withdrawal of Salaita's job offer, however, was not reflective of the university's concern for securing non-domination. By withdrawing the offer, the university enforced a norm of civility under which speaking out in ways that cause offence carries a harsh penalty. To enforce such a norm is to impose a threat of arbitrary interference on one of the most fundamental tools we have at our disposal for securing and enjoying non-domination: freedom of speech. Where such a norm becomes widespread and well-established, those who depend on an income in order to survive (that is, mostly everyone) will become hesitant to speak out publicly for fear of disciplinary action or suspension at their place of work. Where the speech in question itself concerns matters of arbitrary power, both top-down and self-imposed censorship will limit possibilities for contesting threats to freedom, thereby threatening the freedom of us all.

CONCLUDING REMARKS

The version of critical republican civility I present in this chapter provides a standard by which citizens must abide to maintain a free and equal society. Taking the issue of publicly harmful speech as a focal point, the version of critical civility I present aims not toward social peace nor toward disciplinary forms of social control but rather toward securing the conditions necessary for the enjoyment of non-domination. Furthermore, in contrast to forms of civility that call for polite constraint, critical civility demands positive citizen action in response to domination. Abiding by the value of critical civility thus requires that citizens respond to and contest harmful speech in their capacity as bystanders as part of a broader duty to secure the equal freedom of all.

In working out the extent of our responsibilities to respond to harmful speech, critical civility requires that we pay attention to and remain sensitive to context. This critically reflexive approach also demands that we work to predict the potential dominating impact of our responses to harmful speech (or lack thereof) and that we balance our citizen duties against those we have in virtue of the other roles we occupy outside that of citizen, such as those relating to our intimate relationships and our professional lives. A critical republican form of civility thus provides a value with which to guide citizen behavior that avoids the repressive implications of previous accounts of civility and which provides a framework for understanding our positive duties toward fellow citizens, without whom our own freedom would be impossible.

NOTES

1. For further details of the event, see Mackey (2014).
2. Writing in a press release in support of Salaita, the American Association of University Professors (AAUP) argued that, as "extramural" speech, whether "one finds [Salaita's] views attractive or repulsive is irrelevant to the right of a faculty member to express them" and that, as an organization, they have "long objected to using criteria of civility and collegiality in faculty evaluation" due to the threat that it poses to academic freedom (Fichtenbaum and Reichman 2014).
3. Salaita later described his experience with the disciplinary force of "incivility" charges in a 2016 book titled *Uncivil Rites: Palestine and the Limits of Academic Freedom.*
4. One of the most controversial and "uncivil" tweets of Salaita's asked: "At this point, if Netanyahu appeared on TV with a necklace made from the teeth of Palestinian children, would anybody be surprised?" In his analysis of the event, Mohan J. Dutta criticizes the reductive and non-contextual readings of Salaita's comments which led to his losing his position. Describing Salaita's words as a human reaction to the horrific realities of the violence inflicted on the Palestinian people during the war, Dutta points out how "[n]o communicative code is sufficiently adequate in capturing the grotesqueness of the violence. To call for civility in the face of the incivility of settler colonial violence is a grotesque form of incivility" (2021, 50).
5. In his 2014 article "The Civility Wars," Hua Hsu sums up this divide neatly when he states, "For those on the right, civility is political correctness by a different name, while those on the left tend to see it as a way of silencing dissent. What unites these interpretations is a shared suspicion that the rules of civility exist to preserve our hierarchies."
6. Some notable recent works on counterspeech include Langton (2018b), Lepoutre (2017), Howard (2021), Lai (2020), and Fumagalli (2021).
7. The counterspeech literature developed in part from the following well-known contention, delivered famously by Justice Brandeis in *Whitney v. California* (1927) 274 US 357, that "more speech" was preferable to state restriction of harmful speech: "If there be time to expose through discussion the falsehood and fallacies, to avert the evil by the processes of education, the remedy to be applied is more speech, not enforced silence."
8. The counterspeech literature explores how a variety of different actors might feature in responding to harmful speech using "more speech." Some, such as Katharine Gelber (2012) and Corey Brettschneider (2012), argue for state-led, rather than individual-led, counterspeech measures. Their concern with proposals for individual-led counterspeech centers on two main claims: (1) to place expectations upon individual victims and bystanders to respond directly

to verbal attacks is to place an undue and potentially risky burden upon them (see also Vasanthakumar 2020), and (2) given the already unequal relationship between those who use harmful speech and those who are at its receiving end, they contend that it is unlikely that a "bottom-up" approach, especially when pursued by direct victims, will involve the level and kind of authority required in order for the challenge to be effective. While these critiques of citizen-led counterspeech are compelling, I do not think the expressive state-led responses they offer can feasibly be used to counteract the majority of everyday, cumulative sorts of harmful speech which, over time, contribute to unjust social hierarchies. Indeed, while the state should promote expressive respect for all of society's members (see Anderson 1999)—including in direct response to individual cases of harmful speech—there will be many other cases that only citizens themselves can appropriately and feasibly respond to.

9. Counterspeech takes numerous forms and serves a wide variety of goals. Along such lines, Alex Brown (2015, 257) describes counterspeech as "speech that states or explains why and how particular instances of hate speech (or even hate speech in general) are factually incorrect, grossly inaccurate, misleading, lacking in judgement, dangerous, inimical to the values of society, unjustifiable, and so forth, while at the same time falling short of directly attacking or excoriating hate speakers, or lapsing into hate speech."

10. For a good example of collective, coordinated online counterspeech, see Buerger (2021).

11. Ishani Maitra (2012, 116), for instance, argues that silent bystanders to a case of public racist abuse can, even where they strongly disagree with the racist message, inadvertently confer authority on the racist speaker by failing to speak up. Similarly, Lynne Tirrell, in describing the way in which harmful speech "licenses" certain permissibility facts about target groups, contends, "If we do not challenge false assertions, biased presuppositions, and sexist, racist, or other biased speech, we let their licenses stand. Others can easily take them up and run with them" (2019, 2450). Rae Langton, writing on the potential for hearers to "block" attempts by speakers to accommodate unjust norms, argues, "Hearers who do not block will sometimes, through that omission, make a speech act more evil, whether they mean to or no" (2018b, 161).

12. There has been a long-reigning debate on the extent to which we can properly distinguish between republican theory and certain kinds of liberal theory, particularly those from the "liberal egalitarian" perspective. For a compelling analysis of this debate, see Laborde (2013).

13. One of the most provocative elements of the historiography of the republican revival has been a recognition of the deep embeddedness of republican ideals of civic virtue, political participation, and freedom as independence from arbitrary rule within the liberal tradition itself. Re-imagined in this way, we see republican ideals feature as central components in the work of Montesquieu, T. H. Green, and J. S. Mill, among many others. Part of the theoretical work

of revivalists, then, has been to scavenge and rejuvenate these "lost" elements of the tradition as a method of response to the current crises facing liberal democracies today (Sunstein 1988).

14. While the republican project understands freedoms as they are enjoyed by *citizens*, I do not think we need to exclude non-citizens, such as temporary visitors, asylum seekers, and refugees, from our field of concern when it comes to protecting against domination. While there will indeed be certain freedoms not afforded to non-citizens which are afforded to citizens (e.g., voting rights), these will also need to be justified to non-citizens in a way that explains their non-arbitrariness.

15. Importantly, neo-republicans, by grounding their theory in the neo-Roman tradition, distinguish themselves from those who advocate for a neo-Aristotelian form of civic humanism (Laborde and Maynor 2008, 3). Very briefly, while the former is concerned with securing conditions favorable to a society where individuals are free from arbitrary rule, the latter prescribes active citizen involvement in politics as itself a necessary condition for human flourishing. In distancing themselves from the civic humanists, neo-republicans avoid many of the issues associated with the promotion of "thick" civic identities in contemporary pluralistic societies (Pettit 1997, 8).

16. Critics of Salaita might respond at this point that the tweets were not "merely" offensive and were instead instances of either explicit or implicit anti-Semitism. Granting this interpretation, however, does not change the basic point about the disciplinary and dominating nature of certain kinds of civility. On the critical civility approach I put forward, the appropriate and freedom-preserving response to Salaita in this case would still come in the form of public criticism, as opposed to the withdrawal of the job offer.

REFERENCES

Aly, W., and R. Simpson. 2019. "Political Correctness Gone Viral." In *Media Ethics, Free Speech, and the Requirements of Democracy*, edited by C. Fox and J. Saunders. Routledge.

Anderson, E. S. 1999. "What Is the Point of Equality?" *Ethics* 109 (2): 287–337.

Antoci, A., A. Delfino, F. Paglieri, F. Panebianco, and F. Sabatini. 2016. "Civility vs. Incivility in Online Social Interactions: An Evolutionary Approach." *PloS One* 11 (11): 1–17.

Bachvarova, M. 2013. "Non-Domination's Role in Theorizing Global Justice." *Journal of Global Ethics* 9: 173–185.

Berenstain, N. 2020. "'Civility' and the Civilizing Project." *Philosophical Papers* 49 (2): 305–337.

Billingham, O., and T. Parr. 2020. "Online Public Shaming: Virtues and Vices." *Journal of Social Philosophy* 51 (3): 371–390.

Bolotin, L. 2011. "Disability Hate Speech Has No Place Anywhere—Not Even Online." *The Guardian*, November 9. https://www.theguardian.com/commentisfree/2011/nov/09/disability-hate-speech-online.

Bonotti, M., and J. Seglow. 2019. "Self-Respect, Domination and Religiously Offensive Speech." *Ethical Theory and Moral Practice* 22: 589–605.

Bonotti, M., and S. T. Zech. 2021. *Recovering Civility During COVID-19*. Palgrave Macmillan.

Boyd, R. 2006. "The Value of Civility?" *Urban Studies* 43 (5–6): 863–878.

Braithwaite, J., and P. Pettit. 1990. *Not Just Deserts: A Republican Theory of Criminal Justice*. Oxford University Press.

Brennan, G., and P. Pettit. 2004. *The Economy of Esteem: An Essay on Civil and Political Society*. Oxford University Press.

Brettschneider, C. 2012. *When the State Speaks, What Should It Say?* Princeton University Press.

Brown, A. 2015. *Hate Speech Law: A Philosophical Examination*. Routledge.

Buerger, C. 2021. "#iamhere: Collective Counterspeech and the Quest to Improve Online Discourse." *Social Media + Society* 7 (4): 1–17.

Buss, S. 1999. "Appearing Respectful: The Moral Significance of Manners." *Ethics* 109 (4): 795–826.

Calhoun, C. 2000. "The Virtue of Civility." *Philosophy & Public Affairs* 29 (3): 251–275.

Caponetto, L., and B. Cepollaro. 2022. "Bending as Counterspeech." *Ethical Theory & Moral Practice* 26: 577–593.

Celikates, R. 2020. "Radical Civility: Social Struggles and the Domestication of Dissent." In *Debating Critical Theory: Engagements with Axel Honneth*, edited by J. Christ, K. Lepold, D. Loick, and T. Stahl. Rowman & Littlefield.

Cepollaro, B., M. Lepoutre, and R. M. Simpson. 2023. "Counterspeech." *Philosophy Compass* 18 (1): 1–11.

Cloud, D. L. 2015. "'Civility' as a Threat to Academic Freedom." *First Amendment Studies* 49 (1): 13–17.

Costa, M. V. 2013. "Is Neo-Republicanism Bad for Women?" *Hypatia* 28: 921–936.

Dagger, R. 1997. *Civic Virtues: Rights, Citizenship, and Republican Liberalism*. Oxford University Press.

Dagger, R. 2005. "Autonomy, Domination, and the Republican Challenge to Liberalism." In *Autonomy and the Challenges to Liberalism: New Essays*, edited by J. Christman and J. Anderson. Cambridge University Press.

Daly, E. 2015. "Ostentation and Republican Civility: Notes from the French Face-Veiling Debates." *European Journal of Political Theory* 14 (3): 297–319.

Delgado, R., and J. Stefancic. 2019. *Understanding Words That Wound*. Routledge.

Delgado, R., and D. H. Yun. 1994. "Pressure Valves and Bloodied Chickens: An Analysis of Paternalistic Objections to Hate Speech Regulation." *California Law Review* 82: 871.

Dutta, M. J. 2021. "Universities, Civility, and Repression in the Age of New Media: Surveillance Capital and Resistance." In *Civility, Free Speech, and Academic Freedom in Higher Education: Faculty on the Margins*, edited by R. Dutt-Ballerstadt and K. Bhattacharya. Routledge.

Edyvane, D. 2020. "Incivility as Dissent." *Political Studies* 68 (1): 93–109.

Espiritu, E. L., J. K. Puar, and S. Salaita. 2015. "Civility, Academic Freedom, and the Project of Decolonization: A Conversation with Steven Salaita." *Qui Parle: Critical Humanities and Social Sciences* 24 (1): 63–88.

Fichtenbaum, R., and H. Reichman. 2014. "Statement on Case of Steven Salaita." AAUP, August 7. https://www.aaup.org/media-release/statement-case-steven-salaita#.Y9-rOy-l2N8.

Fine, S. 2014. "Non-Domination and the Ethics of Migration." *Critical Review of International Social and Political Theory* 17: 10–30.

Fumagalli, C. 2021. "Counterspeech and Ordinary Citizens: How? When?" *Political Theory* 49 (6): 1021–1047.

Gädeke, D. 2020. "From Neo-Republicanism to Critical Republicanism." In *Radical Republicanism: Recovering the Tradition's Popular Heritage*, edited by B. Leipold, K. Nabulsi, and S. White. Oxford University Press.

Garrau, M., and C. Laborde. 2015. "Relational Equality, Non-Domination, and Vulnerability." In *Social Equality: On What It Means to Be Equals*, edited by C. Fourie, F. Schuppert, and I. Wallimann-Helmer. Oxford University Press.

Gelber, K. 2012. "Reconceptualizing Counterspeech in Hate-Speech Policy (with a Focus on Australia)." In *The Content and Context of Hate Speech*, edited by M. Herz and P. Molnar. Cambridge University Press.

Gourevitch, A. 2013. "Labor Republicanism and the Transformation of Work." *Political Theory* 41 (4): 591–617.

Hare, I. 2009. "Blasphemy and Incitement to Religious Hatred: Free Speech Dogma and Doctrine." In *Extreme Speech and Democracy*, edited by I. Hare and J. Weinstein. Oxford University Press.

Hirvonen, O., and K. Breen. 2020. "Recognitive Arguments for Workplace Democracy." *Constellations: An International Journal of Critical and Democratic Theory* 27 (4): 716–731.

Honohan, I. 2003. *Civic Republicanism*. Routledge.

Howard, J. 2021. "Terror, Hate and the Demands of Counter-Speech." *British Journal of Political Science* 51 (3): 924–939.

Hsu, H. 2014. "The Civility Wars." *The New Yorker*, December 1. https://www.newyorker.com/culture/cultural-comment/civility-wars.

Krause, S. R. 2013. "Beyond Non-Domination: Agency, Inequality and the Meaning of Freedom." *Philosophy and Social Criticism* 39 (2): 187–208.

Laborde, C. 2008. *Critical Republicanism: The Hijab Controversy and Political Philosophy*. Oxford University Press.

Laborde, C. 2013. "Republicanism." In *The Oxford Handbook of Political Ideologies*, edited by M. Freeden and M. Stears. Oxford University Press.

Laborde, C., and J. Maynor. (2008). "The Republican Contribution to Contemporary Political Theory." In *Republicanism and Political Theory*, edited by C. Laborde and J. Maynor. Blackwell.

Laegaard, S. 2011. "A Multicultural Social Ethos: Tolerance, Respect or Civility." In *Diversity in Europe*, edited by G. Calder and E. Ceva. Routledge.

Lai, T. H. 2020. "Political Vandalism as Counter-Speech: A Defense of Defacing and Destroying Tainted Monuments." *European Journal of Philosophy* 28 (3): 602–616.

Langton, R. 2018a. "The Authority of Hate Speech." In *Oxford Studies in Philosophy of Law*, edited by L. Green and B. Leiter. Oxford University Press.

Langton, R. 2018b. "Blocking as Counter-Speech." In *New Work on Speech Acts*, edited by D. Fogal, D. W. Harris, and M. Moss. Oxford University Press.

Lepoutre, M. 2017. "Hate Speech in Public Discourse: A Pessimistic Defense of Counterspeech." *Social Theory and Practice* 43 (4): 851–883.

Lovett, F. 2018. "Non-Domination." In *The Oxford Handbook of Freedom*, edited by D. Schmidtz and C. E. Pavel. Oxford University Press.

Lysaker, O. and H. Syse. 2016. "The Dignity in Free Speech: Civility Norms in Post-Terror Societies." *Nordic Journal of Human Rights* 34 (2): 104–123.

Mackey, R. 2014. "Professor's Angry Tweets on Gaza Cost Him a Job." *New York Times*, September 12. https://www.nytimes.com/2014/09/13/world/middleeast/professors-angry-tweets-on-gaza-cost-him-a-job.html.

MacKinnon, C. 1993. *Only Words*. Harvard University Press.

Maitra, I. 2012. "Subordinating Speech." In *Speech and Harm: Controversies over Free Speech*, edited by I. Maitra and M. K. McGowan. Oxford University Press.

Maitra, I., and M. K. McGowan. 2012. "Introduction and Overview." In *Speech and Harm*, edited by I. Maitra and M. K. McGowan. Oxford University Press.

Matsuda, M. J. 1989. "Public Response to Racist Speech: Considering the Victim's Story." *Michigan Law Review* 87 (8): 2320–2381.

McGowan, M. K. 2012. "On 'Whites Only' Signs and Racist Hate Speech: Verbal Acts of Racial Discrimination." In *Speech and Harm: Controversies over Free Speech*, edited by I. Maitra and M. K. McGowan. Oxford University Press.

McGowan, M. K. 2018. "Responding to Harmful Speech." In *Voicing Dissent*, edited by C. R. Johnson. Taylor & Francis.

McGowan, M. K. 2019. *Just Words: On Speech and Hidden Harm*. Oxford University Press.

O'Shea, T. 2019. "Are Workers Dominated?" *Journal of Ethics and Social Philosophy* 16: 1–24.

Parekh, B. 2006. "Hate Speech." *Public Policy Research* 12 (4): 213–223.

Pettit, P. 1997. *Republicanism: A Theory of Freedom and Government*. Clarendon Press.

Pettit, P. 2012. *On the People's Terms: A Republican Theory and Model of Democracy*. Cambridge University Press.

Pocock, J. G. A. 1975. *The Machiavellian Moment: Florentine Political Thought and the Atlantic Republican Tradition*. Princeton University Press.

Rawls, J. 1996. *Political Liberalism*. Columbia University Press.

Rini, R. 2020. *The Ethics of Microaggression*. Routledge.

Salaita, S. 2016. *Uncivil Rites: Palestine and the Limits of Academic Freedom*. Haymarket Books.

Saul, J. 2019. "Immigration in the Brexit Campaign: Protean Dogwhistles and Political Manipulation." In *Media Ethics, Free Speech, and the Requirements of Democracy*, edited by C. Fox and J. Saunders. Routledge.

Schwarzenbach, S. 1996. "On Civic Friendship." *Ethics* 107 (1): 97–128.

Simpson, R. 2013. "Un-Ringing the Bell: McGowan on Oppressive Speech and the Asymmetric Pliability of Conversations." *Australasian Journal of Philosophy* 91 (3): 555–575.

Skinner, Q. 1998. *Liberty Before Liberalism*. Cambridge University Press.

Skinner, Q. 2008. "Freedom as the Absence of Arbitrary Power." In *Republicanism and Political Theory*, edited by C. Laborde and J. Maynor. Blackwell.

Strossen, N. 1990. "Regulating Racist Speech on Campus: A Modest Proposal." *Duke Law Journal* 1990: 484–573.

Sunstein, C. R. 1988. "Beyond the Republican Revival." *Yale Law Journal* 97: 1539–1590.

Tirrell, L. 2012. "Genocidal Language Games." In *Speech and Harm: Controversies over Free Speech*, edited by I. Maitra and M. K. McGowan. Oxford University Press.

Tirrell, L. 2019. "Toxic Misogyny and the Limits of Counterspeech." *Fordham Law Review* 87: 2433–2452.

Vasanthakumar, A. 2020. "Recent Debates on Victims' Duties to Resist Their Oppression." *Philosophy Compass* 15 (2): 1–8.

Waldron, J. 2012. *The Harm in Hate Speech*. Harvard University Press.

Zerilli, L. 2014. "Against Civility: A Feminist Perspective." In *Civility, Legality, and Justice in America*, edited by A. Sarat. Cambridge University Press.

Online (In)Civility

LAURA D'OLIMPIO, AMY MCPHERSON, AND
RACHEL BUCHANAN

INTRODUCTION

Given how much of our communication is now mediated via technology, we must ask the question about how we can maintain civil relationships online, with both those we know and those we do not. Educating for civility must include a recognition that our social communities and interactions now take place both in person, face to face, as well as online in the virtual sphere. There is no point in arguing one is better or worse than the other, as both have strengths and challenges. But it is certainly the case that online civility may require slightly different skills, while still being supported by additional virtues (both moral and epistemic) than is required by a physical public square. Our concern is that certain features of technology and social media encourage incivility, so our interest in this chapter is to investigate how we might educate children and young people in preparation for civil online interaction. If schooling may play a part in cultivating virtues in appropriate ways, which we believe it can, then this form of

Laura D'Olimpio, Amy McPherson, and Rachel Buchanan, *Online (In)Civility* In: *The Virtue of Civility*.
Edited by: Andrew Peterson, Oxford University Press. © Oxford University Press 2026.
DOI: 10.1093/9780197653791.003.0005

education should be able to adapt to also help foster and support civil online discourse and engagement, if not cyber-phronesis or virtual flourishing.

Online incivility refers to online behavior that can be considered lacking in civility: behaviors characterized by close-mindedness, a refusal to listen to others and to find common ground in discussion, and demonstrating a lack of empathy. Online conduct such as mocking others, being rude, bullying, and being dismissive of discussion can also be considered to demonstrate online incivility. Taking Edyvane's (2012) discussion of political civility as a starting point, it can be understood that online conduct that undermines cohesion, civil discussion, and consensus building can be understood as incivility. While the internet and the rise of social media have been touted as providing users with opportunities for social connection, identity formation, entertainment, information access, and a means of participation in the knowledge economy (Shirky 2009), recent research suggests that the prevailing architecture of the internet is undermining democracy and fostering incivility (Yeung 2018).

With this definition of online incivility in mind, it must be noted that there are challenges to online civility that must be identified before they may be addressed. Therefore, we will commence by exploring some of the ways in which technologically mediated engagement strains the usual social mores and instead encourages epistemic and moral vices that foster incivility. We will consider how online technologies use algorithmically generated timelines and newsfeeds designed to delight or disgust, creating an affective political economy that cultivates political polarization and hostile disagreement. We focus on how the online environment effects the experiences of children and young people in particular, in terms of the way they are exposed to incivility on social media sites and public news forums.

After acknowledging this structural context, we will consider potential individual responses to social media, which may include epistemic and moral vices and virtues (in the mix are courage and cowardice; gullibility and cynicism; open- and close-mindedness; kindness and cruelty). Finally, we will consider whether one of the barriers to civility, in the form of particular epistemic vices that are reinforced online, might be overcome. We are interested in the educative role for inculcating virtues such as civility itself, alongside additional virtues such as epistemic curiosity, tolerance, open-mindedness, compassion, and intellectual humility that also support civil online engagement.

ALGORITHMS AND THE ECHO CHAMBER

Online activity has changed in nature since the normalization of social media participation. Social media platforms such as Facebook are free for users to use; the business model operating is such that users agree "to continuous monitoring of their online behaviour and the collection of digital breadcrumbs thereby generated in return for services" (Yeung 2018, 259). Zuboff (2019) argues that it is very difficult to participate online without interfacing with the supply chains of these digital data flows. Access to users' data and the monitoring of their online activities has fueled the development of "platform capitalism" (Srnicek 2016), where online platforms provide the means for the extraction of users' data (see also Zuboff 2019, who terms this process "Surveillance Capitalism"). The data is used to train machine-learning-generated algorithms. These algorithmic logics generate an algorithmic identity for users by comparison of them with a data set derived from a large population and offering choices (i.e., nudges) that worked with people calculated to be similar to the individual (Cheney-Lippold 2011; Yeung 2017).

Such predictive "smart" technologies were developed by Google (Zuboff 2019), emerged on online gambling sites, and were refined and developed by advertisers using the data scraped from social media networks (Lanier 2018). These predictive analytic-based algorithms select what people see in their social media timelines, what search results are returned to them, what advertisements they encounter online, what viewing and listening suggestions they are offered on platforms such as YouTube or Spotify. In short, such algorithms provide users with a "personalized" online experience across myriad internet applications, generally without users' awareness (Yeung 2018). In 2001, Cass Sunstein warned of the dangers to democracy that come from the "growing powers of consumers to filter what they see" (8). Two decades on, the online world is filtered for consumers often without their knowledge, consent, and understanding—based on algorithmic interpretation of past online activity. The timelines, searches, advertisements, and articles to read are presented to users by technologies designed for "relentless, robotic, ultimately meaningless behavioural modification in the service of unseen manipulators and uncaring algorithms" (Lanier 2018, 23) to keep people spending time online.

Such technologies also have the function of reinforcing the appearance of *similar* things (be they styles; artistic choices, i.e., of music or films; events; consumables, etc.) in our timelines and newsfeeds. Pariser (2011) describes this algorithmic shaping of people's online activity as placing them in "filter bubbles": a process that generates echo chambers that reinforce people's ideological beliefs and increases homophily online, which in turn can reduce people's tolerance for those with different values and political beliefs. The operation of algorithmically generated online content remains largely opaque to internet users. Filter bubbles or epistemic bubbles operate to serve content that users are likely to agree with, increasing the problem of fake news being spread online, as confirmation bias makes it harder for people to discern "real" news from untruths (Resnick

2018; Vosoughi et al. 2018). Meanwhile, echo chambers actively block and seek to discredit views that differ or challenge the prevailing ones held by the group in question (Nguyen 2020). Consider, for example, the anti-vaccination movement (Muric et al. 2021) or conspiratorial-style thinking (Cinelli et al. 2022) that flourishes online and the spread of misinformation that has swayed recent election outcomes such as the United Kingdom's BREXIT Referendum (Dobreva et al. 2020). The structural dependence of online environments upon algorithmically determined content functions as an impediment to online civility. The "social power" of algorithmic systems (Beer 2017, 3) inhibits opportunities for interactions with people holding different views, reflects users' worldview back at them, and may encourage narcissistic tendencies (Yeung 2017, 2018).

ENDORSEMENT AND OUTRAGE: THE AFFECTIVE ECONOMY OF SOCIAL MEDIA

The algorithmically generated online experience not only exposes users to targeted advertising and content designed to keep them online in communities that reflect their values and preferences but also reinforces the online affective economy. An affective economy operates in social media settings; posts that generate feelings of disgust or delight are more likely to be interacted with (Hokka and Nelimarkka 2020; Savolainen et al. 2020). Interaction with a post increases the probability that similar posts will be presented, thereby creating a feedback loop where users continue to be presented with emotive content in their timelines.

Users are rewarded for the creation of such content by the amount of "likes" a given post receives; Sherman et al. (2016, 2018) dub this "quantifiable social endorsement." Their research has shown that positive social reinforcement (in the form of social media "likes" and other forms of engagement) leads to a greater intensity of social media use. Peer endorsement reinforces certain behaviors on social media, and it is posts that elicit emotional responses that are most likely to be interacted with. Through image sharing, commenting, and reacting, internet users can create and sustain connections with others, to feel united and express their political identity, political emotions, and belonging; in many instances, however, such connections are built on a shared exclusion of those considered to be "other" (Ahmed 2004; Hokka and Nelimarkka 2020). Outrage and endorsement serve to reinforce emotive social media posting. These types of posts undermine conditions that foster online civility, and, furthermore, such conditions can lead to moral disengagement in the online environment.

MORAL DISENGAGEMENT IN THE ONLINE ENVIRONMENT

While digital literacy has received significant discussion in relation to children and young people's online behavior, ideas relating to civility and other forms of moral conduct have been neglected. To attend to this, we now explore the ways that children and young people are both exposed to and participate in forms of online incivility, that is, behaviors such as close-mindedness, rudeness, and a lack of empathy that were mentioned earlier. We turn our attention to some of the ways online communication between children and young people can be adversely impacted by forms of moral disengagement. The impact of moral disengagement on young people's online experiences importantly mediates the way they use the space to develop a range of skills that are foundational to civility. This includes experiences such as navigating interpersonal disagreements and cyberbullying, to more overtly political scenarios such as encountering disinformation or actively taking part in online activism and dissent. The range of experiences that constitute young people's online lives (particularly on social media) highlights that this space is a vital, although often under-considered, site where they learn to be civic actors. But due to the characteristics of moral disengagement that thrive in online spaces the question then becomes: How do young people develop the virtue of online civility?

Moral disengagement is a concept emerging from social psychology (see Bandura et al. 1996) that "refers to a family of cognitive processes by which individuals disengage from their own moral responsibilities in order to damage others without experiencing guilt or self-condemnation feelings" (Lo Cricchio et al. 2021, 271–272). This process relies on the established role of morality and moral-based reasoning in both predicting and moderating aggressive and/or transgressive behaviors (Gini et al. 2022). Moral disengagement works primarily through deceiving self-sanctioning behaviors through a range of mechanisms so that "people can de-activate their moral standards and act immorally and/or aggressively without feeling self-reproach" (Lo Cricchio et al. 2021, 274). These mechanisms include diffusion of responsibility, justification of personal anti-social behaviors, cognitive restructuring of aggressive/transgressive behaviors, distortion, or reduction of the impact of harmful conduct, underestimating one's role in causing damage, and dehumanization and/or blaming of victims (Lo Cricchio et al. 2021; Parlangeli et al. 2020).

The concept of moral disengagement has traditionally been used in research to discuss experiences such as schoolyard bullying but has more recently been applied to the virtual world to reflect on related but distinct experiences such as cybergossip and cyberbullying (Falla et al. 2021; Romera et al. 2021). This has required a certain re-thinking of how moral disengagement operates as it is what Runions and Bak (2015, 401) refer to as a "situated process," as moral disengagement is "dependent not only on the characteristics of the individual, but also on the context in which an individual is acting." The internet is understood to produce a unique context for moral disengagement because it facilitates a certain level of disinhibition (Wright et al. 2019). That is, features that characterize online experiences, including invisibility/anonymity, asynchronicity, publicity, and an absence of space and time boundaries, can increase the negative impacts of moral disengagement on victims, perpetrators, and bystanders alike (Lo Cricchio et al. 2021; Wang and Ngai 2020).

To illustrate the way that moral disengagement is used to think about the online environment, it is useful to consider how Bandura et al.'s (1996) seminal work on moral disengagement has been engaged with in this area of study. In this work, Bandura et al. created the Moral Disengagement Scale, which identifies and measures the mechanism involved in this process. Several of the thirty-two items on the scale specifically address expressions of moral disengagement in the online environment. In their study of the relationship between cyberbullying and fake news, Maftei et al. (2022) draw on the Moral Disengagement Scale to highlight the ways online fake news is bound up with and driven by the features of moral disengagement. The items in this study include statements reflecting aspects of moral disengagement such as moral justification ("It is okay to create or distribute fake news if it helps you protect your friends"), dehumanization ("Some people simply deserve to be the subject of fake news that hurts them"), and distorting consequences ("It's okay if you create and/or distribute a little fake news [i.e., a 'small' fake news], because, in the end, it doesn't really hurt anybody") (Maftei et al. 2022, 4). These items capture some of the key mechanisms of moral disengagement and show how they are shaped by the hypercharged environment of online disinformation.

MORAL DISENGAGEMENT AND YOUTH

Moral disengagement in online spaces also has particular impacts on children and young people, with Bauman (2010, 808) positing that "the technological world in which youth socialize may be a social context that promotes moral disengagement." The significant cultural investment of youth in digital technologies and social media has had profound effects on their sense of self, social interactions, and well-being. Navigating the transition to adulthood through digital platforms and virtual interactions means young people are experiencing new ways of constituting their identities (MacIsaac et al. 2018; McGillivray et al. 2016). Due to this, the way moral disengagement structures the virtual world can be especially difficult for this demographic to navigate as they are still developing their social and cognitive skills as well as exploring their own views and testing them against peers, parents, and teachers (Howard et al. 2021; Peterson 2019).

Affective and cognitive empathy, which are normally generated by social cues, can be harder for children and young people to feel and enact in online spaces. As a result of this, Runions and Bak (2015, 402) argue that "[f]or children and youth who are still developing their perspective-taking abilities, this demand on their fledgling perspective-taking skills may be too great, and they may be more likely to fail in taking perspective, and thus in experiencing empathy." This suggests that a hyper-online younger generation operating in an environment that often works to foster moral disengagement may risk developing a set of maladaptive cognitive processes, in part due to their developing moral capacities.

Additionally, the move to online learning during the COVID-19 pandemic significantly increased the role of online spaces in children's and young people's lives and, in turn, opportunities for moral disengagement in the virtual world that is particularly fertile for it. Not only was school conducted virtually but children's and young people's leisure and other social activities were also pushed online. This shift during COVID-19 created more opportunities to navigate the internet and, in turn, exacerbated the existing risks of online spaces including inappropriate content, overuse, cyberbullying, cyberhate, and misuse of personal data (Lobe et al. 2020; Maftei et al. 2022). Attempts to mitigate the potential and impacts of online risk for young people include parental mediation practices, such as limiting access to digital technology, tracking website usage, and cybersecurity (Lobe at al. 2020, 34–39).[1] Young people themselves also make efforts to mitigate risk, including following advice and proactively taking further steps to protect their devices and themselves (43).

The pandemic also increased the creation and consumption of disinformation around the global public response. It created what Cinelli et al. (2020) call an infodemic, "amplifying hate speech, heightening the risk of conflict, violence, and human rights violations, and threatening long-term prospects for advancing democracy, human rights, and social cohesion" (World Health Organization 2020). Online exposure to disinformation, which is the deliberate creation and/or distribution of false or misleading information with the intent to deceive or harm, is a particular issue for children and young people (Howard et al. 2021, 6). The attention given to this issue aligns with the broader socio-cultural interest in the rise of disinformation in media and politics and the subsequent calls for more robust media literacy and e-safety education as well as greater responsibilities being assigned to governments and technology companies in relation to this issue (Howard et al. 2021). Maftei et al. (2022) indicate that the moral disengagement that characterizes online spaces can enhance the spread of disinformation and can then be used as a mechanism of cyberbullying, particularly for young people in comparison to adults. Furthermore, online platforms may generate negative emotions such as feelings of anxiety and anger that occur as a result of seeing fake news online. These negative emotions may drive users to engage with the content and, in turn, drive further algorithmic recommendations to similar content, exacerbating the negative news cycle and associated emotional responses.

RESISTING MORAL DISENGAGEMENT: ONLINE CITIZENSHIP AND YOUTH

Despite the risk that young people face in online spaces, driven by how the virtual world cultivates the conditions for increased levels of moral disengagement, it is essentialist and limiting to conflate these experiences with an inevitable negative outcome. Lobe at al. (2020, 13) emphasize that "experience with risk does not necessarily mean harm. Risk experiences can also be something that utilises coping strategies and strengthens resilience." Howard et al. (2021, 5) propose that agency can be given to young people in this context through policymakers and technology companies implementing child rights–based regulations and "prioritiz[ing] meaningful connections and plurality of ideas for children" in tackling these online risks. This direction is articulated by the Committee on the Rights of the Child (General Comment No. 25, as cited in Howard et al. 2021, 27), which asserts the need to devise proportionate regulation to

> protect children from harmful and untrustworthy content and ensure that relevant businesses and other providers of digital content develop and implement guidelines to enable children to safely access diverse content, recognizing children's rights to information and freedom of expression, while protecting them from such harmful material in accordance with their rights and evolving capacities.

This framing moves beyond attempts to protect children through restriction and monitoring and instead places the onus on online platforms while acknowledging the right of children to have access to this space in a way that provides them with both autonomy and regulatory protections. Ensuring young people have access in this way to the internet is especially important since "[t]heir presence on social media is an important means by which young people can be actively involved in political and civic engagement, even if—or perhaps because—they cannot vote" (Howard et al. 2021, 18). This highlights how a child rights–based approach to online moral disengagement and risk is bound up with civic, democratic imperatives.

Moral disengagement is in tension with conventional concepts and norms of democratic citizenship, highlighting the potential conflicts that arise as children and young people implicitly acquire this form of expression and engagement through online platforms. Political civility is one such characteristic of democratic citizenship that can be hindered by moral disengagement. For Bardon et al. (2022, 4), civility is not only about politeness but also about public mindedness, through which "regard for the broader public improves democratic governance and social coexistence in the long term." Similarly, in his book *Civility and Democratic Education*, Peterson (2019, 7) defines political civility as "how citizens encounter each other and exchange ideas and interests in the public sphere" and asserts that civility is a civic virtue that "requires that we stay engaged with and are attentive to those whose views and actions we fundamentally disagree with." Political civility is considered valuable from a Western liberal-democratic perspective because

> [w]hile civility alone cannot address major structural issues and inequalities—it is not a complete substitute for justice—when civility actually operates it may well help to support the cause of justice through enabling the interests of marginalised and

> disadvantaged groups to be publicised and heard. (Peterson
> 2019, 10)

Peterson does not, however, suggest that civility is the only appropriate mode of political engagement and instead argues that there are some circumstances that call for "justified incivility." He provides the example of racism, arguing that social consensus around a racist view (e.g., public support for a xenophobic immigration discourse) should not be responded to with tolerance and engagement. In this sense, there may be a discrepancy between civil behaviors. In part, this is about "recognis[ing] that political discourse can become overly constrained by norms of civility, thereby ruling out or marginalising those who do not have access to the forms of capital required for 'civil' deliberation" (Peterson 2019, 30). Curzer (2012, 89) supports this position, stating, "A civil person is civil to people who are open-minded enough to be persuadable through civil discourse." Justified incivility can be appropriate in situations outside this framework, provided these engagements are proportionate and can *"only be approached and enacted as a means to an end and not as an end in itself,"* e.g., as a means to reaching a point where civil political deliberation is possible (Peterson 2019, 31, emphasis in original). This conceptualization provides a structure of political interaction in Western democracies, which positions political civility as the most desirable form of engagement and thus one that should be taught as part of democratic education.

However, expressions of moral disengagement, with features which include dehumanization and diffusion of responsibility, clearly make discussions and behaviors associated with political civility difficult. Good faith discourse across political difference in online space is often fraught as it is disrupted by the disengaging features of the online environment as described earlier, which include invisibility/ anonymity, asynchronicity, publicity, and an absence of space and time boundaries. Some research bears out the connection between the internet and incivility, for example, Keller and Askanius's (2020) study of online hate speech in Germany. However, the body of research on this topic is mixed, with other studies showing that uncivil online behaviors are significantly rarer than civil ones, for example, Rowe's (2015) analysis of 498 website comments, which found only 6% of comments were uncivil in nature.

Despite the potential of moral disengagement and online risks such as disinformation, there is evidence that young people have robust strategies to counter incivility and nurture characteristics of democratic citizenship and the virtue of civility in the virtual world. Wang and Edwards (2016) argue that social media provides young people with a challenging space to test and refine their sense of self and interpersonal connections. In contrast to the moral panic that often characterizes discussions of social media and young people, they show how the internet provides youth with a space of opportunity to "practice relationship management" in terms of learning how to establish, practice, and maintain digitally mediated social connections with a range of people (1216–1217). This ability is central to Peterson's (2019) understanding of political civility described above, whereby the exchange of ideas with others is foundational for pursuing democratic ideals. A critical digital citizenship approach acknowledges this connection by encouraging young people to critically reflect on how digitally mediated publics operate and think carefully about their relationship to online risk, communities, and creation (McGillivray et al. 2016). Following this, there is a push in education to create learning opportunities that respond to young people's online lives. For example, teachers are increasingly using social media to help enhance "professional communities of practice [and] learning communities" that can scaffold students' civic development (Johnson et al. 2014, 10, as cited in McGillivray et al. 2016, 727). In addition, there may be more we can do in educational spaces to help cultivate students' epistemic and moral virtues that will foster civility and protect against vices such as incivility both online and offline.

THE ROLE FOR EDUCATORS

We have seen that moral disengagement is a particular problem online, and it can interfere with individuals'—especially young people's— ability to actively and fruitfully engage in their communities. Some of these vital social communities may exist online (either entirely virtual or partly virtual with additional interaction that occurs in person). Thus, the idea of how to activate a sense of citizenship and its associated moral engagement matters to both in-person, face-to-face contexts as well as virtual spaces. We have also noted that the online interaction may be positive, or it may be negative or destructive— much like its in-person equivalents. The systemic structures that are less visible than individual responses have an enormous effect on how such experiences—for the individuals and groups—manifest. Therefore, the responsibility that lies with, for instance, social media companies, software engineers, content creators, and gaming companies is not to be denied. The ethical responsibility on these companies, and on governments to catch up and keep up with technological innovations in order to keep their users safe, is of the utmost importance. This includes appropriate protection of user data, child protection policies, and a duty to raise public awareness about scams and phishing.

While relevant governance and policies must be in place in the first instance, there is also space to consider the responses and actions of individuals and groups online. We operate within a twenty-four-hour news cycle whereby headlines are sensationalized and images are shocking and we are bombarded with these the moment we log online or use social media. Yet, as individuals we may, to a certain extent, choose what we engage with and how, and how we respond to both these narratives and images as well as to other people online: those we may already know and those who are strangers. There is a role, we believe, for educators to help children and young people in learning to cultivate virtuous rather than vicious online responses. Andrew Peterson defines civic virtues and explains the important link between them and a civil society that supports individual and group flourishing. He claims:

> Broadly conceived, civic virtues are worthwhile traits of character necessary for and expressed within social and political associations. As such, civic virtues are particular traits of character that enable citizens to participate well within their democratic community and which, in turn, enable communities to flourish. (2019, 10–11)

When we reflect, as we have done above, on how the spread of misinformation and fake news online is a prevailing influential factor in the creation of echo chambers and the online affective economy, we as educators must consider what we could usefully do to help puncture the creation of close-minded and intolerant—uncivil—spaces online. Alongside citizenship education and the focused cultivation of civility we believe that we need to equip students with the epistemic skills they need to identify and then to critically resist the lure and appeal of fake news and disinformation and their associated campaigns. By fostering epistemic virtues, supported by moral virtues, in the virtual sphere—which is an extension of how we might encourage children to act anyway—this can help create an online environment characterized by civility rather than incivility and by democratic citizenship as opposed to moral disengagement.

EDUCATING FOR ONLINE CIVILITY

Given that online technologies use algorithmically generated time-lines and newsfeeds that are designed to delight or disgust, we have argued that an affective political economy is created that fosters political polarization and hostile disagreement. Individuals may respond to one another and to the news stories and images they encounter online in various ways. The habits we have may see us draw upon epistemic as well as moral vices and virtues: we may be civil or uncivil, courageous, or cowardly; at times we may be gullible or cynical, we may habitually respond with open- or close-mindedness, or with kindness or cruelty. It takes effort to slow down and respond using epistemic and moral virtues rather than vices given the features of, for instance, social media applications that are designed to encourage fast and emotional reactions rather than considered and thoughtful responses.

Educators must try and encourage their students to respond in ways that exhibit the moral and epistemic virtues, to be reasonable, open-minded, and compassionate, while taking care to avoid epistemic vices. Quassim Cassam (2019) describes epistemic vices, such as arrogance, close-mindedness, and dogmatism, as blameworthy character traits, attitudes, or ways of thinking that obstruct efforts to gain, keep, or share knowledge. On this account, there are negative epistemic consequences of epistemic vices for which the moral agent is in some sense responsible—that is, if they are aware of these vices and can possibly change or reduce them. In this way, epistemic vices are to be differentiated from cognitive defects (which one may not be aware of or be able to alter). Epistemic vices and virtues, along with moral vices and virtues, may hinder or help us to understand and gain knowledge, and this is true online as well as offline. There are specific ways such virtues and vices manifest online, and as we have considered above, we must take note of whether they are encouraged or discouraged by the technological tools at our disposal.

Responding carefully and with compassion often takes time: time to pause and consider where another person is coming from and how they might be feeling, or time to think about the potential consequences of our actions or responses. Taking this time to respond may be difficult given that technological tools usually work to push users to *hurry* and respond *instantaneously*, to make fast decisions and react (emotionally) rather than respond (thoughtfully and reasonably). When we do not take this time, we may also forget that we are engaging with and responding to real human beings, who are *like us* in the respect that they too have thoughts and feelings. Because communication online is technologically mediated, people sometimes forget that they are interacting with such real-life others. This is where the idea of the virtues of civility and compassion become of paramount importance. It is not simply critical, analytical, and rational thinking skills that we need good citizens to possess; it is also rational emotions such as compassion and the ability to work and play in collaborative settings alongside others.

One pedagogical tool to support compassionate and reasonable responses to others is dialogical modes of inquiry, particularly as an option to replace debate (D'Olimpio 2020). Dialogical inquiry is aimed at collective seeking of truth, with counter-arguments and their responses acting as a method to substantiate and evidence claims. This approach stands in contrast to debate, a communication style which is adversarial and often framed as winning and, correspondingly, seeking to defeat one's opponents. It is the skills of dialogue rather than debate that can increase civil discourse online.

A specific example of dialogical pedagogy is the philosophical community of inquiry (CoI) practiced by advocates of Philosophy for Children (P4C). A teacher will usually commence a lesson with a provocation such as a text (for example, an age-appropriate story, an object, a video, an image, or a news headline) and students' questions will be sought through a brainstorming session or in pairs. One exercise to help students express and identify philosophical questions is "The Question Quadrant" (Cam 2006). After reading a story, for instance, students may brainstorm questions that emerge from engaging with the text and can then categorize them into one of four spaces on the quadrant designated as "open" or "closed" questions (horizontal axis), or "textual" or "intellectual" questions (vertical axis). A question is considered philosophical if it is open, "deep," and does not yield an immediately obvious answer. Philosophical questions will be those placed within the "open" and "intellectual" quadrant within Cam's Question Quadrant. These questions differ from questions which can be answered by looking in the text (closed, textual), or by asking an expert (closed, intellectual), or by using one's imagination (open, textual). A philosophical question invites contemplation, wonder, and will generate multiple answers, even though some answers will be more reasonable, justified, and sound than others. It is philosophical questioning that is at the heart of a well-functioning CoI, along with trust (D'Olimpio 2016) and an empathetic engagement with others.

After reading through a text and playing an activity such as a concept game (see Cam 2016), for instance, one can use the Question Quadrant (or another method) to draw out philosophical questions focused on the central theme the teacher wishes to explore. After collecting the students' philosophical questions, displaying them, and democratically voting on or deciding upon one to stimulate dialogue, the classroom is arranged into a CoI. The CoI sees participants seated in an inward-facing circle, with the teacher acting as a facilitator of the discussion rather than the authoritative source of all knowledge. This radically alters the traditional role of the teacher whose purpose is not to teach facts which are memorized by students in preparation for testing but, rather, to encourage students to explore ideas and engage in a dialogue for its own sake, using the chosen question as the focal point of the discussion. For example, a CoI may explore whether technology helps or hinders humanity, and various perspectives and examples could be critically explored by the students.

The CoI sees participants willing to critically engage with their own and others' ideas, while compassionately responding to the views of others as they are encountered. Instead of thinking that there are "no correct answers," the philosophical CoI should see participants move further away from the worst answers or arguments and move toward more reasonable, justified ideas. As Splitter (2011, 497) explains:

> Participating in a CoI allows students, individually and collaboratively, to develop their own ideas and perspectives based on appropriately rigorous modes of thinking and against the background of a thorough understanding and appreciation of those ideas and perspectives that, having stood the test of time, may be represented as society's best view of things to date.

While it is true that with quicker access to information than ever previously, citizens are able to be better informed, we are also better at generating echo chambers that serve to reinforce our existing opinions, biases, and assumptions. Equipping students with epistemic virtues such as a critical intellect and epistemic humility should help morally engaged individuals to be motivated to question what they are seeing or hearing, and then seek out further appropriate, academic research in order to debunk conspiracy theories and combat misinformation and fake news (McPherson et al. 2022). The CoI pedagogy is designed to cultivate these critical and dialogical skills, while also offering an experience that prioritizes the rules of civil engagement in the face of diverse points of view, skills and experiences that are needed both online and offline. Cassam is somewhat optimistic (a view he calls "qualified optimism") that we may improve with respect to our epistemic vices (2019, 169). This necessarily involves first recognizing such epistemic vices. Such self-improvement, he claims, relies on the moral agent being motivated to tackle their own character vices as well as being willing and able to make the necessary effort required in the form of self-control. Some, which he labels as "stealthy" epistemic vices, such as implicit biases, are resistant to self-improvement strategies because it is in the nature of the epistemic vice to resist detection and to deprive us of the motivation to eliminate them. Yet, to the extent that we can work to avoid and eliminate epistemic vices, with a view to being more critically engaged, then we should.

This inevitably raises the possibility of education and the role for teachers in assisting with recognizing and striving for improvement with respect to our epistemic vices. Cassam (2019, 120) emphasizes the centrality of the role of education when he states:

> [T]he only hope for a society that cares about knowledge is to equip its citizens with the intellectual and other means to distinguish truth from lies. Education can play a vital role here, especially if it can focus on the development of pupils' critical faculties and epistemic virtues such as rigour and respect for evidence. Only the inculcation and cultivation of the ability to distinguish truth from lies can prevent our knowledge from being undermined by malevolent individuals and organizations that peddle falsehoods for their own political or economic ends.

In a footnote, he adds, "D'Ancona is right to suggest, therefore, that it should be a core task of primary education 'to teach children how to discriminate from the digital torrent' (2017: 114)" (Cassam 2019, 120). Teaching children and young people critical thinking skills and ethics makes a very good starting point to equipping them with the epistemic and moral virtues they need in our techno-logical society, to create a civil online community (Buchanan et al. 2021; D'Olimpio 2018, 2021). A key component of such educa-tion is the chance for students to practice these skills, and this is precisely the benefit of the CoI pedagogy. The students are given opportunities in class to challenge what they see and hear in a constructive way with the aim of seeking truth and gaining knowl-edge, while also understanding that there is room for reasonable disagreement among people. These are the skills that are vital for online civility. This holistic approach to education may be realized in multiple ways, but the teaching of critical thinking skills, or phi-losophy and ethics, is one good way of tackling what is a pressing social issue. Supporting such teaching with dialogical pedagogies, for instance, those favored by proponents of teaching philosophy to children, is one constructive approach designed at cultivating civic-mindedness and the virtue of civility that can be applied in the public sphere, both on- and offline.

Online civility is supported by additional virtues—both moral and epistemic. This is because the online public sphere requires users to be able to discern between what is true and what is manipulated, sensationalized, or false. It requires civic engagement that is marked by an ability to reasonably disagree and to tolerate differing views—and/or to know when to log off and step away when the discussion is too highly charged. One way of developing applicable epistemic vir-tues that support online civility is through the teaching of philosophy which focuses on the development of critical thinking skills and the avoidance of fallacies (flawed argumentation or fallacious reasoning). Such critical thinking skills may also be disseminated throughout the curriculum and manifest in all subjects. While we have highlighted CoI as a means of fostering online civility, other pedagogical strate-gies are also useful when seeking to maximize students' opportuni-ties to practice such techniques, i.e., Socratic dialogue, questioning, student-centered investigation that involves collaborative group work. Such pedagogies may be included in any subject taught in schools, yet such pedagogies find a natural home in the discipline of philosophy (Hand 2018).

By having such epistemic tools at their disposal, young people will be better equipped to be able to navigate the claims and arguments they encounter online. By practicing reasonable and caring dialogue in their classrooms and discussing the ethical and social issues associated with technology and social media, they will then be encouraged to pause and *think* and *consider* rather than simply to react emotionally. This may not be easy, given the technological features we have discussed above, yet if the habit is cultivated it will provide more resilience for those seeking to participate in civil online fora.

CONCLUSION

Given how much time children and young people spend online, we want them to be able to engage in and help create a civil online community, one in which they are safe to explore ideas with others and learn to respect and tolerate diverse people who hold views that differ from their own. The creation and maintenance of such a civil online community relies upon many features central to active citizenship within a democratic society. It will first rely upon governing structures that help to protect everyone, but particularly vulnerable people such as children and young people, online. This may take the form of enforceable policies, safety checks, appropriate labeling (e.g., age ratings), and ethical company practices that do not target youth in unethical ways (i.e., with their advertising). A civil online community then also relies upon educating the general public so that their awareness and understanding of scams, phishing, fake news, etc. is enhanced and community guidelines for responses are set and maintained (this may take the form of moderated online forums, for instance). But then there is also room for individual responses and reactions to what is experienced online, and explicit education for epistemic virtues, which are also supported by relevant moral virtues, is useful. Teaching children and young people epistemic virtues such as being open-minded, critically engaged, epistemically humble, intellectually curious, intellectually tolerant, and seeking evidence for propositions in an effort to recognize justified and substantiated claims helps them to be responsible active citizens in the online world.

In this chapter we have considered the challenges facing us when we seek to promote the virtue of civility online. We have explained how online technologies use algorithmically generated timelines and newsfeeds to create an affective political economy that fosters strong emotions, political polarization, and hostile disagreement. Additionally, social media works to encourage quick, emotional reactions rather than considered compassionate responses to others. Such features of social media are particularly pernicious to children and young people who are increasingly likely to encounter cyberbullying, cyberhate, and inappropriate content online. Added to this is the torrent of misinformation, AI-generated content, and fake news that young users of social media encounter, which they must also navigate as they seek information and facts. In light of the features of online technology that lend themselves to incivility, epistemic vices, and moral disengagement, we have defended a role for educators in teaching the epistemic virtues—supported by moral virtues—that support constructive online engagement by individuals. We acknowledge that this alone is only one part of the solution to addressing online incivility, given the structural features of social media that mediate against civility. Nevertheless, we maintain that epistemic virtues such as criticality, intellectual tolerance, and intellectual humility may be taught, role-modeled, and encouraged in educational spaces, and these are dispositions that are required to support civil online engagement given how quickly online disagreement descends into hostile argumentation. We concluded by briefly detailing pedagogies specifically designed to support the development of such epistemic virtues, such as Socratic dialogue, questioning, and student-centered investigations that are well exemplified in the teaching of philosophy, especially in the community of inquiry.

It is vital that we teach children how to engage critically, ethically, and responsibly online. It is crucial that we educate them to understand that they are engaging in a virtual public space and, as such, their interactions and contributions ought to be civil. The online world crosses national borders and in this way sees us operating as global citizens in a digital realm. For young people who are part of a generation that is immersed in digital technologies, they can make use of technology to mediate many experiences they have, to inform the construction of their identities, to morally engage, and to participate in democratic processes (consider the school strikes for climate rallies and protests as a potent example that were started by a school-age individual, Greta Thunberg, before she was able to legally vote, and her message and action quickly spread to influence the world and school-age children worldwide). In this way, young people's contributions in the virtual sphere make a difference, and we as educators want them to *care* about the effects their actions may have. The role for education to help support online civility must therefore include cognitive components alongside its formative and affective morally educative aspects if we hope to bring it about that our citizens are not only reasonable but also motivated by appropriate dispositions and wish to act in a way that promotes flourishing—not just their own, but also that of the community in which they live, whether that be online or "irl": in real life.

NOTE

1. In light of these concerns, in 2026 the Australian Government enacted a world leading *Social Media Minimum Age Bill*, establishing a minimum age of 16 for access to specified age-restricted social media platforms. The Act provides expanded regulatory authority to require increased transparency and accountability from technology companies, marking a shift from voluntary industry compliance toward enforceable mechanisms for child and youth online safety.

REFERENCES

Ahmed, S. 2004. "Collective Feelings Or, The Impressions Left by Others." *Theory, Culture & Society* 21 (2): 25–42. https://doi.org/10.1177/0263276404042133.

Bandura, A., C. Barbaranelli, G. V. Caprara, and C. Pastorelli. 1996. "Mechanisms of Moral Disengagement in the Exercise of Moral Agency." *Journal of Personality and Social Psychology* 71 (2): 364–374. https://doi.org/10.1037/0022-3514.71.2.364.

Bardon, A., M. Bonotti, S. T. Zech, and W. Ridge. 2022. "Disaggregating Civility: Politeness, Public-Mindedness and Their Connection." *British Journal of Political Science* 53 (1): 308–325. https://doi.org/10.1017/s000712342100065x.

Bauman, S. 2010. "Cyberbullying in a Rural Intermediate School: An Exploratory Study." *Journal of Early Adolescence* 30 (6): 803–833. https://doi.org/10.1177/0272431609350927.

Beer, D. 2017. "The Social Power of Algorithms." *Information, Communication & Society* 20 (1): 1–13.

Buchanan, Rachel Anne, Daniella Jasmin Forster, Samuel Douglas, et al. 2022. "Philosophy of Education in a New Key: Exploring New Ways of Teaching and Doing Ethics in Education in the 21st Century." *Educational Philosophy and Theory* 54 (8): 1178–1197. doi:10.1080/00131857.2021.1880387.

Cam, P. 2006. *Twenty Thinking Tools*. ACER. A modified version of the Question Quadrant retrieved from http://www.philosophyineducation.com/resources/Question+Quadrant.pdf.

Cam, P. 2016. "Basic Operations in Reasoning and Conceptual Analysis." *Journal of Philosophy in Schools* 3 (2): 7–18.

Cassam, Q. 2019. *Vices of the Mind: From the Intellectual to the Political*. Oxford University Press.

Cheney-Lippold, J. 2011. "A New Algorithmic Identity: Soft Biopolitics and the Modulation of Control." *Theory, Culture & Society* 28 (6): 164–181. doi:10.1177/0263276411424420.

Cinelli, M., G. Etta, M. Avalle, et al. 2022. "Conspiracy Theories and Social Media Platforms." *Current Opinion in Psychology* 47: 101407. https://doi.org/10.1016/j.copsyc.2022.101407.

Cinelli, M., W. Quattrociocchi, A. Galeazzi, et al. 2020. "The COVID-19 Social Media Infodemic." *Scientific Reports* 10 (1): 16598. https://doi.org/10.1038/s41598-020-73510-5.

Curzer, H. J. 2012. "An Aristotelian Account of Civility." In *Civility in Politics and Education*, edited by D. S. Mower and W. L. Robison. Routledge.

D'Ancona, M. 2017. *Post Truth: The New War on Truth and How to Fight Back*. Ebury Press.

Dobreva, D., D. Grinnell, and M. Innes. 2020. "Prophets and Loss: How 'Soft Facts' on Social Media Influenced the Brexit Campaign and Social Reactions to the Murder of Jo Cox MP." *Policy & Internet* 12 (2): 144–164. https://doi.org/10.1002/poi3.203.

D'Olimpio, L. 2016. "Trust As a Virtue in Education." *Educational Philosophy and Theory* 50 (2): 193–202.

D'Olimpio, L. 2018. *Media and Moral Education: A Philosophy of Critical Engagement*. Routledge.

D'Olimpio, L. 2020. "Dialogue, Not Debate: How Philosophy Should Help Us to Be Compassionate As Well As Critical." *Eton Journal for Innovation and Research in Education* 4: 57–59.

D'Olimpio, L. 2021. "Critical Perspectivism: Educating for a Moral Response to Media." *Journal of Moral Education* 50 (1): 92–103.

Edyvane, D. 2012. "What Is the Point of a Public Morality?" *Political Studies* 60 (1): 147–162. https://doi.org/10.1111/j.1467-9248.2011.00894.x.

Falla, D., R. Ortega-Ruiz, and E. M. Romera. 2021. "Mechanisms of Moral Disengagement in the Transition from Cybergossip to Cyberbullying: A Longitudinal Study." *International Journal of Environmental Research and Public Health* 18 (3): 1000. https://doi.org/10.3390/ijerph18031000.

Gini, G., R. Thornberg, K. Bussey, F. Angelini, and T. Pozzoli. 2022. "Longitudinal Links of Individual and Collective Morality with Adolescents' Peer Aggression." *Journal of Youth and Adolescence* 51 (3): 524–539. https://doi.org/10.1007/s10964-021-01518-9.

Hand, M. 2018. "On the Distinctive Educational Value of Philosophy." *Journal of Philosophy in Schools* 5 (1): 4–19. https://jps.bham.ac.uk/articles/abstract/10.21913/jps.v5i1.1481/.

Johnson, L., S. Adams Becker, V. Estrada, A. Freeman, P. Kampylis, R. Vuorikari, and Y. Punie. 2014. *Horizon Report Europe: 2014 Schools Edition*. Publications Office of the European Union/The New Media Consortium. https://publications.jrc.ec.europa.eu/repository/handle/JRC90385.

Lanier, J. 2018. *Ten Arguments for Deleting Your Social Media Accounts Right Now*. Bodley Head.

Lobe, B., A. Velicu, E. Staksrud, S. Chaudron, and R. Di Gioia. 2020. *How Children (10–18) Experienced Online Risks During the Covid-19 Lockdown—Spring 2020.* Publications Office of the European Union.

Lo Cricchio, M. G., C. García-Poole, L. W. te Brinke, D. Bianchi, and E. Menesini. 2021. "Moral Disengagement and Cyberbullying Involvement: A Systematic Review." *European Journal of Developmental Psychology* 18 (2): 271–311. https://doi.org/10.1080/17405629.2020.1782186.

Hokka, J., and M. Nelimarkka. 2020. "Affective Economy of National-Populist Images: Investigating National and Transnational Online Networks Through Visual Big Data." *New Media & Society* 22 (5): 770–792. https://doi.org/10.1177/1461444819868686.

Howard, P. N., L. Neudert, and N. Prakash. 2021. *Digital Misinformation/Disinformation and Children.* UNICEF Office of Global Insight and Policy.

Keller, N., and T. Askanius. 2020. "Combatting Hate and Trolling with Love and Reason? A Qualitative Analysis of the Discursive Antagonisms Between Organized Hate Speech and Counterspeech Online." *Studies in Communication | Media* 9 (4): 540–572. https://doi.org/10.5771/2192-4007-2020-4-540.

MacIsaac, S., J. Kelly, and S. Gray. 2018. "'She Has Like 4000 Followers!' The Celebrification of Self Within School Social Networks." *Journal of Youth Studies* 21 (6): 816–835. https://doi.org/10.1080/13676261.2017.1420764.

Maftei, A., A.-C. Holman, and I.-A. Merlici. 2022. "Using Fake News as Means of Cyber-Bullying: The Link with Compulsive Internet Use and Online Moral Disengagement." *Computers in Human Behavior* 127: 107032. https://doi.org/10.1016/j.chb.2021.107032.

McGillivray, D., G. McPherson, J. Jones, and A. McCandlish. 2016. "Young People, Digital Media Making and Critical Digital Citizenship." *Leisure Studies* 35 (6): 724–738. https://doi.org/10.1080/02614367.2015.1062041.

Mcpherson, M., D. Forster, and K. Kerr. 2022. "Controversial Issues in the Australian Educational Context: Dimension of Politics, Policy and Practice." *Asia-Pacific Journal of Teacher Education* 51 (2): 113–127. https://doi.org/10.1080/1359866X.2022.2152310.

Muric, G., Y. Wu, and E. Ferrara. 2021. "COVID-19 Vaccine Hesitancy on Social Media: Building a Public Twitter Data Set of Antivaccine Content, Vaccine Misinformation, and Conspiracies." *JMIR Public Health and Surveillance* 7 (11): e30642. https://doi.org/10.2196/30642.

Nguyen, C. Thi. 2020. "Echo Chambers and Epistemic Bubbles." *Episteme* 17 (2): 141–161. https://doi.org/10.1017/epi.2018.32.

Pariser, E. 2011. *The Filter Bubble: What the Internet Is Hiding from You.* Penguin Press.

Parlangeli, O., E. Marchigiani, S. Guidi, M. Bracci, A. Andreadis, and R. Zambon. 2020. "I Do It Because I Feel That . . . Moral Disengagement and Emotions in Cyberbullying and Cybervictimisation." In *Social Computing and Social*

Media: Design, Ethics, User Behavior, and Social Network Analysis, edited by G. Meiselwitz. Springer.

Peterson, A. 2019. *Civility and Democratic Education*. Springer.

Resnick, B. 2018. "False News Stories Travel Faster and Farther on Twitter Than the Truth." *Vox*, March 8. https://www.vox.com/science-and-health/2018/3/8/17085928/fake-news-study-mit-science.

Romera, E. M., R. Ortega-Ruiz, K. Runions, and D. Falla. 2021. "Moral Disengagement Strategies in Online and Offline Bullying." *Intervencion Psicosocial* 30 (2): 85–93. https://doi.org/10.5093/pi2020a21.

Rowe, I. 2015. "Civility 2.0: A Comparative Analysis of Incivility in Online Political Discussion." *Information, Communication & Society* 18 (2): 121–138.

Runions, K. C., and M. Bak. 2015. "Online Moral Disengagement, Cyberbullying, and Cyber-Aggression." *Cyberpsychology, Behavior and Social Networking* 18 (7): 400–405. https://journals.sagepub.com/doi/10.1089/cyber.2014.0670.

Savolainen, L., D. Trilling, D. Liotsiou. 2020. "Delighting and Detesting Engagement: Emotional Politics of Junk News." *Social Media + Society* 6 (4): 2056305120972037. https://doi.org/10.1177/2056305120972037.

Sherman, L. E., P. M. Greenfield, L. M. Hernandez, and M. Dapretto. 2018. "Peer Influence via Instagram: Effects on Brain and Behavior in Adolescence and Young Adulthood." *Child Development* 89 (1): 37–47. https://doi.org/10.1111/cdev.12838.

Sherman, L. E., A. Payton, L. M. Hernandez, P. M. Greenfield, and M. Dapretto. 2016. "The Power of the Like in Adolescence: Effects of Peer Influence on Neural and Behavioral; Responses to Social Media." *Psychological Science* 27 (7): 1027–1035. https://doi.org/10.1177/0956797616645673.

Shirky, C. 2009. *Here Comes Everybody: How Change Happens When People Come Together*. Penguin.

Splitter, L. 2011. "Identity, Citizenship and Moral Education." *Educational Philosophy and Theory* 43 (5): 484–505.

Srnicek, N. 2016. *Platform Capitalism*. Wiley.

Sunstein, C. 2001. *Republic.com*. Princeton University Press. http://assets.press.princeton.edu/chapters/s7014.pdf.

Vosoughi, S., D. Roy, and S. Aral. 2018. "The Spread of True and False News Online." *Science* 359 (6380): 1146–1151. https://doi.org/10.1126/science.aap9559.

Wang, L., and S. S. Ngai. 2020. "The Effects of Anonymity, Invisibility, Asynchrony, and Moral Disengagement on Cyberbullying Perpetration Among School-Aged Children in China." *Children and Youth Services Review* 119: 105613. https://www.sciencedirect.com/science/article/abs/pii/S0190740920320363?via%3Dihub.

Wang, V., and S. Edwards. 2016. "Strangers Are Friends I Haven't Met Yet: A Positive Approach to Young People's Use of Social Media." *Journal of Youth Studies* 19 (9): 1204–1219. https://doi.org/10.1080/13676261.2016.1154933.

World Health Organization. 2020. *Managing the COVID-19 Infodemic: Promoting Healthy Behaviours and Mitigating the Harm from Misinformation and Disinformation.* https://www.who.int/news/item/23-09-2020-managing-the-covid-19-infodemic-promoting-healthy-behaviours-and-mitigating-the-harm-from-misinformation-and-disinformation.

Wright, M. F., B. D. Harper, and S. Wachs. 2019. "The Associations Between Cyberbullying and Callous-Unemotional Traits Among Adolescents: The Moderating Effect of Online Disinhibition." *Personality and Individual Differences* 140: 41–45. https://doi.org/10.1016/j.paid.2018.04.001.

Yeung, K. 2017. "'Hypernudge': Big Data as a Mode of Regulation by Design." *Information, Communication & Society* 20 (1): 118–136. https://doi.org/10.1080/1369118X.2016.1186713.

Yeung, K. 2018. "Five Fears About Mass Predictive Personalization in an Age of Surveillance Capitalism." *International Data Privacy Law* 8 (3): 258–269. https://doi.org/10.1093/idpl/ipy020.

Zuboff, S. 2019. *The Age of Surveillance Capitalism: The Fight for a Human Future at the New Frontier of Power.* Profile Books.

Civility Across Nations

Challenges and Opportunities for Constructive Dialogue Between Indigenous and Non-Indigenous Peoples in Canada

FRANK DEER AND REBECA HERINGER

INTRODUCTION

Reconciliation, the movement of improving relationships between Indigenous[1] and non-Indigenous peoples while maintaining an understanding of how past events have adversely affected these relationships, may be regarded as a particularly Canadian discussion that is in response to the truths of the country's Indian Residential School experience. Topics such as education, health and wellness, language and culture, and labor market participation are captured in the calls to action that emerged from the final report of the Truth and Reconciliation Commission of Canada (TRC) in 2015 and are intended to address the long-standing concern of how relationships between Indigenous and non-Indigenous peoples may be improved. Central to this concept of reconciliation is the need for fecund

Frank Deer and Rebeca Heringer, *Civility Across Nations* In: *The Virtue of Civility*. Edited by: Andrew Peterson, Oxford University Press. © Oxford University Press 2026. DOI: 10.1093/9780197653791.003.0006 dialogue among all in Canada in an effort to confront historical and ongoing concerns for Indigenous peoples such as racism, poverty, and lack of opportunity. The movement toward reconciliation in Canada exists in an era when such dialogue has proven difficult to establish and maintain. Indigenous and non-Indigenous peoples have experienced difficulty in the creation of opportunities to discuss topics of mutual interest—discussions that might otherwise lead to shared understandings and social harmony. Interaction between these groups has been frequently marked by misunderstanding, mistrust, racism, and violence. It may be assumed that within these interactions for reconciliation, civility[2] may be important for all those concerned. However, the notion of civility and the exercise of civil behavior in the reconciliatory commons may be difficult to achieve given the histories involved—experiences such as forced assimilation and genocide still reside in the consciousness of Indigenous peoples in Canada. This chapter will explore how civility may be difficult to achieve in dialogues of reconciliation. To situate this discussion into the necessary nation-to-nation context, representative episodes of interface will be presented. In responding to the principal questions of the book, consideration will be afforded to how shared histories, colonial structures, and racist legislation have led to challenges to civil discourse.

ON CIVILITY

Since the release of the ninety-four calls to action by the (2015), initiatives to redress the legacy of residential schools and to promote reconciliation have become pervasive in myriad areas of public life such as education, health, justice, and media. Such efforts, however, have not been without critiques, including of the term "reconciliation" itself (Chartrand 2019; Koggel 2018; MacDonald

2019; Madden 2019; Wyile 2018b). Moreover, the pursuit of reconciliation in Canada has not been without challenges. It seems clear that one obstacle in the reconciliatory journey is how civility is resident in exchanges among Indigenous and non-Indigenous peoples. Civility, a term that is frequently used in the Western world, implies the attempt of "protect[ing] individuals and groups from ideas that offend, challenge, and distress" (Clarke and Walker 2021, 3; Berenstain 2020). Civility, as commonly understood, is not a universal value—or indeed virtue—in itself, nor does civility necessarily seek to protect *all* individuals. However, if civility is understood as speech and behavior considered morally adequate to sustain peaceful life in pluralistic societies, then civil discourse ought to be exercised with respect for Indigenous peoples, knowledges, values, and belief systems. As we will argue, such civility has been largely absent from discourses concerning these issues, and the respect that is called for here is essential to the reconciliatory journey.

Historical use of the concept of civility has frequently entailed erasure (of such things as political autonomy, sovereignty, epistemologies), dispossession, and maintenance of oppressive, colonizing structures in order to fulfill colonial agendas. In these terms, any definition of civility "involves a set of normative expectations for behaviour that are classed, racialized, and gendered . . . not only oriented toward maintaining a settler colonial status quo, but [to] construct certain groups as inherently unfit for the space of public discourse" (Berenstain 2020, 311; Gaudet and Martin-Wapistan 2017; Vanthuyne 2021; Wyile 2018b). Civility as the exercise of behavior to establish and maintain peaceful interface may be adduced as a colonizing weapon that may problematize the reconciliatory journey. With such a conceptualization, Indigenous peoples have been perceived as uncivil and thus silenced. Ironically, in the name of "civility," much violence, racism, and all sorts of oppressive speech/behavior have taken place against those who work toward reconciliation

(Bédard 2018; Castleden et al. 2021; Koggel 2018; Madden 2019). Canada might have "generated in its self-narrative a description of a generous, liberal, and progressive society that has overcome its earlier bigotries and prejudices" (Battiste 2019, 125; Exner-Pirot 2018), but if the TRC's calls for action are interpreted and enacted through the colonizer's epistemological lenses, those will be working toward assimilationist ends and simply continue to reify colonizing structures, albeit in disguise (Chartrand 2019; Koggel 2018; Madden 2019; Wyile 2018a).

Rather than try to conform Indigenous values/epistemologies with that of non-Indigenous peoples, our aim with this chapter is to explore where, in the name of "civility" and making the public sphere devoid of dissent, challenges in the pursuit of reconciliation reside but also where opportunities arise when nations seek to foster respectful relationships. Herein, we distill the concept of reconciliation, focusing on some fundamental aspects that appear to be often "forgotten" among non-Indigenous initiatives. Furthermore, by analyzing how "civility" is understood in Indigenous contexts, the opportunities for reconciliation in different spheres of life can become more salient. We demonstrate how fostering respectful conversations, improved relationships, and mutual understanding across nations go beyond the confines of a colonial understanding of "civility" and rather emerge as key to reconciliation regardless of the area.

We are not dismissive of the notion that civility is an important and valued dimension of dialogue, especially among those with differing interests, experiences, and ancestral backgrounds. Ensuring that we are mindful of how our actions and words affect others is important and is done in the service of a society that is, to a reasonable extent, harmonious and flourishing. Civility may provide a strong and culturally relevant frame for social interface that contributes to the public good. However, in settler-colonial states for which generations of racism, subjugation, and genocide by colonial governments and their citizens have traumatized Indigenous peoples, the notion of civil interface must be conceptually aligned with reconciliation—the ongoing journey toward a new relationship among Indigenous and non-Indigenous peoples that maintains awareness of and responsiveness toward their shared and traumatic histories. What this might mean for civility is the importance of honesty and the exercise of respect in dialogue for which such legacies of racism, subjugation, and genocide are real and all too current. It may be important to acknowledge that the sort of civility that is exercised in reconciliatory interfaces can and perhaps should be uncomfortable.

While at times being virtuous (we submit that, for reasons that are cultural in nature, the character of virtue is in the eye of the beholder), civility needs to be regarded with close attention to the contexts in which it may be exercised. Should civility provide a positive veneer of past and current issues for which lack of respect, racism, subjugation, and genocide have been prevalent, then the manner in which civility affects dialogue needs to be considered.

Bonotti and Zech (2021) offer an example of such an issue that is useful to the current discussion:

When American football player Colin Kaepernick began to kneel during the national anthem as a protest against racial and social injustice, US President Donald Trump viewed the action as uncivil and disrespectful. Trump suggested: "You have to stand proudly for the national anthem or you shouldn't be playing, you shouldn't be there, maybe you shouldn't be in the country." He went on: "That's a total disrespect of our heritage. That's a total disrespect for everything that we stand for." . . . Kaepernick faces ongoing accusations of incivility. But his case also raises an important question: should we always be civil? As Kaepernick himself recently reasoned, "when civility leads to death, revolting is the only logical reaction." Sometimes we need to be uncivil in order to highlight injustice and fight against it, especially when other means of doing so are not (or no longer) effective. (37)

In Canada, we have borne witness to similar accusations levied against Indigenous peoples. When traditional ceremonies are held on Canadian city streets in response to social injustice, when attempts are made to initiate searches of municipal landfills because the bodies of Indigenous women are believed to be disposed in them and appropriate end-of-life rituals are desired, the manner through which civility is exercised may be regarded as uncivil by non-Indigenous onlookers. These two examples and others like them might be reduced to episodes of a cultural sort by the non-Indigenous observer, but examples such as these that reflect current reconciliatory activities contribute to dialogue of a reconciliatory sort through the media, in school, college, and university classrooms, and in public dialogue.

The cultural dimension of Indigenous reconciliatory activities is thought of as important by many Indigenous peoples. The cultural mores that are resident in the unique manifestations of Indigenous knowledge, heritage, and consciousness can inform how Indigenous people enter and interface in the reconciliatory commons—those spaces in which reconciliation is discussed, negotiated, and hopefully realized. And if those commons feature the necessary confrontation of traumatic colonial histories and actions, then those cultural mores may govern how Indigenous peoples behave.

WHAT DOES RECONCILIATION ENTAIL?

Reconciliation is not limited to improving relationships among Indigenous and non-Indigenous peoples, but it also entails "Indigenous peoples reconciling with themselves, their communities, and their territories and with the treaties they have formed over millennia with the land, plants, animals, waters—everything around them" (MacDonald 2019, 184; Madden 2019; Wyile 2018b)—which must include substantive restitution (Knockwood 2019). Reconciliation also revolves around settlers critically self-examining and critically engaging with the TRC's calls, for example by challenging logics, discourses, practices, and names (e.g., of roads, parks, and towns) that became normalized as settler identity, and by ensuring the adequate remembrance and commemoration of Indigenous historical leaders (MacDonald 2019; Madden 2019; Wyile 2018a).

Reconciliation requires the unveiling and dismantling of pervasive and ingrained colonizing structures which remain until today (Bédard 2018; Berenstain 2020; Koggel 2018; MacDonald 2019; Madden 2019). Reconciliation requires non-Indigenous peoples to "unlearn what is taught in the official accounts of its history and to learn about the histories of laws, practices, and traditions as told by Indigenous Canadians" (Koggel 2018, 242). It is also more than "merely apologizing or as looking back merely to identify perpetrators and make them accountable for injustices" (245; Wyile 2018b). Apologies, forgiveness, and absolution, if destitute of effective actions to restore Indigenous sovereignty and agency, are empty. As Wyile (2018b) observes, "Indigenous peoples envision transitional justice as 'not a wall but a bridge' that brings history into the present in order to transform understandings about ongoing relationships" (609).

Building this bridge requires a new narrative, one narrated by Indigenous peoples, not by the "benevolent peacemakers" because "a settler mindset of benevolence has had non-Indigenous Canadians erase, dismiss, and marginalize Indigenous collective interpretative resources" (Koggel 2018, 250–251; Exner-Pirot 2018). Reconciliation requires Indigenous *counter-stories* (Madden 2019). Reconciliation requires that settlers will "be not only accepting but also helping to roll back the power of the settler state so that Indigenous peoples have more unencumbered space to exercise self-determination and practise their laws and constitutional orders in ways that work for them" (MacDonald 2019, 191). Reconciliation must seek to restore Indigenous political autonomy and sovereignty, legitimizing Indigenous epistemologies and ensuring that they are active agents in and responsible for shaping their own lives (Exner-Pirot 2018; Frideres 2019; Koggel 2018; MacDonald 2019).

But reconciliation is not a one-way street—it is a shared endeavor (Reimer and Chrismas 2020). As such, reconciliation-as-relationship requires solidarity (especially accountability to Indigenous values), organization (developing effective structures to mobilize the power of Indigenous identity and values), and empowerment (through restoration of connection and the "respect that will emerge as we engage imperial power with dignity in a struggle for justice") (Bédard 2018, 99; Wyile 2018b). As such, reconciliation requires the pursuit of respectful dialogue whereby Indigenous voices are central. In entering into reconciliatory dialogue, individuals must not only respect these issues but also the manner in which they are expressed.

"CIVILITY" TO RESPECTFUL RELATIONSHIPS: INDIGENOUS PERSPECTIVES

From an Indigenous perspective, morally desirable speech and behavior are conducive to holistic balance and harmony, which includes the balance within each individual as well as in their relationships. It may be said that a balanced individual is spiritually, physically, emotionally, and mentally healthy (Barmaki 2022; McGregor 2018). Depending on the situation and ethos in which such holistic approaches are employed, virtuousness is subject to individual discernment and may depend on culturally relevant factors. Civil speech and behavior in such instances are directed to establish such harmony. What is important in situations for which Indigenous culture is prevalent is that respect and honesty inform the sort of civility being exercised. Sometimes the speech and behavior that emerges would be regarded as distasteful by the non-Indigenous onlooker when it is regarded as appropriate by Indigenous peoples.

As the purpose of this chapter is to explore how civility may be resident in and problematized through reconciliatory dialogue, what follows will include a survey of reconciliation in the contemporary Canadian context. Although reconciliation is not a term commonly found in Indigenous languages (Madden 2019), the establishment and maintenance of respectful relationships, harmony restoration, healing, and justice practices have long been central to Indigenous knowledges and beliefs systems, which is why the reconciliatory journey is so familiar to Indigenous communal consciousness. Relationships are the cornerstone of Indigenous cultures and beliefs systems; in these systems, trust and mutual respect are essential, but they do not happen quickly (Althaus and O'Faircheallaigh 2019; Reimer and Chrismas 2020). Respect, more specifically, is pivotal to what may be conceived as an Indigenous view of civility. From an Indigenous perspective, respect is characterized by "honest and genuine relationships and connection with those around you," including what Westerners do not consider as living, such as water (Althaus and O'Faircheallaigh 2019, 105; McGregor 2018). Central to Indigenous perspectives of civility is the notion that offence is not necessarily something to be avoided, especially when overly polite speech and behavior may prevent necessary truth-telling and sharing.

Fundamental to respectful relationships is the art of listening in a non-judgmental way, listening "in a way that people feel heard, and of listening and hearing so that people's views [are] not seen as less significant than the leader's opinion" (Althaus and O'Faircheallaigh 2019, 114) so that others can contribute to decision-making processes. Civility across nations, therefore, necessarily entails respect for the lived reality of Indigenous peoples, their experiences, languages, cultures, and politics. It may be important to note that respectful relationships are not necessarily devoid of dissent. However, when there is respect and trust in one another's intentions, the group can remain united and strong despite disagreements. A respectful conversation is understood as thinking together (Althaus and O'Faircheallaigh 2019). It is characterized by honesty, openness to different views, and genuine care. In a respectful conversation, parties do not seek to manipulate (through faked emotions, for example) and do not engage in belittling remarks or verbal attacks (Barmaki 2022).

Furthermore, it should be noted that dialogue is a self-reflexive and relational approach to healing which "permits us to move beyond duality, to grow in our knowledge and experiences, and to elucidate understanding" (Gaudet and Martin-Wapistan 2017, 98). As such, respectful conversations can challenge systemic structures of shame which have continuously silenced Indigenous peoples (Gaudet and Martin-Wapistan 2017) and are thus essential to restore harmony. Therefore, through sharing and listening, respectful conversations allow the simultaneous process of decolonizing and renewing relationships.

RECONCILIATION THROUGH RESPECTFUL RELATIONSHIPS: CURRENT CHALLENGES AND OPPORTUNITIES

The interactions between Indigenous and non-Indigenous peoples in Canada have been frequently marked by misunderstanding, mistrust, racism, and violence—even in/through places/initiatives that have theoretically aimed at reconciliation. Why? Respectful relationships, from an Indigenous perspective, require reciprocity and respect for agency. It should be noted that respect for agency, or self-control, does not mean self-centered individualism because agency is accompanied by respect for others and their opinions (Barmaki 2022). So, when correctly interpreted, reciprocity and respect for agency can transform institutions and societal practices (Koggel 2018). Conversely, economy, health, and education, among several other areas, continue to reveal disparities between nations and how Indigenous peoples remain marginalized in the settler society (Berenstain 2020; Boksa et al. 2015; Castleden et al. 2021; Cohen-Fournier et al. 2021; Frideres 2019; Long 2022; Madden 2019; Schultz et al. 2021). Colonial structures and racist legislation have continuously led to challenges to respectful relationships because assimilative policies, as "soft rights," are not enough to tackle inequality—these are just "an invitation to *get settler colonialism right instead of ending it*" (MacDonald 2019, 186). "Hard rights," on the other hand are

> exemplified by Indigenous self-determination and the return of lands and waters, are less commensurable with the current structures of the settler state, and they remove settlers' ability to exercise "compassion" and paternalism.... Hard rights focus on the practice of Indigenous rights and the shifting of the power balance. (186)

Indigenous counter-stories will necessarily confront colonizers' narcissism, disrupting mainstream understandings of "civility" and the status quo, politically, economically, and socially (MacDonald 2019; Madden 2019; Manning 2020). This will certainly be uncomfortable to settlers who have taken for granted the power acquired through colonization but is notwithstanding vital to reconciliation.

The following sections explore how the reconciliatory journey may be understood in five distinct areas of reconciliatory concern and how civility may be understood and problematized by participants of reconciliatory dialogue. The areas of land, public sector work, justice, health, and education were inspired by their representation in the ninety-four calls to action of the TRC (2015). The reason for the TRC's focus on these areas is it is these areas of human concern where racism, stereotyping, and further subjugation emerge and affect cross-national relations.

Land

Even after the TRC calls to action were widely disseminated and promoted, land dispossession, disputes, and devastation continue to be at the heart of Indigenous–settler relations in Canada (Madden 2019, 296; McGregor 2018; Zurba et al. 2019). The epistemological mismatch between nations continues to favor the settler colonialist's agenda to the detriment of Indigenous values, knowledge, and experiences. Treaties, for example, must not be interpreted merely through Canadian settler courts for they will continuously fail to comprehend Indigenous legal and governance systems. Reconciliation requires "a systematized process of obtaining sufficient information to understand how much land, and what land, should be set aside in an effort to recognize Indigenous entitlement and sovereignty. Any such process would involve negotiation and partnership with Indigenous nations" (MacDonald 2019, 190; Frideres 2019; Zurba et al. 2019)—that is, intentional and respectful conversations are indispensable. But little to no attention has been given to such discussions in settler courts—and even when conversation does take place, as is the case of Arctic affairs, decisions and policymaking have been top-down, unilateral approaches that ultimately seek to fulfill settler's economic and political interests—interests which most often entail disrespect to what Indigenous peoples perceive as living beings (Exner-Pirot 2018; Frideres 2019; McGregor 2018).

A study conducted by Bozhkov and colleagues (2020) illustrates how, if conducted unilaterally, efforts toward reconciliation will not be necessarily conducive to the understood goals of reconciliation. Engaged in the reconciliation journey, the International Institute of Sustainable Development–Experimental Lakes Area (IISD-ELA) sought to genuinely foster respectful relationships with local Indigenous communities in a freshwater research facility located in northwestern Ontario (Bozhkov et al. 2020). Contrary to Western approaches to research which continuously exploit and misrepresent Indigenous peoples, the IISD project invested time and effort to build respect and trust with individuals from those communities, seeking to gain insight into their understandings of reconciliation and how they perceived the institution's efforts thus far. Indigenous participants observed that a major barrier in the pursuit of reconciliation through that initiative was the lack of the meaningful incorporation of Indigenous values, language, culture. The scientific work remained siloed, and, as a consequence, Indigenous participants observed that reconciliation efforts have been marked by an attempt to "teach" Indigenous peoples, thus dismissing and undermining the legitimacy and adequacy of Indigenous knowledges. Participants thus emphasized the importance of ensuring the comfort of Indigenous peoples in scientific studies like this. It is also vital to meaningfully and actively engage Indigenous knowledge holders (which could take place, for example, by establishing an Indigenous advisory body) in such initiatives to ensure that the values and perspectives of the Indigenous community are thoroughly taken into consideration, not just in a punctual moment (Bozhkov et al. 2020).

The issue of land for Indigenous peoples relates to stewardship, protection, and the intrusive impacts from government and industry. For many nations, land was taken through conquest and never returned. For other nations, land was acquired through unfair treaty arrangements that have been, for the most part, broken by government authorities. The inter-generational trauma that has been experienced by Indigenous peoples as a result of territorial loss, and the disingenuous approach government has had to this issue, have made polite interface difficult for many community members. Civility as it is regarded in this chapter was non-existent on the part of government authorities as they engaged in conquest and dishonest treaty acquisitions. The barriers to achieving what non-Indigenous peoples may understand as civility in the reconciliatory journey may require a perhaps concurrent addressing of these issues related to territorial sovereignty.

Contributing to the Public Sector

In Canada, many instances of Indigenous peoples' workplace relationships with administrators and colleagues have been shaped by disrespect, including in the public sector. Such is evident, for example, through use of racist epithets, inaction from leaders when such instances happen, retaliation when achieving positive outcomes, racist acts intended to end one's career, a tendency to devalue Indigenous skills and to assume the superiority of non-Indigenous knowledge (Althaus and O'Faircheallaigh 2019; Murry and James 2021). Indigenous peoples have struggled with having a voice in their places of work and have felt that their interests are not represented in policymaking (Althaus and O'Faircheallaigh 2019). Efforts toward reconciliation have often been merely strategies adopted by institutions to achieve their narrow band of interests while promoting an acceptable social image (Long 2022). Meaningful and respectful relationships across nations, however, are not established by aggrandized envisioning. Rather, the possibility of such is contingent upon non-Indigenous leaders striving to create opportunities to build common ground with Indigenous employees and making sure their needs and interests are met and adequately represented.

Essential to the development of a reconciliatory relationship are, among other things, appropriate levels of understanding on the part of institutional leaders of Indigenous views of civility—especially with regard to how respectful relationships may be fostered. Indigenous peoples recognize the wisdom of their leaders and are thus genuinely respectful toward them (Althaus and O'Faircheallaigh 2019). Such respect, Althaus and O'Faircheallaigh (2019) point out, "comes from people seeing your character and you living out values that they also hold in high regard" (105). Respect is earned through one's consistent application of shared values, such as taking responsibility for one's mistakes and through showing care for others. More specifically, from an Indigenous point of view, leaders are holistic, balanced, and "walking the talk"; respectful and relational; attentive to the "seven generations" principle and traditional teachings; resilient and persistent; authentic and humble; community focused and diplomatic.

The exercise of civility in the workplace must be understood within the context of respectfulness and the manner through which institutional power is employed. It is important to observe that having a voice in leadership does not mean having power *over* others. An Indigenous view of leadership is starkly different from a Western conceptualization of leadership, which is "hierarchical and one-dimensional, characterized by short-term decision-making, a failure to draw on the knowledge accumulated by earlier generations, and a divorce from the wider natural and spiritual world" (Althaus and O'Faircheallaigh 2019, 133). As an Indigenous-centered path forward, the reconciliatory journey calls for Indigenous leadership, agency, and sovereignty. In order for Indigenous voices to be central and adequately represented in the public sphere, Indigenous peoples must have guidance in the realization of current and future relations which are built through respectful dialogues. It is thus of utmost importance that non-Indigenous leaders become aware of the colonial power structures over which they govern and consider the complex systemic changes and the co-existence of multiple forms of sovereignty that genuine reconciliation requires. Workplace relationships in which such respect and equity are not resident may have difficulty achieving a civility that is honest and fecund. Civility in this realm of endeavor may appear to take on a slightly different character when situated within a work environment in which principles related to such things as respectful workplaces and equity, diversity, and inclusion (EDI) practices may (ostensibly) feature. However, the institutional character of many if not all public sector spaces is only beginning to recognize what is necessary to inter-cultural harmony that is responsive to the tenets of reconciliation. Because of the importance that is rightfully assigned to gainful employment on the part of all Canadians, ensuring that respectful workplace and EDI principles are conditioned in such a way to foster civility that supports reconciliation.

Justice

The under-representation of Indigenous peoples and Nations in the Senate and in the government as a whole (Frideres 2019; Manning 2020) may serve as evidence of how lengthy the reconciliatory journey in Canada will be—especially if we continue to pursue reconciliation through unilateral, colonialist-centered approaches. Without meaningful and respectful dialogue with Indigenous peoples, actions such as the Safe Drinking Water for First Nations Act will only reify mainstream, discriminatory, oppressive structures, policies, and government (Frideres 2019). As Manning (2020) observes, quotas for regional seats are not enough to challenge the current system—Indigenous peoples must have a voice at the center through reserved seats. In the absence of such, negotiations have often led to a sense of distrust, unfairness, and coercion among Indigenous claimants (Frideres 2019).

An Indigenous notion of restorative justice, often enacted through peacemaking circles, evidences the importance and value of respectful relationships, as it envisions healing and restoration and emphasizes respect (for all life forms in the natural world), participation, honesty, empowerment, empathy, accountability, and mutual understanding (Barmaki 2022; Frideres 2019; Knockwood 2019; McGregor 2018). An Indigenous view of justice, therefore, is not captured by colonial frameworks. Reconciliation will not develop in such a justice system by trying to make Indigenous perspectives into colonial frameworks, for any conduct which leads to world unbalance is perceived as unjust (McGregor 2018). Only when Indigenous values, knowledges, and culture are honestly accepted as legitimate and worthy will respectful conversations, negotiations, and policymaking begin to emerge.

Civility in this area of social concern relates to how existing stereotypes have emerged related to Indigenous dependence upon the Canadian social welfare system as well as the overrepresentation of Indigenous people in Canada's justice system. Such stereotypes with direct connection to issues of dependence and criminal activity have conditioned civility in reconciliatory dialogue in negative ways. It is situations such as these that support the notion that collective confrontation with historical truths associated with such stereotypes may be important. The final report of the TRC (2015) asserts that the lack of historical knowledge has led to how Indigenous peoples are reflected in public discourse and policy. The way many in the public have regarded Indigenous people has reinforced racist attitudes and has fueled civic distrust between Indigenous and non-Indigenous people. Understanding the historical truths associated with Indigenous people can play an important part in the reconciliatory process. As the TRC final report offered, "To build for the future, Canadians must look to, and learn from, the past" (2015, 114).

Health

Not only is there is a pervasive lack of accessible mental health services to Indigenous peoples in remote areas around the country, but there is also a lack of Indigenous mental health training for Indigenous and non-Indigenous workers (Boksa et al. 2015; Castleden et al. 2021). Cohen-Fournier and colleagues (2021) emphasize that much of the conflict that arises in healthcare stems from epistemological mismatches across nations which continually favor mainstream worldviews to the detriment of Indigenous values and concerns. As a consequence, Indigenous values and understandings of wellness, holistic health, and healing practices are not adequately translated in mainstream services, and stigma and discrimination remain, posing further barriers to Indigenous peoples when seeking health support (Boksa et al. 2015; Cohen-Fournier et al. 2021; Schultz et al. 2021). Indigenous relational and holistic conceptions of health are not comprehended by a Western individualist approach to well-being. "Recognizing and respecting these differences," Cohen-Fournier et al. (2021) note, "is a first step toward meaningful dialogue and reconciliation" (777).

While it is not uncommon to hear settlers' discourses of willing to "do the right" thing, claiming to feel uncomfortable to engage with Indigenous traditions due to lack of expertise has led to inertia and, consequently, the continuing disrespect toward Indigenous peoples' ways of being (Castleden et al. 2021). Therefore, besides the urgent need to reach remote communities and to provide mental health training to Indigenous workers, non-Indigenous health practitioners can play a major role in the pursuit of reconciliation through at least two commitments: refraining from responding based on stereotypes and ingrained beliefs and rather taking the time to understand Indigenous clients' views, perspectives, and values, and seeking to engage in respectful collaborations with Indigenous healers and knowledge holders in order to unlearn/relearn approaches to public health (Boksa et al. 2015; Castleden et al. 2021; Schultz et al. 2021).

In Canada, health concerns are one of the more politically charged aspects of ongoing reconciliatory dialogue. One of the more pressing aspects of the Canadian Indigenous experience is linked to health and well-being. Aspects of the issue of health and well-being for Indigenous peoples in Canada is related to access and being appropriately served by the publicly funded health sector. As many Indigenous peoples still inhabit their traditional territories—many of whom still live within the government-imposed reserve system that was intended to subjugate Indigenous peoples and control such things as access to government services—access to health services is limited and has led to terrible instances of racism in the accessing of such services. The outworking from this aspect of the Canadian Indigenous experiences is continued reference in public dialogue to how Indigenous peoples are, to many Canadians, not equal members of the Canadian mosaic. The racism and stereotyping that emerge about Indigenous peoples because of their health problems and their perceived burden on the public health systems have affected civil discourse.

Education

The concept of civility has surely become ubiquitous in academic settings in recent decades. Although educational institutions such as universities are described as safe spaces for expression and discussion, such "civility" has led universities to become stronger sites of colonialism, oppression, and silencing of Indigenous peoples, including Indigenous students, faculty, and staff. Berenstain (2020) argues that civility functions in academia as "as an epistemic sleight of hand by silencing dissent and quieting speech while simultaneously pretending to promote and value the very things they are cautioning against" (326). What features on many campuses that support this claim are the frequent occurrences of anti-Indigenous racism, trivialization of Indigenous scholarship, and lack of support for Indigenous engagement activities of the sort that are provided to other areas of academic endeavor.

Clarke and Walker (2021) note that reconciliation and academic freedom may not always be able to coexist—several instances in which "academic freedom" took precedence left Indigenous peoples in Canadian universities feeling angry, hurt, unsafe, attacked, and uncomfortable. Episodes in Canadian universities such as misuse of Indigenous knowledge by non-Indigenous scholars, trivialization of Indigenous histories and experiences, and cultural appropriation committed by non-Indigenous scholars and universities—all in the name of scholarship—are examples of how the two may not be able to co-exist.

In a similar vein, institutional attempts toward reconciliation can be seen through the tokenistic acts of indigenizing the university, such as through hiring Indigenous scholars while not providing them support to articulate their worldviews and undervaluing Indigenous ways of knowing (Bédard 2018; Castleden et al. 2021; Schmidt 2019). As Bédard (2018) observes, the reality of Indigenous scholars has been either having to remain "in the cupboard" or facing all sorts of lateral violence from their faculties, administrators, or the university community. Such lateral violence, Bédard notes, could include "outright rejection of participation in Indigenization efforts, isolation, lack of support, verbal or physical assaults, and sabotage, to name a few" (92). Drawing from her own experience, Bedard expands:

Having witnessed other colleagues' efforts with design and implementation of Indigenization, I can report Indigenous participants are often strategically isolated within their faculties and the university community, ignored or avoided by faculty unreceptive to change, receive insufficient staffing requirements, are underfunded, and face verbal attacks, belittling, and dismissals. (92)

As such, the commonly sought goal of indigenizing the academy requires decolonizing oppressive structures, which includes (but is not limited to) university governance, policies, curriculum, and spaces. But programs and faculties will not be transformed with settlers' bureaucracy blaming, apathy, and inaction (Castleden et al. 2021). Reconciliation will not be achieved if Indigenous peoples are continually made to demonstrate the legitimacy of their knowledges, epistemologies, and ways of being. Conversely, through respectful relationships, Indigenous knowledges can be "recognized within the university society as a valid means of understanding and expressing the world" (Bédard 2018, 87)—a goal that can be pursued even by an individual non-Indigenous faculty member (Schmidt 2019).

A major roadblock to the reconciliatory journey has also been posed in the area of academic research. Perceived as "the sciencification of racism," research has become a dirty word among Indigenous peoples because scholarship in this area is seen as most often disruptive and does not offer an opportunity for mutual learning or bona fide collaboration (Bozhkov et al. 2020; Brunger and Wall 2016; Chapman and Schott 2020; Murphy et al. 2021). Genuine community-engaged research takes time; it is not achieved through institutional dialogue (Bozhkov et al. 2020)—certainly a disposition that contrasts with the neoliberal focus on efficiency. Research that genuinely seeks to empower Indigenous peoples must not be led by the researcher's agenda nor even institutional ethical assumptions (Brunger and Wall 2016)—a commitment that will certainly challenge colonial racism and neoliberal individualism. Relationship building and knowledge co-production require mutual respect. Therefore, power imbalances such as "the institutional hierarchy of research, as well as political factors that influence how information is used," must not be overlooked (Chapman and Schott 2020, 934). Research that truly aims at enhancing Indigenous self-determination requires respectful dialogue to understand a local community's values, needs, and interests (which will look different across nations) and must *thoroughly* centralize and engage Indigenous voices from the early stages of designing a study until knowledge from that study is disseminated (Brunger and Wall 2016; Chapman and Schott 2020; Murphy et al. 2021). Ultimately, it is the Indigenous community who must decide *if, when,* and *how* research is to take place—a disposition that certainly requires commitment and humility from all parties. Once this commitment is made and adhered to, a sort of civility that may be apprehended by all involved may be possible.

Such concerns are certainly germane to the education sector. Especially given the under-representation of Indigenous teachers in the public school system, non-Indigenous school leaders have a major role to play (Osmond-Johnson and Turner 2020; Wotherspoon and Milne 2020). In countries like Canada for which Indigenous issues have become more developed, there is an urgent need for curriculum review/development, policies, professional development, and support for assessment and pedagogical practices that are culturally adequate (Madden 2019; Schaefli et al. 2018; Wotherspoon and Milne 2020). For such endeavors, educators must seek to develop meaningful and respectful relationships with the community, working in collaboration with Indigenous leaders, parents, and community members (Osmond-Johnson and Turner 2020; Schaefli et al. 2018). Meaningful collaboration, however, will not be achieved through punctual, partial, "convenient" efforts. Embracing Indigenous values will require time, ongoing dedication, and willingness to disrupt the status quo rather than sporadically trying to fit fragments of Indigenous values in the curriculum or policies so as to portray schools/educational systems as being committed to reconciliation. As Wotherspoon and Milne (2020) observe, despite the pervasiveness of recognition in policy frameworks across jurisdictions that it is important to include Indigenous values in education, "educational practices that build on Indigenous cultural knowledge and orientations continue to be overwhelmed by content, individualized orientations to learning and outcomes, and measurable attributes grounded in Western knowledge and perspectives" (10). A genuine commitment to reconciliation through education requires the challenging of colonial power structures and neoliberal agendas—a responsibility that must take precedence over a merely market-driven, individualistic rationale for education. It requires the sincere willingness to *learn from* Indigenous peoples, not merely teach them.

We've devoted more time to this section on education because of the importance that is assigned to it in the Final Report of the TRC (2015). As the commissioner of the Commission repeatedly stated during his commission's work and afterward: *education got us into this mess, and education will get us out.* Although much of what is resident in the Final Report's calls to action focuses upon prescribed action on the part of various governmental and non-governmental institutions, the fundamental intention with the work of the Commission is to condition a conversation on reconciliation that is not just institutional in nature but relates to public dialogue on the Indigenous experience. It is through education that children, youth, government employees, and members of the public will be better equipped to enter discussions of a reconciliatory nature that is marked by civility. Canadians have borne witness to such attempts at dialogue in the absence of the appropriate knowledge and orientations—those attempts have often featured racism and stereotyping that has problematized the path toward reconciliation.

FINAL THOUGHT: CIVILITY AND THE RECONCILIATION MOVEMENT

The perennial problems among human beings that can lead to consideration of how civility may be established and encouraged in the civil commons are not lost on Indigenous peoples in Canada. If, as was discussed earlier, civility ought to be understood as behavior (including speech) that is considered morally adequate to sustain peaceful interface in those commons in which plurality of perspective is resident, then necessary attention ought to be afforded to the fundamental purposes, interests, and/or trajectories that reflect activity in those commons.

In the case of how Indigenous peoples are situated in settler nation-states such as Canada, the fundamental trajectory that is supposed to inform societal betterment is that of reconciliation. Central to the reconciliatory journey, as affirmed by the TRC (2015), is truth. Discovering truth, apprehending its meaning and applicability, debating its details, and allowing those truths to be subject to development are necessary aspects of the reconciliatory process.

Confronting truth in a reconciliatory ethos can be difficult. The realities of past interfaces—interfaces marked by racism, maleficence, and genocide—can affect and has affected relations between Indigenous and non-Indigenous peoples, and the effects of past harms still reside in the consciousness of many. Confronting these past harms is difficult for all involved. When apologies are made and firm purposes of amendment are declared—usually by governments and religious institutions—they are often made/declared after the difficult task of confronting these harms has been navigated. And the offering of an apology in which responsibility for past harms is acknowledged should not signal an end to the reconciliatory journey. Past harms can leave significant and inter-generational scars for all involved.

One point in this discussion merits restating—cultural dimensions of civility that are held by some in reconciliatory dialogue may affect how civility is apprehended. As most conversations on the topic of civility demonstrate, there is importance assigned to politeness, courtesy, and a sort of kindness that reflects a desirable moral standard. There are, as intimated here, cultural mores that are associated with civility as a means of managing peaceful interface that are so tacitly understood that they don't bear mentioning. It is, for instance, understood to be civil for university students to enter a classroom, sit in an orderly fashion as the classroom and its furniture allow, and face the instructor in a way that demonstrates that they are paying attention to the lecture. Students may yield to custom when they wish to contribute to the class by raising a hand, awaiting a pause in the instructor's lecture, or other tacitly accepted way to enter the discussion. This is civil behavior on the part of the students, but it is also respectful and, insofar as it is in line with the tacitly accepted manner in which students behave as members of a classroom community, it is cultural. From the early stages of formal education, individuals are enculturated to behave in desired ways in learning spaces. The respect that is expected of students toward their teachers/instructors is a part of this enculturation. Culture and its relationship to civility is an important consideration. When the culture that accompanies civil behavior is a departure from that which is widely expected, misunderstandings may emerge.

In participating in scholarly events at Canadian universities, as one of the authors (Deer) often does, it is frequently the case that such events, be they lectures or conference sessions, are attended by a diverse academic audience. Many demographic categories might be reflected in the audience, but it is almost always the case that there are very few or any Indigenous audience members. Yet Deer, an Indigenous member of the Kanien'keha'ka ("Mohawk") nation, leads such events in accordance with his background, his customs, his views on *civility*. Instead of politely tapping the head of the micro-phone or lightly tapping his ceramic coffee cup with a spoon, he says aloud "Kontióhkwa!" (a Kanien'keha word that generally means "group" or "those assembled") sharply in order to command the attention of those present. It is clear that, according to those present at such events, this means of gaining attention to those assembled is rude. Unnecessarily abrupt. Uncivil.

The term "Kontióhkwa" is one that is used to gain the attention of people in gatherings. It is also, when appropriate, the first word of the Ohén:ton Karihwatéhkwen (this may be taken to mean "words before all else") address, a customary recitation that commences any gathering. Concern has been shared regarding the nature of this way of commencing an event or lecture. It is unclear if it is the abruptness that some attribute to it or that it is in a language that most don't understand. But this custom is exactly that—a common means for a Kanien'keha'ka to start an event or lecture. If fact, many Kanien'keha'ka may regard it as inappropriate to commence a gather-ing in any other way.

As stated herein, the reconciliatory journey is one that challenges us to create a new relationship in which such things are respected across cultures, and an understanding of each other's histories, experi-ences, and approaches to cross-cultural interface is essential. In order to enter into and justly contribute to this journey, dialogue across cultures is essential. This will involve confronting difficult histories, truths, and all our respective contributions toward discord, racism, subjugation, and genocide. Civility can and should be regarded, at some level of principle, as an important aspect of our reconciliatory dialogues. But when such dialogues explore some of the most trau-matic experiences imaginable and the inaction of others (e.g., gov-ernment) to redress injustices, civility may not only be put to quite a test, but the cultural understandings of how reconciliatory dialogues ought to progress can be contested. Civility may be understood as virtuous, but the place that respect and truth have in reconciliatory dialogue is essential. If our well-being is affected by our relationships with others in the societal commons, then it is important to ourselves and our fellow citizens to be mindful of our behavior. However, the orientation toward civility ought not adversely affect the journey toward reconciliation as well as that toward moral truth. Honest, reasoned conversation that is appropriately inclusive of requisite perspectives is necessary toward the understandings essential to reconciliation.

NOTES

1. In this chapter, the term "Indigenous" refers to the First Nations (Indian), Inuit, and Métis peoples of Canada and related territories.
2. Herein, the term "civility" will refer to speech and behavior considered morally adequate to sustain peaceful life in pluralistic societies.

REFERENCES

Althaus, C., and C. O'Faircheallaigh. 2019. *Leading from Between: Indigenous Participation and Leadership in the Public Service.* McGill-Queen's University Press.

Barmaki, R. 2022. "On the Incompatibility of 'Western' and Aboriginal Views of Restorative Justice in Canada: A Claim Based on an Understanding of the Cree Justice. *Contemporary Justice Review* 25 (1): 24–55. https://doi.org/10.1080/10282580.2021.2018654.

Battiste, M. 2019. *Decolonizing Education: Nourishing the Learning Spirit.* UBC Press.

Bédard, R. 2018. "'Indian in the Cupboard': Lateral Violence and Indigenization of the Academy. In *Exploring the Toxicity of Lateral Violence and Microaggressions: Poison in the Water Cooler,* edited by C. Cho, J. K. Corkett, and A. Steele. Springer International. https://doi.org/10.1007/978-3-319-74760-6.

Berenstain, N. 2020. "'Civility' and the Civilizing Project." *Philosophical Papers* 49 (2): 305–337. https://doi.org/10.1080/05568641.2020.1780148.

Boksa, P., R. Joober, and L. J. Kirmayer. 2015. "Mental Wellness in Canada's Aboriginal Communities: Striving Toward Reconciliation." *Journal of Psychiatry & Neuroscience* 40 (6): 363–365. https://doi.org/10.1503/jpn.150309.

Bonotti, M., and S. T. Zech. 2021. *Recovering Civility During COVID-19*. Palgrave Macmillan.

Bozhkov, E., C. Walker, V. McCourt, and H. Castleden. 2020. "Are the Natural Sciences Ready for Truth, Healing, and Reconciliation with Indigenous Peoples in Canada? Exploring 'Settler Readiness' at a World-Class Freshwater Research Station." *Journal of Environmental Studies and Sciences* 10 (3): 226–241. https://doi.org/10.1007/s13412-020-00601-0.

Brunger, F., and D. Wall. 2016. " 'What Do They Really Mean by Partnerships?' Questioning the Unquestionable Good in Ethics Guidelines Promoting Community Engagement in Indigenous Health Research." *Qualitative Health Research* 26 (13): 1862–1877. https://doi.org/10.1177/1049732316649158.

Castleden, H., M. Darrach, and J. Lin. 2021. "Public Health Moves to Innocence and Evasion? Graduate Training Programs' Engagement in Truth and Reconciliation for Indigenous Health." *Canadian Journal of Public Health* 113 (2): 211–221. https://doi.org/10.17269/s41997-021-00576-7.

Chapman, J., and S. Schott. 2020. "Knowledge Coevolution: Generating New Understanding Through Bridging and Strengthening Distinct Knowledge Systems and Empowering Local Knowledge Holders." *Sustainability Science* 15 (3): 931–943. https://doi.org/10.1007/s11625-020-00781-2.

Chartrand, L. 2019. "Mapping the Meaning of Reconciliation in Canada: Implications for Métis-Canada Memoranda of Understanding on Reconciliation Negotiations." In *Braiding Legal Orders: Implementing the United Nations Declaration on the Rights of Indigenous Peoples*, edited by J. Borrows, L. Chartrand, O. E. Fitzgerald, and R. Schwartz. Centre for International Governance Innovation.

Clarke, P., and K. Walker. 2021. "Does 'Civility' Threaten Academic Freedom at Canadian Universities?" *Education Law Journal* 30 (1): 1–39.

Cohen-Fournier, S., G. Brass, and L. J. Kirmayer. 2021. "Decolonizing Health Care: Challenges of Cultural and Epistemic Pluralism in Medical Decision-Making with Indigenous Communities." *Bioethics* 35 (8): 767–778. https://doi.org/10.1111/bioe.12946.

Exner-Pirot, H. 2018. "Friend or Faux? Trudeau, Indigenous Issues and Canada's Brand." *Canadian Foreign Policy Journal* 24 (2): 165–181. https://doi.org/10.1080/11926422.2018.1461667.

Frideres, J. 2019. *Arrows in a Quiver: Indigenous–Canadian Relations from Contact to the Courts*. University of Regina Press.

Gaudet, J., and L. Martin-Wapistan. 2017. "Learning Through Conversation: An Inquiry into Shame." In *Power Through Testimony: Reframing Residential Schools in the Age of Reconciliation*, edited by K. Vanthuyne and B. Capitaine. UBC Press.

Knockwood, C. 2019. "Rebuilding Relationships and Nations: A Mi'kmaw Perspective of the Path to Reconciliation." In *Braiding Legal Orders: Implementing the United Nations Declaration on the Rights of Indigenous Peoples*, edited by J. Borrows, L. Chartrand, O. E. Fitzgerald and R. Schwartz. Centre for International Governance Innovation.

Koggel, C. 2018. "Epistemic Injustice in a Settler Nation: Canada's History of Erasing, Silencing, Marginalizing." *Journal of Global Ethics* 14 (2): 240–251. https://doi.org/10.1080/17449626.2018.1506996.

Long, B. 2022. CSR and Reconciliation with Indigenous Peoples in Canada." *Critical Perspectives on International Business* 18 (1): 15–30. https://doi.org/10.1108/cpoib-12-2017-0096.

MacDonald, D. 2019. *The Sleeping Giant Awakens: Genocide, Indian Residential Schools, and the Challenge of Conciliation.* University of Toronto Press.

Madden, B. 2019. "A De/Colonizing Theory of Truth and Reconciliation Education." *Curriculum Inquiry* 49 (3): 284–312. https://doi.org/10.1080/03626784.2019.1624478.

Manning, S. 2020. "The Canadian Senate: An Institution of Reconciliation?" *Journal of Canadian Studies* 54 (1): 1–24. https://doi.org/10.3138/JCS.2019-0003.

McGregor, D. 2018. "Mino-Mnaamodzawin: Achieving Indigenous Environmental Justice in Canada." *Environment and Society* 9 (1): 7–24. https://doi.org/10.3167/ares.2018.090102.

Murphy, K., K. Branje, T. White, et al. 2021. "Are We Walking the Talk of Participatory Indigenous Health Research? A Scoping Review of the Literature in Atlantic Canada." *PloS One* 16 (7): 1–28. https://doi.org/10.1371/journal.pone.0255265.

Murry, A., and K. James. 2021. "Reconciliation and Industrial-Organizational Psychology in Canada." *Canadian Journal of Behavioural Science* 53 (2): 114–124. https://doi.org/10.1037/cbs0000237.

Osmond-Johnson, P., and P. Turner. 2020. "Navigating the 'Ethical Space' of Truth and Reconciliation: Non-Indigenous School Principals in Saskatchewan." *Curriculum Inquiry* 50 (1): 54–77. https://doi.org/10.1080/03626784.2020.1715205.

Reimer, L., and R. Chrismas, eds. 2020. *Our Shared Future: Windows into Canada's Reconciliation Journey.* Lexington Books.

Schaefli, L., A. M. C. Godlewska, and J. Rose. 2018. "Coming to Know Indigeneity: Epistemologies of Ignorance in the 2003–2015 Ontario Canadian and World Studies Curriculum." *Curriculum Inquiry* 48 (4): 475–498. https://doi.org/10.1080/03626784.2018.1518113.

Schmidt, H. 2019. "Indigenizing and Decolonizing the Teaching of Psychology: Reflections on the Role of the Non-Indigenous Ally." *American Journal of Community Psychology* 64 (1–2): 59–71. https://doi.org/10.1002/ajcp.12365.

Schultz, A., T. Nguyen, M. Sinclaire, R. Fransoo, and E. McGibbon. 2021. "Historical and Continued Colonial Impacts on Heart Health of Indigenous Peoples in Canada: What's Reconciliation Got to Do with It?" *CJC Open* 3 (12): S149–S164. https://doi.org/10.1016/j.cjco.2021.09.010.

Truth and Reconciliation Commission of Canada. 2015. "Calls to Action." https://
ehprnh2mwo3.exactdn.com/wp-content/uploads/2021/01/Calls_to_Acti
on_English2.pdf.

Vanthuyne, K. 2021. "'I Want to Move Forward. You Can Move Forward Too.'
Articulating Indigenous Self-Determination at the Truth and Reconciliation
Commission of Canada." *Human Rights Quarterly* 43 (2): 355–377. https://
doi.org/10.1353/hrq.2021.0023.

Wotherspoon, T., and E. Milne. 2020. "What Do Indigenous Education Policy
Frameworks Reveal About Commitments to Reconciliation in Canadian
School Systems?" *International Indigenous Policy Journal* 11 (1): 1–29. https://
doi.org/10.18584/iipj.2020.11.1.10215.

Wyile, H. 2018a. "'The Currency That Is Reconciliation Discourse in Canada':
Contesting Neoliberal Reconciliation." *Studies in Canadian Literature* 43 (2):
121–143. https://doi.org/10.7202/1062918AR.

Wyile, H. 2018b. "Towards a Genealogy of Reconciliation in Canada." *Journal of
Canadian Studies* 51 (3): 601–635. https://doi.org/10.3138/jcs.2017-0021.r1.

Zurba, M., K. F. Beazley, E. English, and J. Buchmann-Duck. 2019. "Indigenous
Protected and Conserved Areas (IPCAs), Aichi Target 11 and Canada's
Pathway to Target 1: Focusing Conservation on Reconciliation." *Land* 8 (1): 1–
20. https://doi.org/10.3390/land8010010.

The Hidden Source of Civility

PAUL W. LUDWIG

INTRODUCTION

I will argue that civility requires motivation, a reason for citizens to want it. Neither morality nor rational interest is a sufficient motivator, at least not currently. What motivates civility is actually civic friendship, although the latter is under-theorized in liberalism, and in fact citizens and theorists alike are often unaware that it is operating. Just as we have preferential feelings toward fellow members of other groups we belong to, we have preferential feelings toward those in our own nation-state. This civic friendship is not, primarily, a goal or ideal but rather a factual condition of functioning societies. Its feelings provide us with a motive to be civil; where the feelings wane, civility wanes. Thus the revival of civility today requires patching up our civic friendship. In the political philosophy of Aristotle, the psychology of friends—particularly of friends who have quarreled—holds out some hope for such a patching-up and for the revival of civility.

Paul W. Ludwig, *The Hidden Source of Civility* In: *The Virtue of Civility*. Edited by: Andrew Peterson, Oxford University Press. © Oxford University Press 2026. DOI: 10.1093/9780197653791.003.0007

THE INADEQUACY OF OTHER, MORE OBVIOUS MOTIVATIONS TO BE CIVIL

Like other virtues, civility requires motivation. Why be civil? What motivates us to be civil or to practice civility toward people we encounter? For a few individuals, virtue is its own reward. The further question, "But why do you wish to be virtuous?," seems obtuse to them, much as a young person exercising to improve the beauty of her body, if asked the analogous question, "But why do you wish to be beautiful?," would consider the question meaningless. Perhaps a sociologist might be able to dig deeper; there might be social factors determining what "virtuous" even means, just as bodily beauty has social determinants prescribing, say, a slenderness not always fashionable in ages past. On such a theory, civility, too, could cease to be virtuous, given different social determinants—perhaps determinants in a society like ours. Uncivil behavior, heckling or badgering, perhaps "trolling," in recent parlance, might come to seem a badge of honor, a worthwhile practice and, in the limit, a virtue. In an extremely polarized society, *partisan* virtues might come to the fore: such virtues would not be civil in the sense of "citizenly" or "among citizens." Partisans might be surprised at the suggestion that they should be more civil; civility might seem weak rather than excellent: accommodationist, caving in, and therefore, in the end, shameful. Of course, such partisans could be mistaken in their belief that partisan excellences are true virtues. To be a virtue, an excellence might require a greater universality than mere partisanship could provide. But that consideration highlights a tension in the concept of "civility" itself: its etymology, at least, implies that civility extends merely to citizens. There is no suggestion that civility extends beyond citizens, to foreigners—at least, not in the language itself. Any extension we might wish to make, to include foreigners, would need to be motivated and argued for. What motivates us to be civil? Does it have something to do with our polity, our citizenship?

A public policy approach to the question might differ greatly from the approach in philosophical ethics. An economist, for example, might naturally begin from self-interest, arguing that we are all in the same boat, and, if we do not wish to drown, we had each better do our part to keep the boat afloat. A Kantian ethicist, by contrast, might insist that a self-interested civility—that is, civility practiced for any reason other than duty—is no true civility, no true virtue, at all. *Fiat officium, pereat mundus.*[1] The economist places a higher premium on realism. Because very few people, the economist reasons, find virtue to be its own reward, self-interest might motivate a larger number. Your civility will benefit me but not out of the goodness of your heart; rather, an enlightened self-interest will guide you. This economical view of virtue runs up against a problem of its own. The partisan spoken of above *is* acting in his own interest. He helps his friends and harms his enemies. To be sure, he also contributes to a larger, longer-term disaster. But a societal disaster, like climate change, is slower to develop and further in the future than the battles he currently fights. To see the bigger picture requires enlightenment, an intellectual virtue, much in the way that, to see civility as its own reward requires a person who is already virtuous. Instead of presupposing moral paragons, like the Kantian ethicist does, or intellectual paragons, like the economist does, should we not presuppose people with no virtue "beyond what private citizens are capable of," nor an education beyond the reach of ordinary human nature and luck?[2] Intelligence and morality are virtues that "we should pray for," but not that we should expect. Today's dearth of civility shows this problem clearly: if people were intelligent enough to be civil, or moral enough to be civil, they would be civil. But they are not. Today's citizens are more interdependent economically than at any time in history. If they (we) could perceive that our mutual benefit depends on civility, we would be civil. Yet we are failing to be civil. It is as if we do not know our own interest. In this way, we have exhausted two possibilities. Civility's primary motivation is not morality or self-interest.

In contrast to both the Kantian ethicist and the economist, my own lens is political philosophy, in particular the philosophy of Aristotle. The quotations above come from his treatise on politics. Aristotle values realism instead of the Platonic idealism he criticizes, but he also believes in virtue. Unlike the Kantian moralist, Aristotle believes in motivated virtue: there are reasons why one would wish to be virtuous; some of those reasons may be self-seeking without utterly overthrowing the whole notion of virtue. Beauty—wanting to be fine or noble in one's character—is one of those motivations. However, Aristotle is also keenly aware that virtues require infrastructure. The conditions on the ground in a given society have much to do with what *citizen* virtue, in particular, becomes. Aristotle seems equally at home speaking of citizen virtues in a polity with a broad-based franchise (which we would call democratic) as he is speaking of restricted-franchise regimes (aristocracies, timocracies, oligarchies) that we tend to lump together as being simply unjust. Different excellences come to the fore in different regimes.[3] He also believes in a human nature that stays constant across the regimes, a nature with diverse potentialities that come out under different conditions. Aristotle would never agree with a modern economist who wished to reduce all motivation to self-interest, for example. Self-seeking is one potentiality of man; there are others.

Political philosophy, on this view, attempts not to be reductive. But political philosophy also wishes to affect political practice. With an important topic like civility, we cannot be content with such a broad view that it gives us no practical help becoming civil or helping others to increase civility. Political philosophy is a practical discipline, not just a theoretical one. Moreover, the subject of political philosophy is human behavior. Unlike a discipline such as biology, where a species does not change its behavior merely because it over-hears biologists talking about it, humans do sometimes modify their behavior in response to the ideas that trickle down from social science into practice. Political philosophy thus has the power to elevate and to lower: reductive ideas such as "every motive is, at bottom, merely _______ (fill in the blank: self-interest, will-to-power, etc.)" can lower the tone of a society. By the same token, a high-minded philosophy has the power to elevate, but only if citizens find it believable.

One way of staying tethered to reality is to confess that civility, as a virtue, is pedestrian. Civility is not exciting or glamorous. In fact, civility is boring. Try to excite a child about the virtue of courage by telling her a story of derring-do. Even great acts of moderation or self-abnegation such as Jesus's fasting forty days in the wilderness elicit awe and respect. But civility? Let us not kid ourselves. Civility lacks glamour. Grand virtues are choiceworthy because they inspire us. What is inspiring about civility? Civility asks only that we get along with others, speak politely, for the purposes of mutual benefit, such as in deliberation or debate. Even archaic virtues such as the princely virtues of liberality or clemency, which we scarcely recognize as virtues any more, encountering them only in history or fiction—even these can inspire. Civility lacks the cachet of princely virtue, in part because civility is a virtue of weakness: the prince does not need to speak civilly (because he can command the floor, or the chair, at whim). By contrast, we democrats need each other to be civil because we all lack the prince's power always to have our say. I must act civilly toward you, in part, to earn from you the civility I need if I am ever to get to have a few minutes on the podium. This self-interested quality of civility detracts from its greatness. Saintly virtues, too, are often virtues of weakness: humility, meekness, mercy, spiritual poverty. Yet disciples of such virtues perceive that turning the other cheek is not an easy or natural thing to do. They perceive that lashing out, fighting back, is much more common. It requires strength of soul to practice humility. Does civility require any analogous strength? Civility is not self-sacrificial. Saintly virtues set aside power, ruling it out of court. Civility begins in powerlessness, having little to lay aside or to sacrifice. By being civil, I sacrifice my ability to raise my voice, to say what I *really* think, for example to be insulting. This is not an inspiring sacrifice.

In all these ways, civility's motivation remains hidden. We need civility, we want civility, but most of us would secretly prefer others practiced it while we went on talking just as much and as loudly as we please. This last aspect of course is shared with many virtues. As Mordred sings in *Camelot*, "Fidelity is only for your mate!" But even marital fidelity is far more inspiring than civility. Fidelity is part of romantic love, something most of us value very highly. We admire fidelity, and we feel bad when we violate it.

I will argue that love and friendship play a role in civility. *Civic* friendship is actually the prime mover of civility. Citizens are civic friends, and just as personal friends do not wish to offend one another, citizens *qua* citizens have an analogous desire not to offend. Friends wish to benefit each other, and in an analogous way, citizens have a desire to be benefactors. Civic friendship provides a motive for good behavior of various kinds. Having potential friends everywhere creates moral observers in whose sight people do not wish to be caught practicing ethical vices (cf. Smith 1982, 25 [I.i.5.5], 259 [VI.iii.46]). Incivility is one of these vices, and civility can be thought of as a benefit that we confer on fellow citizens. The following two sections will argue that civic friendship is a realistic way of looking at politics; civic friendship is a factual condition more than it is an ideal. I realize that these claims must sound very dubious and will require a correspondingly heavy lift on my part. Given our current incivility, the civic love I am alleging must be very weak indeed! Certainly, we observe civic friendship today more often in the breach. Where civic friendship wanes, civility wanes. But the final section will offer some hope for renewal, arguing that there is reason to believe our current incivility stems from disappointed civic friendship rather than from the disappearance of civic friendship.

CIVIC FRIENDSHIP: DEMONSTRABLY REAL BUT UNAPPRECIATED

Just as we have preferential feelings toward fellow members of other groups we belong to, we have preferential feelings toward those in our own polity. Americans, for example, care more about fellow Americans than they do about foreigners, all other things being equal. Let us separate arguments that civic friendship is a fact from arguments that it is good. Americans are joined in their favoritism by Canadians (who prefer Canadians to Americans), by Japanese (who prefer Japanese to Canadians), and by practically every other country on earth. The fact of this national favoritism gets obscured not by other facts but by our morals: since it is wrong, many feel, to show favoritism, we tend to deny that we do it. What we deplore in jingoistic fellow-citizens, we attempt to squelch in ourselves. Notice, however, that this moral argument is a poor argument for the existence or nonexistence of the feelings. The facts that belligerent nationalism could follow from such feelings, that inequality could ensue from favoritism, and that populists have recently exploited these preferences prove nothing about their nonexistence. They prove the opposite: if such feelings did not exist, no belligerence or inequality could follow from them, for there would be nothing to exploit. To take a specific example, the fact that out-sourcing of jobs was exploited by an American president says a lot about how powerful the feelings opposing out-sourcing are (see, e.g., Chiarella and Lynch 2018). The feelings exist and must be reckoned with, not only by populists but by responsible statesmen. Like many aspects of civic friendship, the issue of out-sourcing transcends the ordinary Left-Right binary: people of diverse commitments concede that the out-sourcing of jobs has backfired, if not economically then at least politically. Out-sourcing is in bad odor because it violates the preference that ordinary citizens have for fellow citizens (I claim). Majorities of Americans, for example, think the country should take care of its own citizens first and that wealth creation should benefit Americans more than foreign nationals.

The desire for border controls and strict scrutiny of asylum applications is a second example. Citizens literally value themselves and their fellows more than they value outsiders; shared humanity is not enough. Paul Collier (2018, 194–198) documents societal unwillingness to help the less fortunate *when the latter include recent immigrants* as opposed to fellow citizens. The fact that this unwillingness violates other norms such as charity and hospitality argues for its strength, not its weakness or nonexistence. If a political passion—favoritism for fellow citizens—can override such high virtues, it is a force to be reckoned with. Here, too, this national favoritism can be whipped up into anti-immigrant fervor by unscrupulous demagogues. Does that mean it is a fact or not? How can something that is not the case be whipped up?

At this point, many readers will ask me to please just stop. Civic friendship? If this is what I mean by friendship, then it is simply evil. So far, we have argued only for the existence and reality of civic friendship, but friendship is intimately bound up with goodness. So, let us transition to the moral question. There are moral arguments in favor of favoritism. Consider other groups we happen to belong to. Families show favoritism, too. Just as, when push comes to shove, most of us will favor our own children over someone else's children, citizens, too, favor their own. Families that did not favor their own members over outsiders would not remain families for long. They would not be viable. Therefore, favoritism within moral limits is a healthy condition of families. By analogy, nations that did not favor their own members over outsiders would not remain nations for long. They would not be viable. Therefore, favoritism within moral limits is a healthy condition of nation-states. Family love is exclusive. Civic friendship is exclusive, too. In fact, all friendships are exclusive— civic friendship is no outlier in this regard. To reject exclusivity in friendship is to reject friendship.

Notice, too, that favoritism holds favorites to a higher standard. Fellow citizens share citizen virtues (in our liberal-democratic case, commitments to freedom and equality) that we do not share with international trading partners, for example. International trading partners, Aristotle writes, do not care that each other "should be a certain way" or that they be good in their characters (1944, 3, 1280b2–9; Ludwig 2020, 238–241). Citizens do care about character. John Cooper interprets:

> Americans take pride . . . not just in accomplishments, but even more in the qualities of mind and character that (are presumed to have) made them possible. . . . [They] definitely do not want [fellow citizens] to be small-minded, self-absorbed, sleazy. What their fellow-citizens are like matters to them personally, it seems, in ways that the personal qualities of the citizens of a foreign country do not, because they feel . . . that [it] somehow reflects on themselves. (1999, 367–368; Ludwig 2020, 241–242)

It is a longer argument, but these merely civic virtues are, for Aristotle, relative to regimes—democratic virtues differ from aristocratic ones—and they rarely if ever constitute full ethical virtue. Instead, citizens of liberal democracies, for example, care deeply that their fellow citizens share beliefs about freedom and equality. We do not care, or not nearly as much, that Belarusian or Chinese citizens share our beliefs. One source of our current polarization is the worry that our fellow citizens do *not* share such beliefs. The final section will return to the question whether failure to live up to such standards has produced some of the anger in our incivility.

The two senses of favoritism—concern for well-being and concern for civic virtue—go together. Some unity, some cohesion, is necessary to form a group at all. The reality is probably that preference for one's own groups is natural, while the extension of affection to far-flung groups is derived. Concentric circles of care might begin small, close to the self, expanding outward to include others but weakening as they expand.[4] Aristotle, the great theorist of civic friendship, also believed in international friendship. He recognized that a cross-border, low-grade friendship exists between all persons, between "human and human" (Aristotle 1934, 8.1, 1155a19–22). Many readers will still wish to ask why these cosmopolitan feelings cannot be as strong as our parochial ones. What causes one friendship to be stronger than another?

We have so far spoken only of feelings. What *causes* those feelings? If civic friendship were merely a feeling, feelings can be changed or exchanged for other feelings. Opponents of civic friendship or those troubled by its favoritism may believe it possible to combat such feelings, whether by laws, institutions, economic incentives, or education. Aristotle argues that citizens' friendly feelings—our favoritisms—have causes. Friendship is always based on something shared in common. The amount or importance of what is shared in common determines the closeness of the friendship that results, the intensity of the feelings (Aristotle 1934, 8.9, 1159b25–1160a8; 8.2–3, 1155b17–1156b32). The things shared in common are preeminently goods, although Aristotle is willing to define the good analogically to include utilities and pleasures, which are not simply good, the way moral and intellectual virtues are. Friends who share true virtues in common have a perfect or highest kind of friendship. People who share nothing more than the enjoyment of getting together with each other at the pub are also friends, on his view: a lower, lesser type of friendship based on pleasure alone. And finally, if I have nothing more in common with my neighbor than our mutual wish to share lawn tools, we are also friends "by analogy" with the higher kinds; we are friends based on utility, a (relative) good. Friendship is a natural and normal result of shared utility, just as it is with the higher goods. I cannot help liking the neighbor with whom I share, favoring him over others who live on my street. Unless, of course, I share a greater good in common with them. And unless, of course, I have a falling out with my useful neighbor, since friendship is prone to angry feelings of betrayal—more on that in final section. On this view, I certainly may become personal friends with a foreigner and prefer him to fellow citizens. International friendships become personal friendship when we come to share more with certain foreign nationals than we do with random fellow citizens we happen to meet. Fellow citizens are civic friends because they share utilities, i.e., goods loved for their usefulness. Thus, compared with friendships of virtue and friendships of pleasure, civic friendship meets only a rather low bar of friendship. Why call this relation a friendship at all?

Aristotle is keenly aware that civic friendship is weaker than personal friendship. When asking "How many friends should we have?" he narrows the number down to pairs and very small groups, "except in the civic sense [of friend]" (1934, 9.10, 1171a12–20). Civic friendship is not personal friendship but an analogy to personal friendship. The ancient polis did not qualify as a friendship in the full sense of the word, for Aristotle; it was much too big to qualify as a friendship except in the civic sense. Such considerations go some way toward refuting the commonplace assumption that the polis was small enough for everyone to be friends, but the modern state is too big.

What utilities do civic friends share? The common defense is one such shared utility. The regime or constitution is another (Aristotle 1934, 9.6, 1167a27–34; Ludwig 2020, 253–257, 267–268). Like defense, our regime is a utility (rather than a good for its own sake) because we like it primarily for what it has done for us, or what we hope to gain from it. There is an element of self-interest in our embrace of a political system. Because humans have reason, we cannot truly share, with others, a political system unless we, and they, agree about it. Liberal democracy is a regime or constitution, though not necessarily a written document such as the U.S. Constitution; rather, the regime refers to the distribution of offices that such written documents spell out—in the U.S. case, it includes the separation of powers, sovereign people, and representative (not direct) democracy. Its citizens love the liberal-democratic regime to the extent that it secures liberty and equality. In turn, the regime acts as a regimen, quietly shaping the citizens under it, forming them. For example, living in the United States changes people—the regime reliably churns out citizens of a recognizable American type, often stamped in high relief on us, enough to provoke comedy. But it is a type that esteems freedom and equality. Recent immigrants sometimes lack the obvious "stamp," but their children, who grow up in the United States, often have it to a remarkable degree. Not coincidentally, Americans tend to like this kind of person—the type they themselves belong to. This stamp or impress of the regime on citizens gives further reasons to feel an affinity or predilection for fellow citizens. We recognize and respond to a type. In this way, civic friendship creates a self-sustaining cycle. Citizens who believe in the worth and truth of liberal democracy esteem it. Citizens who esteem the same thing have reason to esteem—or feel affinity for—each other. These are some of the causes of the preferential feelings that might otherwise seem arbitrary or unfair.

To return to international friendship: because a foreigner I meet does not share with me such great utilities—a regime and common defense—we two tend to feel more distant from each other than do fellow citizens. However, if he and I get to know one another and begin sharing some greater good in common, we often develop feelings for each other that override the preferences of civic friendship. The fact that we cannot quantify, in advance, how much of one shared good will override another shared good is not an argument against civic friendship, unless it is also an argument against all ethics that fail to be reductive.

In addition to the above moral considerations, Aristotle strengthens the factual case for civic friendship by adducing and analyzing four conditions that create differing instances of it. Remarkably, each of these conditions has a modern analogue under liberal democracy, and, in some cases, liberal-democratic versions are more robust than the ancient versions were. However, all is not well, as readers will have already suspected; his analyses show where we need work to improve in our own, modern societies. A list of the conditions producing civic friendships that Aristotle analyzes includes a preponderant middle class (almost always lacking in the ancient polis), proliferation of small associations (anathema in Plato's *Republic*, as for most ancient lawgivers), an economy of reciprocity (win-win, as opposed to zero-sum, exchanges are vastly more prevalent in modern markets than in ancient), and honors for civic benefactors (Ludwig 2020, 15–16). Each of these features deserves a lengthy treatment, but the following brief analyses will suffice to show how each produces civic friendships. Agreement on the regime, with which we began, is key to them all; where agreement suffers, these further instances of civic friendship suffer, too.

CONDITIONS PRODUCING CIVIC FRIENDSHIP (AND THEIR RECENT DECLINE)

One of the conditions for civic friendship is a predominant middle class. Aristotle's "best-practicable" regime (as opposed to his "best regime" of *Politics* 1944, 7–8, an aristocracy based on virtue, which seldom if ever comes into existence; compare 4, 1295a25–31) bases itself on a middle class. This middle-class regime, "polity," assumes no virtue "beyond what private citizens are capable of," nor an education beyond the reach of ordinary human nature and luck, as we saw earlier. It is "a life the majority can participate in and a regime that most cities can share." He writes:

> When some are envious, others contemptuous, nothing is further from civic friendship and political community. For community is a friendly thing. . . . The city wishes, at least, to be made up of equal and similar people as much as possible. (Aristotle 1944, 4, 1295b6–26; Ludwig 2020, 236–239)

The middle-class regime keeps people as similar and equal as possible; the regime is a mix between democracy (i.e., direct-vote democracy, a bad regime in his opinion) and oligarchy, in which only the wealthy can vote. Each major faction—the many poor and the few rich—naturally want their party's signature regime, democracy or oligarchy. In polity, by contrast, a middle class grows large enough either to outweigh each faction or to throw its weight to whichever side will prevent the emergence of either extreme. Importantly, this preponderant middle class was almost never achieved in the ancient world. Civic "friendship" in the polis meant an uneasy truce between the two ordinary factions: the people and the wealthy.[5] Today, by contrast, nearly all liberal-democratic citizens are middle class. The middle class vastly outnumbers the upper and lower classes. The recent challenge is that the tech revolution and certain financial policies have strained this condition for civic friendship.

The modern innovation that created the middle class is related to the second condition of civic friendship Aristotle analyzes: an economy of reciprocal favors. In the ancient world, it was almost impossible to rise up out of poverty. That is because peasant economies, based on fixed parcels of land, were zero-sum. One person's gain was always someone else's loss. Aristotle overcomes this fault by making monetary transactions into exchanges of favors. By loaning money to someone starting a business, for example, an investor becomes a benefactor conferring a favor. Ideally, the beneficiary reciprocates later, attempting to put the original benefactor in his debt. An upward spiral of goodwill, perhaps even a competition to benefit each other, ensues. Crucially, each citizen feels honored by the money he receives, and this honor Aristotle likens to a civic kind of love: money is a measure of their civic friendship (1934, 9.1, 1163b30–1164b3; 8.13, 1162b16–34). But to the extent the ancient economy remained zero-sum, these commercial friends may have gained at the expense of fellow citizens. Only with the rise of liberal markets did wealth creation really take off,[6] and we no longer think (or need to think) of ourselves as exchanging favors to have win-win exchanges. Alien as Aristotle's analysis may seem, it continues to point out aspects of human nature that our economists would do well to keep in mind. With the globalization of the economy, the commercial traffic that *citizens* used to share (alongside the common defense and their regime) has gradually transformed into a giant market in which citizens have no better status than foreigners. This violates the concentric circles of care, jumping past the national circle to get to the outer circles. At a time of off-shoring lower-middle-class jobs, the wealth created by the computer technology and financial industries was disproportionately earned by people with elite advantages. The more unequal the classes became, the more the economy ceased to be (or at least to seem) win-win and began looking rigged. Worthless endeavors, at which elites had advantages, such as rent-seeking and lobbying the government, came to seem more lucrative than creating wealth through invention and creating value through exchange. People lost faith that the economy offered them a fair chance. The "capture" of various parts of the economy by monopolies and monied interests as well as by governmental set-asides contributed to this perception. This movement from win-win assumptions back to zero-sum assumptions has made liberal democracies more divisive, like the ancient polis with its factions of rich and poor. Citizens who do not prosper, Aristotle can tell us, feel not merely deprived economically but dishonored. For Aristotle, wages confer honor, the civic analogue of love, and he agrees with one of the founders of capitalism about the honor inherent in work (Ludwig 2020, 217–221; Smith 1982, 50 [I.iii.2.1]; cf. 212–213 [VI.i.4]). Wages affect more in the human heart than mere self-interest.

Proliferation of small associations is a third condition of civic friendship. Cultivating associations is important because associations are actually instances of civic friendships—a facet of Aristotle's theory that shocks the sensibilities of readers who think civic friendship must always extend to all citizens equally. But a natural result of the concentric circles of care is that citizens must form groups that prefer fellow members to those outside it, though the latter, too, are fellow citizens. Why call these groups *civic* friendships, then—why not call them sub-civic, if they do not extend to citizens as a whole? Each of the associations Aristotle lists has a public function that integrates at least some of its members into the larger whole: fraternal organizations based on the ancestral clans that originally came together to form villages and cities; marriage alliances (intermarriages between opposing groups); committees or guilds that sponsored religious festivals; and, finally, the shared activities of public amusements or leisured pastimes. "This sort of thing is the work of friendship; for the choice to live together is friendship," he concludes (Aristotle 1944, 3, 1280b30–1281a10).

Aristotle is practically unique among ancient theorists and lawgivers in permitting—and even encouraging—these smaller associations. Any association smaller than the overall polis was suspected of undermining it. The regimes most admired in antiquity, such as Sparta, attempted to stamp out all affinities except that for the citizen body; even families were suspect for their nepotism and favoritism. Families were legally weakened at Sparta and Thebes; Plato's *Republic* completes their idea by abolishing the family entirely. For Plato and for these actual Greek cities, sub-civic groups are the diametric opposite of civic friendship (Plato 1937, 464c–d, 424a; Aristotle 1944, 2, 1262b8–15). As was the case with his middle class, Aristotle's preference anticipates developments in the modern world, under liberal democracies, where a private sphere has opened up in which voluntary joining is encouraged, and associations have proliferated beyond count.

Here again, work is needed to revive associational health today: participation in labor unions, political parties, charities, service organizations, social clubs, and bowling leagues, not to mention small town councils and neighborhoods, passed its zenith in the first half of the twentieth century. Administrative centralization, individualism, and even prosperity have hurt participation in groups. All of these groups making up the fabric of a nation-state are civic friendships, and all of them can be revived, but it will take policies specifically tailored to fostering them and perhaps even specifically aware of their value as instances of civic friendship. Aristotle lists one further condition for civic friendship to flourish, but since it bears directly on our current incivility, we fold it into the final section.

HOW INCIVILITY DERIVES FROM DISAPPOINTED CIVIC FRIENDSHIP

The source of civility, civic friendship, hides in plain sight because liberalism has no theory of civic friendship. Born of the wars of religion, liberal theory is rightly conscious of the harm that unity can promote, not merely when citizens behave with collective selfishness but when too many citizens cohere too well around a shared ideal or idol. As a result, the passions and practices of civic friendship have undergone re-descriptions in modern thought: what is actually a desire to help others gets relabeled as "self-interest rightly understood" (Ludwig 2020, 154–160), and citizens' desire to become noble benefactors is denigrated as being "patronizing." Benefaction and especially society's rewards—honors—for benefactors happen to be Aristotle's fourth and final condition for civic friendship. Healthy societies reward civic benefactors (Ludwig 2020, 248–250). As if to anticipate our liberal-democratic worries, he is acutely aware that civic benefactors have big egos, push for their own way, and get angry at ingratitude. Their anger, in fact, turns out to be paradigmatic of all friendship. The beauty of this part of Aristotle's theory is that it offers an encouraging explanation of our current incivility.

A brief foray into Aristotle's psychology of friends in their attempts to benefit each other will show how relevant his analysis continues to be in our current context. Doing good to others generates love—not in the receiver but in the giver (Aristotle 1934, 9.7, 1167b16–1168a27). Doing good is active and productive, while receiving good is passive. The active lover realizes and instantiates himself in the recipient, creating a stake in the other person that he owns. He has made an improvement in the life of the beneficiary; a part of him now resides in another self, who is his handiwork, and he loves that part of himself through his natural self-love. He also loves the nobility of his deed, which continues to reside in the beneficiary. Thus, benefactors naturally love their beneficiaries more than beneficiaries love them back, despite the fact that ethically, the beneficiary owes more love in gratitude. The more citizens feel they have benefited society, the more ownership over it they feel, and their care and concern rise accordingly. Military veterans, for example, have often made deep investments of self—blood, time, a limb, or a lifetime with some other disability—and come to feel proprietary rights over the society they believe they have benefited. What happens when the beneficiary is ungrateful as Aristotle says naturally happens, or even casts the gift back in their teeth? Their resulting anger is the flip side of their previous love.

Aristotle boldly theorizes that all friendly feelings actually derive from our angry and self-assertive faculty of soul (1944, 7, 13287b38–1328a17; Ludwig 2020, 43–52). For evidence, he asks us to consult our experience when we feel anger at being slighted. Our anger is kindled more when friends and relatives hold us in contempt than when strangers do. The important difference between strangers and friends is love. Therefore, the greater anger is somehow connected to the greater love. His prime example of friendly feeling collapsing into anger is the disappointed benefactor. Benefactors get angry at the injustice of their intimates because "in addition to suffering harm, they think they are deprived—by people who they believe owe them one—of a benefaction" (Aristotle 1944, 7, 1328a8–15). These intimates "owe them one" because the disappointed benefactor previously benefited them. Elsewhere Aristotle describes the benefactors as engaging in precisely the sort of reciprocal competition in conferring benefits that we earlier saw Aristotle encourage commercial friends to engage in.[7] Benefactors wish to be noble by giving freely, no strings attached, yet egoistic strings remain and become obvious when they feel betrayed. Any ingratitude is perceived as a slight from a beneficiary who "owes them one." Military veterans are merely among the more obvious examples of this psychology. All friendships have this problem; even the best friends are vulnerable to slights by their friends, according to Aristotle's psychology. The feature is simply a shortcoming of our passional being.

How does this psychology of friendship relate to incivility? Consider your feelings about "the other side" in today's polarized situation. Fear probably plays a role in your feelings. But anger is more common. In Aristotle's theory, anger often stems directly from the psychology of friendship: namely, from the feelings of betrayal that occur when friends quarrel. Do you feel disappointed in the other side, perhaps even betrayed? In the U.S. context, a very prevalent thought is "They call themselves Americans, and this is how they behave!" Once again, Aristotle's analogue is family love: "Harsh are the wars of brothers" and "Those who have loved greatly will hate greatly, too" (1944, 7, 1328a16–17). To what extent is our current anger owing to a prior love (preference, favoritism, affinity), which goes unrecognized because of liberal-theoretical blinders, but which exists nonetheless, and which comes to sight, today, mainly in disappointment? As we saw earlier, civic friendship holds fellow citizens to higher standards—just like family love does. If the familial analogy is right, the very anger that seems to prove civic friendship weak or nonexistent may actually be evidence that it exists and continues to play a role. For example, blue-collar Americans today feel betrayed by elites, who (they think) prefer cosmopolitanism to citizenship. Elites today feel disappointment with blue collars, who often hold "deplorable" opinions about freedom and equality. To disagree about such fundamentals as liberty and equality—the bases of the regime—is to endanger the regime agreement that is the key to all civic friendships. Readers who come to believe that civic friendship is a fact must judge for themselves whether optimism is justified by today's anger (that is, if we had ceased caring that fellow citizens "should be a certain way," we would not *be* angry with them), or whether civic friendship is indeed about to disappear with the waning of regime agreement. Incivility is consistent with both.

My own opinion is that our current incivility shows signs of this family-like betrayal. The war between progressives and conservatives has become so intense that each side defines itself in opposition to the other. Even where they used to agree, they cannot agree. The fact that one party embraces some opinion *means* that the other has to disavow that opinion. This is a nearly childish negation, the kind of thing we usually see mainly in families, for example when spouses divorce. The sheer negativism stands out in high relief against the fact that, in the U.S. case, the populist wings of both parties actually agree on many issues. Their common ground is startlingly large, but neither side can admit it exists.[8] The hatred of family members who have quarreled, far from being evidence they do not love each other, is evidence that they do—or at least did. Sometimes they never patch it up. But sometimes they do. It is heartening to think that even our worst incivility might be a symptom not merely of our decline but also of our resources for finding civility again. People concerned to revivify and bolster the virtue of civility, if the foregoing argument is correct, can find resources in the same flawed, passional nature of human beings that currently exacerbates our divisions. The anger that animates us now is not simply opposed to friendship but related to it. We could not, on this theory, even be friendly beings, if it were not for our ability to get angry. Not every instance of anger is an instance of disappointed friendship, but many of them are. We have some grounds for hoping our current anger is such an instance: civic friends disappointed in one another, feeling betrayed. One practical lesson Aristotle can teach us, in our attempts to increase civility, is the paradox that those who give the gift of civility also unwittingly place themselves in the position of benefactor. My civility to my opponents is effectually a benefit I bestow; if they fail to reciprocate civility back to me, I automatically become a disappointed benefactor, on this view, feeling angry and betrayed—the opposite of what my civility was aiming at. The bigger picture for civility and for its prognosis is that greater civility can be expected to follow from a healed civic friendship and, moreover, that civility, while laudable in itself, might lack a sufficient motivation, if civic friendship is left out of account.

NOTES

1. "Let there be duty, though the world perish."
2. This and the following quotation come from Aristotle, *Politics* (1944, 4, 1295a25–31), discussed below.
3. On mere citizen virtues, as opposed to full ethical virtues, see the argument in the following section, especially the discussion of Cooper 1999.
4. See Nussbaum with Respondents (1996, 9). The image of concentric circles comes from Hierocles the Stoic, although I use the image more naturalistically, rejecting his ethical counsel to "draw the circles—concerning the behavior that is due to each group—together in a way, as though toward the center, and with an effort to keep transferring items out of the containing circles into the contained." The fragment is preserved in Stobaeus, *Anthology* 4.84.23; see Ramelli (2009, 91).
5. Oligarchic factions swore oaths, according to *Politics* (Aristotle 1944, 5, 1310a9–11), such as "I will be ill-disposed toward the people, and I will plot whatever evil for them I can."
6. McCloskey (2011) estimates that wealth underwent a seventeen-fold increase.
7. Aristotle (1934, 4.3, 1124b10–17); see the discussion in the previous section
8. Common ground: in 2024, the Trumpian wing of Republicans and Bernie Sanders's wing of Democrats agreed that globalization was a mistake, each wishing to limit competition when it hurt blue-collar workers. Both have swore off the wars of choice which aimed to spread democracy at gunpoint. Crucially, Republicans joined Democrats in being worried by inequality. Last, both wanted to break up Big Tech monopolies and to rein in their surveillance of citizens. That was a great deal of agreement to ignore merely because the other side, too, was saying it. Since that time, however, Trump himself has reversed these positions in a number of crucial instances.

REFERENCES

Aristotle. 1934. *Nicomachean Ethics*. Translated by H. Rackham. Harvard Loeb.

Aristotle. 1944. *Politics*. Translated by H. Rackham. Harvard Loeb.

Chiarella, Tom, and James Lynch. 2018. "The Last Shift: What Really Happened to Those Carrier Jobs That Trump Saved?" *Popular Mechanics*, May 15. https://www.popularmechanics.com/technology/infrastructure/a20066498/carrier-factory-donald-trump-jobs/.

Collier, Paul. 2018. *The Future of Capitalism*. HarperCollins.

Cooper, John M. 1999. "Political Animals and Civic Friendship." In *Reason and Emotion*, 356–77. Princeton University Press.

Ludwig, Paul W. 2020. *Rediscovering Political Friendship: Aristotle's Theory and Modern Identity, Community, and Equality.* Cambridge University Press.

McCloskey, Deirdre. 2011. *Bourgeois Dignity.* University of Chicago Press.

Nussbaum, Martha, with Respondents. 1996. *For Love of Country: Debating the Limits of Patriotism.* Edited by J. Cohen. Beacon Press.

Plato. 1937. *Republic.* Translated by P. Shorey. Harvard Loeb.

Ramelli, Ilaria. 2009. *Hierocles the Stoic: Elements of Ethics, Fragments, and Excerpts.* Translated by D. Konstan. Society of Biblical Literature.

Smith, Adam. 1982. *The Theory of Moral Sentiments.* Edited by D. D. Raphael and J. L. MacFie. Liberty Fund.

Is Civility Always a Virtue?

On the Toppling of Edward Colston's Statue

AURÉLIA BARDON, MATTEO BONOTTI, AND
STEVEN T. ZECH

INTRODUCTION

On May 25, 2020, Minneapolis police officer Derek Chauvin murdered George Floyd when he knelt on Floyd's neck for over nine minutes despite the victim's pleas for help and repeatedly informing the officer he could not breathe. Floyd's death, along with other high-profile Black deaths at the hands of (often White) police officers or vigilantes, generated public outrage and sparked a wave of protests in the United States in the summer of 2020 (Edgar and Johnson 2024). Similar mass mobilizations took place across the globe and included broader demands to address instances of contemporary and historical racial injustice. Protests often coalesced around sites of commemoration, and in one high-profile incident, participants in a Black Lives Matter demonstration in the United Kingdom defaced and toppled a statue of Edward Colston and rolled it into the Bristol harbor. Many

Aurélia Bardon, Matteo Bonotti, and Steven T. Zech, *Is Civility Always a Virtue?* In: *The Virtue of Civility*.
Edited by: Andrew Peterson, Oxford University Press. © Oxford University Press 2026.
DOI: 10.1093/9780197653791.003.0008

of the protesters viewed the Colston statue as embodying and celebrating a history of slavery and British colonialism, others saw its toppling as the actions of a lawless mob (Moody 2021), and judges ruled that it was a "violent act" (BBC News 2022). These accounts are not mutually exclusive and each contains some degree of truth. While the four primary protagonists prosecuted for criminal damage in toppling the statue were ultimately acquitted, there are ongoing debates about the nature and appropriateness of their actions that have implications for future cases.

A decision about the fate of the Colston statue falls in the realm of contentious politics and took place following prior efforts to remove the statue and amid ongoing debates about other monuments. Contentious politics entails individual or collective actors making claims that bear on the interests of others and often involves the government as a target, initiator of claims, or third party (Tilly and Tarrow 2015, 7). Instances of contention are usually characterized by some level of coordinated effort to advance those claims through institutional and noninstitutional means. In the context of controversial monuments, we saw mass mobilization through popular protest and frequent counter-mobilizations, as well as moments of contention in the political arena and media. In addition to the Colston statue, recent episodes of contentious politics related to controversial monuments have taken place with the "Rhodes Must Fall" campaign to "decolonize" education in South Africa (Schulz 2019), numerous efforts to engage with Aboriginal "frontier" history and White "settlement" in Australia (Scates 2021), and efforts to confront a legacy of slavery and White supremacy in the southeastern United States (Benjamin et al. 2020), among others. These moments of contention have raised important questions. How should we memorialize and engage with history? When large segments of the population view statues as controversial, how do we judge people's arguments and actions during subsequent moments of contentious politics? And, ultimately, what should we do about these monuments?

In this chapter we argue that civility provides a useful lens through which to analyze and make judgments about words and actions related to controversial monuments. From a normative political philosophy perspective, the civility concept simultaneously captures an aspirational view of human behavior and how we *ought* to behave in a world characterized by frequent disagreements, as well as a framework to make judgments about contentious political issues (Bonotti et al. 2024). Civility can provide guidance when we evaluate what debates, actions, and policies might look like around contentious political issues, and help stimulate productive ways to reflect on and (re)evaluate history.

This chapter proceeds in four parts. First, we unpack the concept of civility, identifying its different (sub-)dimensions and examining the relationship between them. Second, we provide an overview of the events that led to the toppling of Edward Colston's statue in Bristol on June 7, 2020. Third, we conduct an analysis of empirical data that aims to show how different forms of civility and incivility manifested in U.K. parliamentary debates following the statue's toppling. More specifically, we collected and analyzed Hansard records referring to the toppling of the statue between June 7, 2020, and December 19, 2023, using content analysis to evaluate the kinds of arguments against the toppling provided by different British MPs in Parliament and how these arguments relate to different (sub-) dimensions of (in)civility (and their intersections). We consider three main lines of argument against the toppling of Colston's statue, which we refer to as the "vandalism," "democracy," and "retain and explain" arguments. We show that the "vandalism" and "democracy" arguments, as well as a broad version of the "retain and explain" argument, constitute instances of surface-level politeness or surface-level civility, prioritizing either civility as politeness or justificatory civility over moral civility. However, we also argue that a narrow version of the "retain and explain" argument can be interpreted instead as a genuine expression of disagreement regarding what moral civility requires and how it should be achieved. We conclude by returning to a discussion of two central points about civility. Civility is an aspirational concept that provides some guidance about ideal or preferred speech and actions, and the multidimensional nature of civility provides a useful framework to make judgments about behaviors in contentious politics.

CIVILITY, VIRTUE ETHICS, AND CONTENTIOUS POLITICS

Civility is widely considered a virtue, i.e., an admirable trait of character and something which provides guidance for how we should act.[1] The behaviors or attitudes associated with civility, such as being polite, respectful, or attentive, are therefore considered desirable. But virtues are not always the morally correct guide for action. As Hursthouse and Pettigrove (2023) write, certain character traits, "despite being virtues, are sometimes faults."

Consider, for instance, the case of honesty. Honesty, i.e., saying what is true instead of lying or deceiving, is a moral virtue. Yet, saying something just because it is true is also not always the right thing to do. Honesty can be in tension with other values such as kindness, empathy, or considerateness. When something is true but also happens to be hurtful (e.g., "Your new haircut looks terrible") or a form of non-constructive criticism (e.g., "Your essay does not make any sense"), then being honest is not a desirable behavior. The same is true of other virtues, such as courage or fidelity, and, in this chapter, we argue that it is true of civility as well. That civility is a virtue, then, does not tell us that being civil is always the right thing to do or that being uncivil is always morally objectionable. Whether it is morally permissible to disregard the norms of civility depends on a number of other considerations. To illustrate this point, we distinguish between several (sub-)dimensions of civility and incivility. This disaggregation of civility and incivility is key to understanding what kinds of (in)civility really matter.

The growing literature on civility distinguishes two main dimensions of this virtue, which we call "civility as politeness" and "civility as public-mindedness." On the one hand, civility is sometimes understood as a virtue associated with etiquette and good manners. Being civil here means conforming to "generally agreed upon, often codified, social rules" (Calhoun 2000, 260). The specific rules themselves might vary over time or from one society to another (Kekes 1984; Sinopoli 1995), but the point is that they codify what ought to be done (or what should be avoided) if we want to express to others that we recognize them as co-members of society with whom we must coexist. For instance, civility as politeness tells us how to behave in everyday social interactions with others in a way that conveys to them that we recognize them "as enjoying a certain standing in relation to the problem of sociation" (Edyvane 2020, 95). It also tells us how to behave in more challenging scenarios, such as when we deeply disagree with someone: we should listen to what they have to say, we should not interrupt them, and we should avoid dismissive language or language that is considered inappropriate or offensive. In this sense, civility as politeness is necessary to make disagreeing possible and tolerable, "even—and especially—in the absence of actual respect or affirmation" (Bejan 2011, 417), and it works as a "lubricant" (Boyd 2006, 871) for social cooperation.

On the other hand, civility is also sometimes treated as a political concept, i.e., as a virtue that applies to us as citizens in the context of liberal democratic politics (Edyvane 2017; Meyer 2000). Political civility thus understood is "bound up with the idea of an association of citizens, and includes cognate ideas of the civic, the civil, and the civilian; it concerns one's status and duties as a member of a political community, as a citizen with certain rights and responsibilities" (Edyvane 2017, 345). This is what we call civility as public-mindedness, which is characterized by an attitude of giving proper weight and recognition to others as free and equal members of society. For this reason, civility as public-mindedness is often considered a core liberal value (Boyd 2006, 863; Meyer 2000, 79; Rawls 2005, 217; Sabl 2005, 219). The distinction between civility as politeness and civility as public-mindedness matters in part because the latter is more demanding than the former: one can be perfectly polite and conform to socially established rules without recognizing others as free and equal.

It is also important to distinguish further between two sub-dimensions of civility as public-mindedness. We call the first sub-dimension "justificatory civility": it focuses on the duty to provide public reasons to justify political decisions. This idea was famously introduced by Rawls in *Political Liberalism* as the "duty of civility" (2005, 217) and, for most liberal political philosophers today, this is what civility is mainly about. Being civil in this sense means that one should not refer to reasons that others cannot be expected to understand. Reasons that are directly and necessarily based on comprehensive doctrines, for instance, are typically considered non-public reasons and, consequently, seen as reasons that one should not refer to in the justification of state action (Bardon 2018, 659–660; Quong 2011, 270). To fulfill one's duty of civility, one should instead appeal to reasons that are based on political values that can reasonably be expected to be shared by others as well as generally accessible guidelines of inquiry, that is, "principles of reasoning and rules of evidence in the light of which citizens are to decide whether substantive principles properly apply and to identify laws and policies that best satisfy them" and "the methods and conclusions of science when these are not controversial" (Rawls 2005, 224). This restraint in public justification is necessary to adequately respect others as free and equal: only when state action is justified by public reasons can others be recognized in their status as free and equal co-legislators.

But there is another, distinct sub-dimension of civility as public-mindedness, which we call "moral civility." This kind of civility does not focus on the justification of state action but on the deeper moral commitments that are expressed in people's actions and speech. Being civil in this sense means recognizing others as free and equal by refraining from infringing upon their individual rights and equal civic standing. It is this sub-dimension of civility as public-mindedness that comes the closest to the value of respect (Christiano 2012, 113). When we are acting civilly in this sense, we *communicate* to others that we respect them as our equals: it is this communicative aspect that distinguishes moral civility from respect, which is not necessarily a communicative act. Indeed one can be respectful without communicating it and therefore without being morally civil (Calhoun 2000, 261–262).

It is important to distinguish between civility as politeness, justificatory civility, and moral civility, because one is not necessarily civil, or uncivil, on all three (sub-)dimensions at the same time (Bardon et al. 2023)—and the failure to be civil on any (sub-)dimension is not necessarily morally objectionable. In fact, although civility in general is a virtue, being civil on all three (sub-)dimensions is not always the only permissible (or desirable) course of action. To understand this, it is important to see that the different (sub-)dimensions of civility do not share the same objective. All three (sub-)dimensions communicate some kind of respect toward others, but the kind of respect displayed by complying with norms of politeness is very minimal: when we are polite, we signal to others that they are co-members of society, but not necessarily that they are *free and equal* members of society. Alternatively, the two (sub-)dimensions of civility as public-mindedness communicate a much more demanding understanding of respect: justificatory civility and moral civility send the message to others that they are recognized as free and equal members of society. Whether civility is required and whether incivility is sometimes permissible therefore depends on which (sub-) dimension(s) of civility is (are) at stake: one could be polite without being public-minded, and one could be public-minded without being polite; one could also exhibit justificatory civility without being morally civil, and one could be morally civil without exhibiting justificatory civility. Cases in which an individual is civil or uncivil along all (sub-)dimensions are easy to assess, but oftentimes this is not what happens. Of all possible combinations, two are particularly worthy of our attention: surface-level politeness/civility and critical impoliteness/incivility.

First, *surface-level politeness and surface-level civility* combine, respectively, compliance with established norms of politeness or compliance with rules of public justification, on the one hand, with moral incivility, on the other hand. An instance of surface-level civility might include the case of "polite Nazis" (Tiso 2017), who may strategically use politeness to appear superficially reasonable and respectful, but who at the same time advance political agendas that fail to recognize the free and equal civic standing of members of certain groups; i.e., they violate moral civility. Politeness is usually a virtue, but not in such a case when it helps to cover up moral incivility.

Second, *critical impoliteness and incivility* combine the advancement of liberal democratic values demanded by moral civility with, respectively, a violation of the norms of politeness or of the rules of public justification. Acts of dissent or disobedience will sometimes be considered impolite when they violate established norms of politeness, but they might do so while advocating for respecting others as free and equal, and so communicate a fundamental commitment to liberal and democratic values. This is what Edyvane describes as "incivility-as-dissent": "instead of functioning as a one-off challenge to a particular institutional failure, incivility-as-dissent more often consists in recurring practices of small-scale rebellion inspired often by a nebulous sense of injustice" (2020, 105; see also Delmas 2018). Similarly, the Rawlsian example of abolitionists permissibly appealing to religious reasons to justify the abolition of slavery (Rawls 2005, 249) can be interpreted as a case of critical incivility: the violation of the rules of public justification becomes acceptable because it aims at denouncing the incompatibility of slavery with equal respect for all. There are also acts that could be considered as promoting certain aspects of moral civility while violating others at the same time: this is arguably the case when climate activists engage in violent or other criminal acts in order to put pressure on governments to tackle climate change (Bonotti et al. 2024)—a goal that arguably communicates respect for others as free and equal (cf. Zellentin 2015).

Surface-level impoliteness/civility and critical impoliteness/ incivility matter precisely because they reveal the complexity of the value of civility. It is this complexity that illustrates how civility is not always a virtue. On the one hand, surface-level impoliteness/ civility could do more harm than good by helping to conceal serious injustice, in which case being civil in the politeness or justificatory sense is not a desirable course of action and should not be considered praiseworthy. On the other hand, critical impoliteness/incivility can be justified as a means to a greater good, in which case being uncivil in the politeness or justificatory sense might be a permissible course of action, one that is not necessarily blameworthy. What ultimately matters is not simply the compliance with norms of civility but which norms exactly one is complying with, and for what purpose. Civility, then, provides a useful lens through which to approach cases of contentious politics. Keeping in mind the complexity of the value of civility and the various ways in which (sub-)dimensions of (in)civility can be combined is necessary to evaluate actual controversies carefully.

THE COLSTON CASE

The fate of the Edward Colston statue in Bristol had been mired in controversy leading up to and following its defacement, toppling, and tossing into the Bristol harbor during the June 7, 2020, Black Lives Matter protests. A "Countering Colston" campaign spearheaded numerous initiatives prior to the statue's unauthorized removal, seeking to confront the public celebration of controversial figures like Colston who profited from the slave trade and instead to provide a more truthful history, to commemorate and mourn those who suffered and died as a result of the slave trade, and to celebrate courageous figures who fought for abolition and emancipation instead.[2] A year following the incident at the harbor, the city's "We Are Bristol" History Commission engaged with the public about the future of the Colston statue and its plinth. As part of this engagement, the History Commission conducted a survey with nearly fourteen thousand respondents weighing in on whether the statue should be placed in a museum, what should be in the plinth space, and how they felt about the statue being pulled down. The History Commission's report found that 80% of Bristol residents thought that the statue should be displayed in a local museum, 71% supported adding a plaque to the plinth describing events on June 7, 2020, and 65% of residents felt positive about the statue being pulled down (Burch-Brown et al. 2022, 8–13). These responses were generally consistent across ethnicities, but there were considerable differences across age categories, with younger people expressing more positive feelings about the statue's removal than older respondents, and women being more positive about removal than men.

The History Commission report unpacked many of the reasons behind respondents' positive and negative feelings about the statue's removal. Many of the positive feelings about the removal stemmed from the views that Colston should not be celebrated because of his role in transatlantic slavery, that the council had previously failed to act despite a concerted campaign, and that the statue's removal would send to residents a message about racial progress and the fostering of a more inclusive community. Many of the negative feelings came about because of the illegal and undemocratic nature of the statue's toppling and the general erasure of history (Burch-Brown et al. 2022, 14–15). The Commission's work raises important questions about how we ought to memorialize and engage with history.

Despite the satisfaction some activists might feel in removing statues of historical figures deemed *personae non gratae* in contemporary political and social climates, there might also be some hidden downsides to overly zealous efforts (Wells 2020). There are clear tensions present in divergent views on statue removal as the public grapples with finding a balance between confronting and better understanding the past while taking care to avoid an erasure of history. Citizens of Bristol erected the statue 174 years after Colston's death in 1895 to celebrate some of his virtuous and philanthropic actions, like providing money for hospitals, schools, and churches, but it is certainly difficult to view those actions apart from Colston's central role in the horrors of the transatlantic slave trade (Moody 2021; Nasar 2020).

Politicians and the public have a range of options at their disposal when deciding what to do about contentious monuments, which might include preserving (without alteration), removing, (re)contextualizing, or reclaiming such monuments (Burch-Brown 2022). In practice, this might involve inaction or a concerted effort to preserve the status quo; removing the monument through legal or extralegal means; or the alteration of a monument, for example by including a counter-narrative or putting it in dialogue with an alternative perspective. In the U.K. context, the government has provided some guidance for the "custodians of commemorative heritage assets" when faced with calls to remove monuments and other contested heritage from public view. Options might include to retain, to retain and explain, or to relocate the asset (Gov.UK 2023).

Image 1. Statue of Edward Colston. The monument was erected in 1895, and on June 7, 2020, the statue was defaced, toppled, and thrown into Bristol harbor during the George Floyd protests. (Wikimedia Commons, statue by John Cassidy, photographed by Simon Cobb, June 24, 2019).

CIVILITY IN PARLIAMENT: THE COLSTON CASE IN THE U.K. HANSARD RECORDS

Having provided an overview of the civility concept and of the events that led to the toppling of Edward Colston's statue in Bristol on June 7, 2020, in this section we offer an analysis of empirical data that aims to show how different forms of civility and incivility manifested in U.K. parliamentary debates following the statue's toppling. More specifically, we collected and analyzed Hansard records referring to the toppling of the statue between June 7, 2020, and December 19, 2023, using content analysis, in order to evaluate the kinds of arguments against the toppling provided by different British MPs in Parliament and how these arguments relate to different dimensions of (in)civility (and their intersections). In our analysis, we found three main lines of argument against the toppling of Colston's statue. We will show that two of these arguments—what we call the "vandalism" and the "democracy" arguments—as well as a broad version of the third, "retain and explain" argument, constitute instances of surface-level politeness or surface-level civility, prioritizing either civility as politeness or justificatory civility over moral civility. However, a narrow version of the "retain and explain" argument, we will explain, can be interpreted instead as a genuine expression of disagreement regarding what moral civility requires and how it should be achieved. We examine each of these arguments in turn.

The Vandalism Argument

One of the most common arguments advanced by British (especially Conservative) MPs against the toppling of Colston's statue was centered around the idea of vandalism, i.e., the intentional and violent damaging of the statue. For example, the then Conservative Home Secretary Priti Patel highlighted several times how the use of violence and vandalism to remove Colston's statue (and any statues more generally) is always unacceptable. For instance, Patel argued:

> Violent activity can never be regarded as a legitimate form of protest. I do not just expect those who engage in violent activity to face the full force of the law; importantly, we should ensure that those who have a legitimate voice are heard through the right means. . . . It is not for mobs to tear down statues. (Priti Patel, Home Secretary, June 8, 2020)

Patel's views were echoed by other Conservative MPs, such as Orpington MP Gareth Bacon:

> [V]andalising monuments to the heroes who defeated fascism, defended our freedoms and ended slavery in the United States does absolutely nothing to further the cause of equality. (Gareth Bacon [Orpington] [Con], June 8, 2020)

These and other similar statements capturing the vandalism argument condemned the fact that Colston's statue had been covered in graffiti, damaged, toppled, and pushed into the Bristol harbor.

We consider this argument an instance of surface-level politeness, using civility as politeness to undermine civility as public-mindedness. In other words, for defenders of the vandalism argument, it does not matter when and why vandalism is used, or what it is meant to express: for them it is simply always wrong to vandalize, because vandalism violates norms of civility as politeness.[3] This position, however, neglects the fact that acts of vandalism can sometimes be driven by the intention to advance moral civility, i.e., to communicate to others that we respect them as free and equal persons, for example by challenging laws and institutions that deny their free and equal status—in the case of Colston's statue, the institution of slavery, with which Colston was deeply associated. The vandalism argument therefore assumes either that politeness is as important as moral civility or that it is wrong to violate politeness in the name of moral civility. In both cases, it denies that critical impoliteness (i.e., the use of impoliteness to advance moral civility) can ever be justified.

The Democracy Argument

A second line of argument that we identified in our content analysis of the U.K. Hansard records relates to democracy or, more precisely, to the protesters' failure to use democratic processes in order to advance their political goals. Once again, the then Home Secretary Priti Patel was among those advancing this criticism, via statements such as the following:

> We live in an open society and in a democracy. We have the means and mechanisms to bring statues down and to change society in the way we wish. (Priti Patel, Home Secretary, June 8, 2020)

> Whether we are talking about a statue or any other type of memorial, people should work through the correct democratic processes, with local authorities and the right individuals, to achieve the change that they want to see. (Priti Patel, Home Secretary, June 8, 2020)

This view was echoed by other prominent Conservative politicians. For example, Baroness Williams of Trafford articulated the democracy argument in the following way:

> With regard to the destruction of the statue of Edward Colston, both noble Lords have condemned the violence, and neither are sorry to see the back of a slave trader. I can understand

those points but there is a broader point about doing things in a democratic and peaceful way. Actually, that statue could have been removed years ago, had it been done in a democratic way. (Baroness Williams of Trafford, Minister of State, Home Office [Con], June 9, 2020)

My Lords, the Colston statue is in Bristol, and therefore is a matter for the elected representatives of Bristol to deal with democratically. If people are not happy with the democratic process in Bristol, they can do something about it at the ballot box. (Baroness Williams of Trafford, Minister of State, Home Office, June 9, 2020)

The democracy argument, we contend, is an instance of surface-level civility, which involves using justificatory civility to undermine moral civility.

This claim, however, requires some clarification. Justificatory civility, we explained earlier, is normally associated with the idea of public reason, i.e., the view that political decisions ought to be justified by appealing to reasons that all members of the public are likely to understand and accept at some level of idealization. Employing democratic means per se may not be *sufficient* to guarantee compliance with justificatory civility. After all, decisions about the removal of statues could be made via majoritarian democratic mechanisms such as referendums without necessarily engaging in the process of public reasoning that justificatory civility requires. However, while not sufficient, promoting change via the democratic process is *necessary* to realize the idea of justificatory civility—i.e., the exchange of public reasons to justify political decisions about statues (and about any other policy issues) is possible only if those participating in this process are committed to democratic institutions and procedures. In other words, public reasoning would be meaningless and fruitless under an authoritarian leader or if most citizens believed that change can and should be pursued via violent protest. Those who defend the democracy argument against the toppling of Colston's statue therefore appeal to the value of justificatory civility in an indirect way, in the sense that they emphasize the importance of creating the democratic preconditions for justificatory civility.

According to the defenders of the democracy argument, therefore, no matter what the objective of a publicly relevant act is, it must result from a democratic process. For them, the absence of a commitment to democratic institutions and procedures constitutes a violation of justificatory civility which is always problematic, even when the undemocratic act aims to advance moral civility. In summary, the democracy argument assumes either that justificatory civility is as important as moral civility or that it is wrong to violate justificatory civility in the name of moral civility. In both cases, it denies that critical incivility (i.e., the use of justificatory incivility to advance moral civility) can ever be justified. By doing so, the argument neglects an important point: democracy can sometimes fail to advance moral civility. Several MPs pointed this out during the debate around the Colston statue:

> My right hon. Friend has quite properly said that residents should lobby local authorities to raise principled objections to offensive statues, but Bristolians have lamented the inconsistent response of their local authority. Will my right hon. Friend consider publishing guidance not to determine outcomes but to create uniform principles, so that law-abiding citizens who object to statues can feel sure that their complaints are heard? (Laura Farris [Newbury] [Con], June 8, 2020—1)

> My Lords, is the Minister aware that one of the causes of the protest and the pulling down of the Colston statue in Bristol was the failure to act on previous lawful representations about that

statue and the frustration caused? . . . Will the Government ever learn to start listening to peaceful representations, particularly from elected Members? (Lord Foulkes of Cumnock [Lab Co-op] [V], June 9, 2020—2)

[T]he people of Bristol have in fact tried to get rid of that statue many times, and democracy failed in that case. (Baroness Jones of Moulsecoomb [GP] [V], June 9, 2020—2)

Local people in Hackney were appalled. I spoke to Jermain Jackman today, who chairs the Hackney Young Futures Commission, and he told me: "When the statue of Edward Colston in Bristol was pulled down, the Government called the protests out for not allowing the democratic process. However, Hackney allowed and followed a democratic process, consulting the local community, which was overwhelmingly in favour of having it removed. However, the Government put pressure on the board and ignored the will of the people." (Alex Sobel [Leeds North West] [Lab/Co-op], October 20, 2020—7)

All these statements highlight the fact that trying to realize moral civility via democratic means—which are a manifestation of justificatory civility—can sometimes fail. In such cases, violating democratic norms by engaging in critically uncivil behavior may be desirable and even necessary, a point which defenders of the democracy argument neglected or dismissed.

The Retain and Explain Argument

The third main line of argument against the toppling of Colston's statue that we identified in our analysis of the U.K. Hansard records is the "retain and explain" argument. According to this view, Colston's statue (and controversial statues more generally) should not be removed but rather preserved, and the role (both positive and negative) of the public figures portrayed by such statues explained and contextualized in their society's history and culture.

Once again, we can find the argument being raised by Conservative MPs. For example, Lord Ribeiro stated:

My Lords, do not take down statues; take down racism. These were the words of Sir Geoff Palmer, Scotland's first black professor and currently emeritus professor of life sciences at Heriot-Watt University. I agree with these sentiments and believe that the statues should remain, but they should have a clear description attached detailing the contributions made by the subjects and how they achieved their wealth and status. . . . We should leave the statues where they are but explain why they are there. Will my noble friend undertake to do this? (Lord Ribeiro [Con] [V], June 15, 2020)

This argument, however, was also echoed outside the Conservative Party. For example, two MPs from the Scottish National Party (SNP) defended a similar position, criticizing the protesters who had vandalized and toppled Colston's statue:

Does the Home Secretary agree with the leading human rights activist Professor Sir Geoff Palmer that we cannot erase parts of history and that a more honest narrative is needed about memorialised figures in the slave trade as a crucial step in our journey to becoming a fair and inclusive society? (Owen Thompson [Midlothian] [SNP] [V], June 8, 2020)

Many Elizabethan British heroes used violence to enhance their wealth. Does the Home Secretary agree that violence is never part of the solution, but if we can educate our citizens in where we have been, what we have done and to whom, that will provide the basis for an equal and humane society? (Douglas Chapman [Dunfermline and West Fife] [SNP] [V], June 8, 2020)

The "retain and explain" argument, as an alternative to the toppling of the statue, could be interpreted in two ways: a broad one and a narrow one.

According to the *broad* interpretation, the "retain and explain" argument constitutes an instance of surface-level politeness or surface-level civility, i.e., of the use of politeness (i.e., retain rather than topple) to undermine civility as public-mindedness or of justificatory civility (i.e., explain) to undermine moral civility. If interpreted in this way, the "retain and explain" argument—like the vandalism and democracy arguments previously examined—denies that critical impoliteness and critical incivility can ever be justified.

There is, however, a second *narrow* interpretation of the "retain and explain" argument. According to this interpretation, the argument is not an instance of surface-level politeness or civility undermining moral civility, but rather *an expression of disagreement regarding how moral civility should be advanced*. More specifically, according to this narrow interpretation, the "retain and explain" approach allows one to advance moral civility without needing to violate civility as politeness or justificatory civility. Since it rejects toppling, and therefore vandalism, the "retain and explain" approach does not entail a violation of civility as politeness, and since it does not fail to comply with the democratic process, which is a precondition for justificatory civility, it does not violate the latter either. Furthermore, based on the narrow interpretation, the provision of information on (or next to) the statue helps to advance moral civility, e.g., by explaining in what sense the person portrayed by the statue might have violated the status of certain people as free and equal (a violation of moral civility), and what a society should do in order to prevent similar violations of moral civility in the future.

If interpreted in this way, the "retain and explain" argument does not suggest that civility as politeness and/or justificatory civility are as important as moral civility, or that critical impoliteness and incivility can never be justified. Instead, its key message is that under certain conditions—which apply to the case of Colston's statue, and perhaps of other similar statues—the best way of promoting moral civility is not by removing a statue but by retaining and providing information about it. Of course, some people may still disagree with the view that this is the best way of advancing moral civility by providing information, and that removal may be more effective at achieving this goal. For example, Liberal-Democrat member of the House of Lords Baroness Hussein-Ece highlighted:

> My Lords, it is ironic that the removal last week of the statue of slave trader Edward Colston has provided more information about Britain's role in the Atlantic slave trade than any history lesson in our schools. (Baroness Hussein-Ece [LD] [V], June 15, 2020—3)

But despite these kinds of disagreements, it is still plausible to interpret the narrow version of the "retain and explain" argument as a genuine attempt to advance moral civility in ways that align with civility as politeness and justificatory civility rather than as a way of prioritizing civility as politeness or justificatory civility over moral civility.

CONCLUSION

The analysis conducted in this chapter, combining normative political philosophy with qualitative content analysis, has revealed that the virtue of civility can provide an important critical lens for understanding and evaluating contemporary debates about contentious statues and monuments. We focused especially on the statue of Edward Colston in Bristol, which was defaced, toppled, and thrown into Bristol harbor during the George Floyd protests on June 7, 2020. By conducting a content analysis of the U.K. Hansard records referring to the toppling of the statue between June 7, 2020, and December 19, 2023, we found three main lines of argument against the toppling of Colston's statue. We argued that two of these—what we called the "vandalism" and the "democracy" arguments—as well as a broad version of the third, "retain and explain" argument, constitute instances of surface-level politeness or surface-level civility, prioritizing either civility as politeness or justificatory civility over moral civility. However, we also explained that a narrow version of the "retain and explain" argument can be interpreted instead as a genuine expression of disagreement regarding how moral civility should be achieved.

We hope that our analysis has shown that civility is an aspirational concept that provides some guidance about ideal or preferred actions and behaviors, including in the context of contentious politics. More specifically, we believe that three important conclusions can be drawn from our analysis.

First, the multidimensional nature of civility that we outline provides a useful framework to make nuanced judgments about actions and behaviors in contentious politics (and beyond). It shows that promoting civility does not always require an alignment between its three dimensions—sometimes it is permissible (and desirable) to violate civility as politeness and/or justificatory civility in order to promote moral civility, as in the case of critical politeness and critical incivility. Of course, in some cases full alignment between the three dimensions *is* possible, as in the case of the narrow interpretation of the "retain and explain" argument. However, as we discussed, one should not consider this the sole (or even the best) way of realizing civility, especially in the realm of contentious politics. Importantly, when power asymmetries exist, violating norms of politeness and/ or justificatory civility may be the only suitable and effective way for certain individuals and groups to make themselves heard and challenge morally uncivil norms and institutions.

Second, and relatedly, our multidimensional framework also offers an important critical tool for evaluating apparently civil arguments and discourse that might conceal uncivil motives. As we saw in the case of the "vandalism" and "democracy" arguments, as well as of the broad version of the "retain and explain" argument, what might appear as genuine defenses of civility often conceal instead what could be interpreted as a commitment to (or, at least, an unwillingness to question or challenge) deeper forms of incivility. Adopting a more critical approach to evaluating these kinds of discourses—and doing so by combining normative with empirical approaches—is, we believe, an important contribution of our analysis.

Third, and finally, our analysis can also offer useful guidelines for policymakers and citizens engaging in public debate and decision-making about contentious statues and monuments, and other policy issues. More specifically, it can provide the foundations for developing citizens' competencies in making judgments about these issues, e.g., via civics and citizenship education. Furthermore, it can also contribute to the design of philosophically informed consultation and community engagement forums (e.g., citizens' assemblies and other types of deliberative forums), which can help to improve collective decisions about contentious policy issues, and which take the virtue of civility seriously in increasingly polarized societies.

NOTES

1. This section builds and expands on material from Bardon et al. (2023).
2. For more on the Countering Colston campaign, see the various resources on the website https://counteringcolston.wordpress.com/.

3. In this sense, we consider vandalism different from violence targeting people, which constitutes an instance of moral incivility, communicating disrespect for others as free and equal persons (Bardon et al. 2023). We acknowledge that some extreme forms of vandalism may border on moral incivility (Bonotti et al. 2024; see also Bardon et al. 2024), however, we set these borderline cases aside here.

REFERENCES

Bardon, Aurélia. 2018. "Two Misunderstandings About Public Justification and Religious Reasons." *Law and Philosophy* 37: 639–669.

Bardon, Aurélia, Matteo Bonotti, and Steven T. Zech. 2024. "Civility, Contentious Monuments, and Public Space." In *The Self, Virtue, and Public Life: Interdisciplinary Perspectives*, edited by Nancy E. Snow. Routledge.

Bardon, Aurélia, Matteo Bonotti, Steven T. Zech, and William Ridge. 2023. "Disaggregating Civility: Politeness, Public-Mindedness and Their Connection." *British Journal of Political Science* 53 (1): 308–325.

BBC News. 2022. "Bristol Colston Statue Toppling Was 'Violent Act,' Say Judges." September 29. https://www.bbc.com/news/uk-england-bristol-63059300.

Bejan, Teresa M. 2011. "The Bond of Civility: Roger Williams on Toleration and Its Limits." *History of European Ideas* 37 (4): 409–420.

Benjamin, Andrea, Ray Block, Jared Clemons, Cheryl Laird, and Julian Wamble. 2020. "Set in Stone? Predicting Confederate Monument Removal." *PS: Political Science & Politics* 53 (2): 237–242.

Bonotti, Matteo, Steven T. Zech, and Alexander Faehrmann. 2024. "Civility and Environmental Politics." *Political Studies* 73 (1): 347–369.

Boyd, Richard. 2006. "The Value of Civility?" *Urban Studies* 43 (5–6): 863–878.

Burch-Brown, Joanna. 2022. "Should Slavery's Statues Be Preserved? On Transitional Justice and Contested Heritage." *Journal of Applied Philosophy* 39 (5): 807–824.

Burch-Brown, Joanna, and Tim Cole, with Edson Burton, Nigel Costley, Steve Poole, Shawn Sobers, and Estella Tincknell. 2022. *The Colston Statue: What Next? We Are Bristol History Commission Short Report*. Bridging Histories.

Calhoun, Cheshire. 2000. "The Virtue of Civility." *Philosophy & Public Affairs* 29 (3): 251–275.

Christiano, Thomas. 2012. "What Is Civility and How Does It Relate to Core Democratic Values?" In *Civility and Democracy in America: A Reasonable Understanding*, edited by Cornell W. Clayton and Richard Elgar. Washington State University Press.

Delmas, Candice. 2018. *A Duty to Resist: When Disobedience Should Be Uncivil*. Oxford University Press.

Edgar, Amanda Nell, and Andre E. Johnson. 2024. *The Summer of 2020: George Floyd and the Resurgence of the Black Lives Matter Movement.* University Press of Mississippi.

Edyvane, Derek. 2017. "The Passion for Civility." *Political Studies Review* 15 (3): 344–354.

Edyvane, Derek. 2020. "Incivility as Dissent." *Political Studies* 68 (1): 93–109.

Gov.UK. 2023. "Guidance for Custodians on How to Deal with Commemorative Heritage Assets That Have Become Contested." Department for Culture, Media and Sport and Lord Parkinson of Whitley Bay, October 5. https://www.gov.uk/government/publications/guidance-for-custodians-on-how-to-deal-with-commemorative-heritage-assets-that-have-become-contested.

Hursthouse, Rosalind, and Glen Pettigrove. 2023. "Virtue Ethics." In *The Stanford Encyclopedia of Philosophy*, Fall ed., edited by Edward N. Zalta and Uri Nodelman. https://plato.stanford.edu/archives/fall2023/entries/ethics-virtue/.

Kekes, John. 1984. "Civility and Society." *History of Philosophy Quarterly* 1 (4): 429–443.

Meyer, Michael J. 2000. "Liberal Civility and the Civility of Etiquette: Public Ideals and Personal Lives." *Social Theory and Practice* 26 (1): 69–84.

Moody, Jessica. 2021. "Off the Pedestal: The Fall of Edward Colston." *Public History Review* 28: 1–5.

Nasar, Saima. 2020. "Remembering Edward Colston: Histories of Slavery, Memory, and Black Globality." *Women's History Review* 29 (7): 1218–1225.

Quong, Jonathan. 2011. *Liberalism Without Perfection.* Oxford University Press.

Rawls, John. 2005. *Political Liberalism.* Exp. ed. Columbia University Press.

Scates, Bruce. 2021. "Set in Stone? Dialogical Memorialisation and the Beginnings of Australia's Statue Wars." *Public History Review* 28: 72–89.

Schulz, Johannes. 2019. "Must Rhodes Fall? The Significance of Commemoration in the Struggle for Relations of Respect." *Journal of Political Philosophy* 27 (2): 166–186.

Sinopoli, Richard C. 1995. "Thick-Skinned Liberalism: Redefining Civility." *American Political Science Review* 89 (3): 612–620.

Tilly, Charles, and Sidney Tarrow. 2015. *Contentious Politics.* 2nd ed. Oxford University Press.

Tiso, Giovanni. 2017. "On Polite Nazis and the Violence of Speech." *Overland,* December 6. https://overland.org.au/2017/12/the-violence-of-speech/.

Wells, Andrew. 2020. "Introduction: Is It Wise to Decolstonize?" *Patterns of Prejudice* 54 (5): 473–483.

Zellentin, Alexa. 2015. "Climate Justice, Small Island Developing States and Cultural Loss." *Climatic Change* 133: 491–498.

Civility, Listening, and the Cultivation of Sustained Attentiveness

ANDREW PETERSON

INTRODUCTION

In his first speech after the 2020 U.S. presidential election the candidate for the Democratic Party—and soon to be next president of the United States of America—commented on the fractured and uncivil nature of political discourse. What is perhaps most notable about Joe Biden's remarks are not that they offer a particularly compelling or insightful analysis of the then (and, perhaps even more so, current) U.S. political context. Rather, it is that such expressions are nothing new. In fact, it is now commonplace for politicians, other public officials and commentators, academics, and citizens more generally to bemoan levels of political incivility in contemporary liberal democracies and to advocate for more civil and productive forms of political discussion that seek to bridge fractured divides.

Andrew Peterson, *Civility, Listening, and the Cultivation of Sustained Attentiveness* In: *The Virtue of Civility*. Edited by: Andrew Peterson, Oxford University Press. © Oxford University Press 2026.
DOI: 10.1093/9780197653791.003.0009

Yet, persistent "crises" of civility raise the specter that more civil forms of discourse, while not necessarily unobtainable, are certainly very difficult to attain. While there is some agreement about the goal—broadly speaking, for better informed, more constructive, and mutually engaged political dialogue—there is less clarity about how this goal might be attained. In other words, diagnoses of the problem and general prescriptions for a solution are commonly cited, but improved civic dialogue has not resulted. Moser (2024), for instance, states that "polarization in society arises from the deepening divisions between individuals with differing opinions, values, and beliefs," and that polarization and the lack of civility are "fuelled by a need for more meaningful communication and a growing unwillingness to engage with perspectives that differ from our own." Such statements raise the question, however, of precisely how more "constructive"—or, more to the point for this chapter, more virtuously civil—dialogue can be cultivated.

In some quarters—ranging from corners of public life to classrooms in schools—better quality political conversations are viewed as dependent on having in place particular rules to be understood and followed. Yet, even a rudimentary consideration of rules for quality political conversations readily suggests that though not *unimportant*, rules of conduct are insufficient for developing the forms of civil political discourse so desired. In other words, if civil discourse, and the civility on which it depends, were a matter solely of following certain rules[1] or guidelines, the task would be somewhat easier and straightforward—requiring, that is, little more than (1) well designed and easily understandable rules and (2) a shared commitment to those rules by those involved. But civility on most readings, and certainly when conceived as a virtue, runs much deeper.

This said, civility is not an altogether straightforward virtue. It remains the case, therefore, that developing a deeper understanding of central component elements of civility would hold some value, including for thinking through how civility stands as a virtue and how civility might be cultivated in education. One such disposition, which is the focus of this chapter, is the disposition of "sustained attentiveness." Broadly construed, sustained attentiveness is a form of listening embodied by a willingness and ability to remain concerned with listening to, engaging with, monitoring, and evaluating the interests and concerns of others through dialogue.[2] As it is presented in this chapter, sustained attentiveness requires of citizens that they track (historically, culturally, economically, and politically) the interests of their fellow citizens as best they can—a not altogether easy and straightforward undertaking. A suggestion in this chapter is not only that sustained attentiveness will lead to better and more civil conversations but also that sustained attentiveness strengthens civility as a virtue important for *political and moral relationships between citizens*. This latter concern is important because, for some, civility is a rather weak virtue lacking the depth and humanity of other virtues, while also being synonymous with outdated and/or oppressive designations of etiquette and "acceptable" behavior.

Following this introduction, this chapter is divided into four main sections. In the first section, some initial comments are offered about the definition of civility that underpins this chapter and its subsequent focus on listening and sustained attentiveness. In the second section, the focus turns to civic listening and to what might be termed a "crisis of listening." In the third section, sustained attentiveness as a particular form of learning—a form that aligns with civility as a virtue—is introduced and advanced. In the fourth, and final, main section some thoughts about educating sustained attentiveness (and by extension the virtue of civility) are given. Before moving to the substantive content of this chapter one final clarification needs to be made. The focus of this chapter is on civic listening, sustained attentiveness, and civility within specifically offline dialogical contexts. There may well be other contexts in which sustained attentiveness is also important (such as engaging with traditional media or social media), but these are outside of the scope and available space of this chapter.

CIVILITY AS A POLITICAL *AND* MORAL VIRTUE

Following others (see, for example, Boyd 2013; Curzer 2012; Laden 2019; Shils 1997; Zurn 2013), I understand there to be two main forms of civility—*everyday civility* and *political civility*. The former refers to politeness, manners, and being courteous in everyday life and in engagements with others. The actions of a civil neighbor, for instance, might include saying good morning, not being noisy, and even lending a hand in times of need. These are worthwhile and positive actions that will be guided by social norms and customs, but are not in and of themselves virtuous. Political civility relates to how citizens engage with each other and discuss ideas and interests within public life. Political civility might be cast in rather limited and superficial ways, concerned, that is, with following certain rules for political discourse that fall short of deep engagement with their fellow citizens. On such accounts, civility might be viewed as an important, but shallow, political virtue. The form of political civility I have in mind, however, runs much deeper and necessarily involves a moral, as well as political, connection between citizens. Civility is relevant to the various and wide social associations in which citizens engage and places important civic and moral obligations on citizens. In previous work (Peterson 2019), which I seek to extend in this chapter, one such obligation is the need for citizens to stay engaged with and be attentive to other citizens whose views and actions they disagree with. This obligation—a key burden of democratic citizenship—does not play a role in everyday citizenship or in accounts that ascribe a more limited role and amoral role to political civility.

In that earlier work, I distinguished between two distinct but related components of political civility. First, there is *civil conduct* which concentrates us on how citizens engage in interactions, including in civic discourse, with fellow citizens, that is, whether they enter dialogue with a commitment to honest and free interchange, to open-mindedness, to empathizing and sympathizing with the views of others, and to at least seeking some resolution and forging of common ground where ideas and interests conflict. As Edyvane (2017, 348) suggests, civic conduct can be viewed as a political and social "lubricant." Second, there is *civic friendship* between citizens that recognizes and further supports the existence of political and moral bonds and relationships between citizens that are vital for the stability and health of democratic communities— bonds, that is, of mutual *fellow-feeling* and *well-wishing* between citizens. When civic friendship is invoked we are reminded that civility is impacted by whether and how citizens understand and enact their relationships to their fellow citizens—including whether and how they listen.

The civic conduct and civic friendship that are central to and for civility are also mutually reinforcing. As Boyd (2006, 865) suggests, having "a sense that we are all part of one moral collectivity or public can only exist when we are in the habit of treating one another in ways that observe the formal conditions of civility." On such a reading, civility stands not only as a *political* concept but one that has a core *moral* element and purpose. In other words, civility is a strength of character that enables citizens as citizens *and* human beings to participate well and in concert with others within their democratic lives and communities. Being civil in the political sense I have outlined here involves thinking, feeling, deliberating, discerning, and enacting the right course of action in situations where civility is involved and is required—including when and how to *listen* to others.

THE PERILS OF POLARIZATION: A CRISIS OF LISTENING?

Political polarization is a fact of life in contemporary democracies, and polls suggest that citizens are concerned about the negative impacts of polarization and would welcome less polarized civic discourse and communities.[3] While literature and commentary on the perils of polarization have been concerned largely with the nature and tone of speech, over recent years some increased attention has been paid to the act of listening. This identification of the importance of listening in political discourse is not necessarily a completely new feature of literature on democracy. In his classic defenses of democracy and participatory politics, Benjamin Barber has written of the necessity of "civic listening," suggesting that "the public not only has a voice, but an ear: the skills of listening are as important as the skills of talking" (1998, 118) and that "talk as communication . . . involves receiving as well as expressing, hearing as well as speaking, and emphasizing as well as uttering" (2003, 174). In his earlier work, Barber (1984, 356) situated civic listening at the core of the participatory citizenship required for strong democracy, arguing that the participation

> that characterizes strong democracy attempts to balance adversary politics by nourishing the art of listening. "I will listen" means to the strong democrat not that I will scan my adversary's position for weaknesses and potential trade-offs, nor even that I will tolerantly permit him to say whatever he chooses. It means, rather, "I will put myself in his place, I will try to understand, I will strain to hear what makes us alike."

Yet, listening remains an under-examined and -appreciated concept in public life and civic theory (including theoretical ideas of civility). Not only has listening received far less attention that speaking, but when attention is paid to listening the focus tends toward "the passive form of the verb, the right 'to be listened to,' rather than the active form, 'listening.'" meaning that listening receives most attention "as part of the dialectic relationship between speaking and listening rather than as an active citizenship practice in its own right" (Schmoll 2021, 88). Writing in 2012, Dobson spoke of listening as the "new democratic deficit," an epithet that remains fitting today.

Listening is not just an act(ions) but can also refer to a disposition. With this recognition our focus shifts to not just whether we *participate in an act* of listening, but whether we are *motivated* and *disposed* to listen to the views, interests, and perspectives of others—including those with whom we disagree. While current literature on civility and political discourse has shown more interest in *what* and *who* is being listened to (witness, for example, the wide attention paid to the perils of populism, echo chambers, and fake news), placing explicit focus on civic listening as a disposition central to, and *for*, civil discourse brings into focus questions concerning *whether*, *why*, and *how* we are (or indeed are not!) listening.

It is, perhaps, the dominance of listening as an *act* or *process*, rather than as a *disposition*, that has led to a crisis of listening which is intimately bound with political polarization. This crisis comprises two main elements. First, that citizens are no longer listening to different perspectives and, second, that even when citizens engage in the act of listening the form taken is superficial, performative, and, as Kasriel (2023, 9) suggests, "transactional." Transactional listening, which stands in stark contrast to sustained attentiveness as a form of listening that is introduced in the next section, can be understood as primarily concerned with conveying information, primarily in a one-sided way and with narrow and expedient goals. A critical, and democratic, problem when listening is transactional is that interlocutors "talk past" each other or unduly prioritize their own speech acts over and above truly connecting with those of others.

This lack of democratic listening is both a symptom and a cause of political polarization. Relevant here is the fairly consistent finding in empirical studies that disagreeing groups of citizens "tend to see each other as motivated by self-interest and ideology" and are "unwilling to hear or recognize the truth" (Bruneau and Saxe 2012, 855). Furthermore, and linked to this gap between citizens, listening (or the *lack* thereof) holds a synergistic relationship with other crucial features of democratic life, including levels of trust, community, and service. In its global survey, the 2017 Edelman Trust Barometer (Edelman 2017, 33) found that 53% of people reported that they "did not regularly listen to people or organizations with whom they often disagree." In their 2023 report, Edelman found that 65% of people reported that the "lack of civility and mutual respect today is the worst I have ever seen" and that "the social fabric that once held [their] country together has grown too weak to serve as a foundation for unity and common purpose" (2023, 22). When asked "if a person strongly disagreed with me or my point of view," only 30% said they would help that person if they were in need, only 20% that they would be willing to live in the same neighborhood, and only 20% that they would be willing to have them as a coworker (23).

Before progressing to consider sustained attentiveness as a form of listening as a core component of the virtue of civility, it is also worth noting that democratic listening is not solely a concern for democratic theorists and philosophers (nor, indeed, for those interested in education for democratic citizenship, which is the focus of the last main section of this chapter). Many politicians and public figures have pronounced the importance of listening in democratic life. Recently deceased former U.S. president Jimmy Carter, for instance, positioned listening to Americans as a central element of his presidency, leading some to suggest that Carter stands as a "case study in listening leadership" (Stillion Southard and Wolvin 2009, 141). More recently, speaking in 2019 in the context of polarization following the United Kingdom's withdrawal from the European Union, then MP and now podcaster and public intellectual Rory Stewart (BBC, 2019) explained:

> I have been going up to Wigan, which is a safe Labour seat, going up to Warrington, and again and again people keep saying to me "are you not going to get abused? Are people not going to shout at you?" In fact what happens is that sometimes there are disagreements but actually people are unbelievably polite . . . and they are also very very courteous. I think if there is a challenge to our society, one big challenge above all, it is to heal divisions. We are now split . . . we have got to find our way to the common good. . . Getting to that common ground is about understanding particular details. And understanding particular details is about listening and sorting things is about acting.

This reflection from Stewart highlights in implicit terms two crucial points regarding the relationship between listening and civility as a virtue. First, that listening is a precondition for appropriate action. That is, citizens can only act appropriately (or, perhaps more accurately, are more likely to act appropriately) if they have truly listened to their fellow citizens. Second, that listening brings us closer as citizens, developing bonds and connections that are looser and more frayed when listening does not occur.

LISTENING AND SUSTAINED ATTENTIVENESS

Just as the notion of civic listening is not new, neither is the idea that certain forms of listening are more apt for civil, democratic conversation than others. More democratic and connected forms of listening have, indeed, found some expression in democratic theory and in response to the polarization prevalent in democracies today. Engaged forms of listening have been characterized variously as "deep listening" (Kasriel 2023, 9), "active listening" (Moser 2024), "empathetic listening" (Andolina and Conklin 2021), and even now online "social listening" (Stewart and Arnold 2018, 85). The term I prefer and seek to set out in this section is listening as *sustained attentiveness*. Though bearing some similarities with other forms of engaged listening, a focus on sustained attentiveness does, in my view, enable a clearer sense of how listening not only comprises an important component of being civil but is intimately connected to—and is a precondition of—civility as a virtue. In short, through the commitment to and practice of sustained attentiveness, citizens can better conduct civil conversations and also be brought into closer relation with their fellow citizens.

The idea that engaged forms of listening enable humans to connect on a deeper and more human level than more narrow forms of listening has found favor in therapeutic and psychological literature, but has not been considered in any real detail in current literature on civility as a virtue. The essence of the position advanced can be elucidated initially through reflecting on the following words from Naomi Rachel Remen (2006, 143):

> I suspect that the most basic and powerful way to connect with another person is to listen. Just listen. Perhaps the most important thing we ever give each other is our attention. And especially if it's given from the heart. When people are talking, there's no need to do anything but receive them. Just take them in. Listen to what they are saying. Care about it. Most times caring about it is even more important than understanding it.

In this passage, listening is conceived as an active and engaged process through which one builds and evidences care for the other and their humanity. In facing the challenges of political polarization and the value of truly deliberative conversations, Moser (2024) reflects that "when individuals are willing to listen, they open themselves to understanding the motivations, fears, and aspirations underlying diverse perspectives. This empathetic approach is a cornerstone of overcoming polarization." In their response to polarization, Kasriel (2023, 10) speaks of the "need to cultivate an openhearted attention" and to "learn how to focus that attention towards others, acknowledging to ourselves the speaker's humanity." Listening is not a passive disposition or act. Rather, the listener needs to work hard to engage the speaker and to shape what the speaker is saying and what is revealed in conversation (Parker 2010).

To listen in this way and to provide others, including those with whom we disagree, our attentiveness is not a disposition that can be tokenistic, fleeting, or partial. To be truly democratic and to hold the possibility of virtue, a citizen's attentiveness to others needs to be sustained and dedicated. Without *sustained* attentiveness, it is unlikely that citizens will form the understanding or the bonds required to connect with others so important for "coaxing out the interests of others through sensitivity and tact" (Kingwell 1994, 211). This coaxing requires not just an immediate desire to know and understand the interests of others, but a desire to stay with these interests, tracking how they change and are impacted by ongoing dialogue, events, and vicissitudes.

Eschewing current misrepresentations of sympathy, in a previous text (Peterson 2017) I considered the value and importance of a sympathetic disposition for engaging with others and for forging moral and civic relationships. Counter to common understandings and usages today, I contended—and contend here—that the act and condition of sympathy is fundamental to listening. Though sympathy is more commonly associated with suffering and the virtue of compassion, there are important reasons for bringing sympathy into the conversation about sustained attentiveness. First, because a good deal of the most divisive matters that polarize citizens today involve suffering to some greater or lesser extent (and here the idea that sympathy is an appropriate response to a wider range of situations than compassion is relevant [Snow 1991]). Second, because the quality of sympathy, or offering a sympathetic ear, provides a model and basis for opening ourselves up to be able to listen and engage with a wider range of matters, experiences, and interests. The broad understanding of sympathy that I have in mind encompasses a recognition, an affinity (Garber 2004), and an identification (Konstan 2014) with another person. It is in recognizing, developing affinity, and identifying with others, which can happen truly only when we listen properly, that citizens can draw others closer to their circle of concern, reducing distance between citizens and allowing citizens to consider their shared human frailties and possibilities. Philosophy and literature abound with eloquent elucidations of this idea of which two will serve to exemplify here. First, John Donne's poem "For Whom the Bell Tolls":

> No man is an island,
> Entire of itself.
> Each is a piece of the continent,
> A part of the main.
> If a clod be washed away by the sea,
> Europe is the less.
> As well as if a promontory were.
> As well as if a manor of thy friend's or of thine own were.
> Each man's death diminishes me,
> For I am involved in mankind.
> Therefore, send not to know
> For whom the bell tolls,
> It tolls for thee.

Second is the following oft-cited passage from Rousseau's ([1762] 1979, 224) *Émile* in which this recognition of common humanity and human fragility is to the fore:

> Do not, therefore, accustom your pupil to regard the sufferings of the unfortunate and the labors of the poor from the height of his glory; and do not hope to teach him to pity[4] them if he considers them alien to him. Make him understand well that the fate of these unhappy people can be his, that all of their ills are there in the ground beneath his feet, that countless unforeseen and inevitable events can plunge him into them from one moment to the next.

A further aspect of sympathy, which some ascribe now to empathy too but with less secure philosophical lineage, is that sympathy can act as an important motivator for attending to the needs of others (see, for example, Eisenberg 1986; Sverdlik 2008; Kristjánsson 2014). The motivational work sympathy undertakes would seem to be crucial for the cultivation and sustenance of fellow feeling between citizens.

Before moving to consider the formation of sustained attentiveness through education, it is worthwhile spending a little time considering two potential criticisms—both of practical relevance—that are likely to confront the sustained attentiveness I have advocated for here. Moreover, because of the moral closeness that I have ascribed to sustained attentiveness, if accurate the criticisms would cause serious problems for civility *as a virtue*. The first criticism could run something like the following: in all, or certain, situations sustained attentiveness places too heavy a burden on citizens, requiring them to engage with and listen to other citizens whose views are confronting, oppressive, or worse. Such a concern is particularly pointed when power inequalities (whether historical or current) are apparent between interlocutors. There are no conclusive arguments that will fully appease those who might raise this criticism. That said, active and participatory forms of citizenship (particularly of the civic republican variety that I have advocated for previously [Peterson 2011]) *do* place particular and not insignificant burdens on citizens, which in turn might impact more heavily on certain citizens than others. In a democracy citizens must, however, listen to the views with which they disagree if they are to (1) seek to understand them and (2) seek to address them (in whatever form such address might take, whether it be to challenge, seek to change, or reconcile with their own views, for instance). Of course, the establishment of safeguards is important to help to protect those who have been wrongly subjugated in the past and/or present and to provide support for the cognitive and emotional challenge that sustained attentiveness brings for those involved. So too, there might be some situations in which the weight of oppression or the rawness of events is so strong that the burden of sustained attentiveness would be too heavy to reasonably expect of citizens.

This first potential criticism, then, is better understood as a warning to be heeded, worked through, and mitigated, rather than being fatal for sustained attentiveness. In facing this first criticism, it might also be useful to have recourse to Howard Curzer's (2012, 84) *Aristotelian Account of Civility* in which he suggests that "civil people act and feel rightly when encountering people espousing differences." Not only is it the case that citizens will be better able to perceive and judge how to act and feel rightly if they listen, but also—and more to the point here—that acting rightly may under particular circumstances involve removing oneself from engaging in dialogue and listening if harm (or, at least, too much harm) will result from said engagement.

The second potential criticism of sustained attentiveness is the concern that sustained attentiveness could serve to *deepen*, rather than reduce, division and polarization. In other words, that through truly listening to others with whom they disagree, citizens will come to realize that polarization runs even deeper than they had thought. As with the first potential criticism, it is unlikely that sufficient reason or evidence can be provided to say that the deepening of division might never occur and could never be the case. However, there are reasons for considering that such cases are likely to be limited (and certainly less than the narrowing of division). Consider the following, for example, from a report from surveying research on polarization in the United States:

> Most partisans hold major misbeliefs about the other party's preferences that lead them to think there is far less shared policy belief. This perception gap is highest among progressive activists, followed closely by extreme conservatives: in other words, the people who are most involved in civic and political life hold the least accurate views of the other side's beliefs. (Kleinfeld 2023, 1)

Given that the perception gap is (1) based on major misbeliefs and (2) is widest for those most politically active, it is hard to think how a form of listening that focuses on sustained engagement and bringing citizens closer together could serve to *further* what are already deep divisions. Certainly, psychological theories such as contact theory (Allport 1979) suggest that positive interactions between groups is beneficial in reducing difference if certain conditions (such as equality of status) operate. Of course, this response is not in and of itself compelling—far from it. As such, other evidence is required. With that in mind, there is now a fairly wide and cross-disciplinary evidence base that entering into genuine dialogue and listening with other citizens serves to narrow, rather than widen, divisions. In their work on citizen deliberation, Jacobs et al. (2009, 82) found that citizens were not fixated on "winning or losing" and instead were genuinely committed to working together to talk, listen, and, where possible, find areas of agreement. Studies in political science on contexts of deeply divided societies and broader work in social psychology similarly attest to the role of listening in bringing citizens closer together (see, for example, Dembinska and Montambeault 2015; Itzchakov et al. 2017; Wahl 2021; Zhou and Fredrickson 2023). While not completely rebutting the second criticism, there are grounds for being cautiously optimistic about the democratic and moral potential of sustained attentiveness for the civil conduct and civil bonds necessary for the virtue of civility.

EDUCATING SUSTAINED ATTENTIVENESS IN HIGH SCHOOLS

Just as with democratic citizenship itself, sustained attentiveness will not develop without intentional, deliberate, and careful cultivation. There are, of course, many forms and spaces of education within which sustained attentiveness might be learned, and it is the case that engagement *in* sustained attentiveness is a necessary form *of* such learning. In this final main section, I focus on one such space—high schools.[5]

The idea that listening is an important element of civic learning in schools is not new and has found some representation in recent curricular reviews and reports. Interestingly, this representation has perhaps been more clear and consistent in the United States than in my own context of England, where listening has more typically been added as an adjunct or counterpart to talking or speaking (see, for example, Oracy Education Commission 2024). In contrast, in the United States there has been a stronger focus on listening as a separate civic disposition in its own right within civic education. One major American report, for example, contends that "competent and responsible citizens share four common traits," one of which is to exhibit "moral and civic values," including being *"willing to listen to alternative perspectives"* (Campaign for the Civic Mission of Schools 2011, 11, emphasis in original). More recently, the extensive National Academy of Education report "Educating for Civic Reasoning and Discourse" advocates the importance of cultivating a "disposition to listen to and consider contrasting points of view" (2021, 4). The report positions the benefits of listening in the following way:

> Listening has epistemic benefits. It can help us to see what we are missing or not sufficiently appreciating about an issue or its impact. Listening also has benefits for the manner in which we relate to each other. Active listening is ethical and relational in that it is a way of treating others as political equals, respecting them as individuals, and perhaps enabling relationships to form. Listening can help us to see that others have reasoned beliefs, many of which are worthy of our time and consideration, and may even come to influence our own beliefs. It can help us to see our shared humanity and our shared fate as well as appreciate our real and enduring differences. (39)

Pedagogically, classroom rules for discussion (such as not speaking over each other) might act as an important stage in clarifying for students certain actions or constraints while they support listening (Crocco et al. 2017). As noted earlier in this chapter, however, rules are insufficient on their own to foster the commitment, motivation, and civic identity needed for sustained attentiveness and which move us from more limited forms of civil discourse to forms that recognize and seek to further foster more bonds between citizens. For those moral bonds to be recognized and developed, students need to be brought into community with others—their peers, their teachers, members of their communities—through appropriate and supported forms of dialogue in which listening is prioritized and scaffolded.

Bringing students into community with each other in this way requires the careful cultivation of listening communities. Here, the community of inquiry central to philosophy in schools acts as one leading pedagogical practice and caring community to provide meaningful opportunities for students to practice and learn sustained attentiveness. As D'Olimpio (2018) suggests, when constituted properly, communities of inquiry foster trust and allow participants to engage in deliberative reflective exploration of the ideas and perspectives being shared. One leading writer on philosophy in schools, Laurance Splitter (2011, 497–498), has also pointed to the collective nature of communities of inquiry through which participants recognize themselves, other participants, and the collective by understanding oneself as "valuing self-worth through one's associations," through "recognising that others also seek this sort of self-worth," and through understanding that "self-appreciation and appreciation for others are interdependent and mutually reinforcing."

These sentiments hold resonance for cultivating sustained attentiveness given the mutuality I have suggested exists between attentiveness and fellow feeling. Philosophy in schools teacher Pablo Muruzábal Lamberti (2018) suggests that through communities of inquiry, students become "apprentices of listening."[6] As noted already in this chapter, listening—and certainly listening as sustained attentiveness—is as much a collective endeavor as it is an individual one. Moreover, listening is a complex and an active activity. When we are attentive to a speaker, we engage not just with what they are saying but with a range of other matters, including what we may know about them (including, does what they are saying fit with what we already know about them? How does what they are saying relate to the ongoing dialogue?). So too, we engage with our own thoughts and ideas about what is being said (including, how does what they are saying align or differ from my own views? What questions would I like/need to ask to better understand the speaker's views), as well as other perspectives of which we are aware (including, how does what they are saying accord with or contradict other perspectives of which I am aware? With which other ideas and perspectives does the perspective of the speaker align?). Through being attentive to what is being said, students are involved in a learning process of constantly navigating between ideas they are hearing, ideas they hold, and ideas they know from other sources.

Though this process is inherently complex, we cannot (and contra some therapeutic forms of listening) attend properly to what is being said without *at the same time and as part of the process* navigating, juxtaposing, comparing, contrasting, assessing, evaluating and—crucially—connecting with others. As Lamberti puts it:

[L]istening presupposes a certain degree of sovereignty to think freely. Listening should not mean one stops thinking one's own thoughts. This could be the case when a student is required to obey his or her teacher and does what (s)he is being told, which by definition sabotages any attempt to philosophize. Based on the above, one could assert that there are multiple sources one taps into when listening; there are more voices to be heard than the one speaking at a given time and space, making the art of listening a polyphonic activity.

In their discipline-leading work, Hess and McAvoy (2015) report that effective deliberative practices in school classrooms were best supported through a range of whole-school and curricular practices, including flexibility to examine issues, intentional planning, cultivating diversity, and a supportive whole-school environment. These authors also demonstrate the expertise of teachers in supporting student learning through highlighting apt moments and aspects of dialogue, including opportunities for meta-communication about positive and less positive aspects of the conversation. Through participation in well-supported and reflective deliberation and such careful and skillful teaching, students in Hess and McAvoy's study gained confidence in discussing controversial and sensitive political issues and showed more interest in *listening* to perspectives that differed from their own. The meta-analysis referenced here is likely to be strengthened, educationally speaking, through explicit consideration of the aim(s) of listening, the nature of listening, and what obligations for listening citizens have, the role and character of the listener, and the connection and relationship between listeners and speakers.[7]

CONCLUSION

Writing in 1973, Mount offered the following, pointed reflection about civility:

> In the flourishing city, civility is part of the air we breathe. We no more trouble to analyse it than we take a chemical sample of the atmosphere when we lean out of the window on a summer morning. The mere presence of a debate on civility is therefore a sign that the city is in danger—or at least that people fear so. (31)

Though specifically about civility, the condition Mount identifies could well be applied to civic listening today. In this chapter I have argued that sustained attentiveness as a form of civic listening is not only an important component of civility but is a necessary component of civility as a virtue. Sustained attentiveness enables citizens to examine and answer important questions about civic life and the purposes of civic life, questions that could not be answered by citizens alone nor by citizens conversing only with those with views similar to their own.

Moreover, and in simple terms, sustained attentiveness not only serves as a form of civil conduct but is vital for civil fellow feeling, and is so for at least two main reasons. First, in helping citizens to understand others and to understand their views, their interests, their fragilities, and their goals in life and why these goals are important to them. Second, when citizens truly listen and are attentive in doing so the bonds that tie us—bonds that have become increasingly frayed—are strengthened. There are also likely to be other civic benefits—for civility and for civic understanding and participation more generally—from sustained attentiveness, the redistribution of civic knowledge (Schmoll 2021). Yet, as with other aspects of civility, and with civility itself, current trends in public dialogue and conversations paint a rather bleak picture for civic listening. Whether the current crisis of civic listening can be reversed remains to be seen, but such a reversal will unlikely occur without citizens truly committing to staying attentive to the other citizens and without citizens conceiving attentiveness as a condition of fellow-feeling within a democratic community.

NOTES

1. There is not sufficient space in this chapter to detail in full what a rule-based approach to civil conversation consists of, but sets of rules for civil discourse can easily be found online. See, for example, American Bar Association (n.d.).
2. My position here can be differentiated from that of Beatty (1999), who argues that good listening is itself a moral and intellectual virtue. My view is that sustained attentiveness is a particular form of listening vital for the virtue of civility.
3. See, for instance, Frankovic (2024); Newport (2023); Pew Research Center (2023); Duffy et al. (2019); National Centre for Social Research (2024).
4. Translations of Rousseau use the term "pity" to refer to what here I am referring to as sympathy; see Peterson (2017) for a fuller explanation.
5. I use the term "high school" here as a catch-all term for schooling from the ages of eleven to sixteen.
6. It is important to note, and accept, that the term "apprentice of listening" suggests that there are, or might be, masters of listening, and it is not altogether

clear that there is an abundance of masters of listening in public life today. This means that teachers are faced with the challenging task of seeking to find examples and exemplars which can serve as educational guides and, if possible, as role models for students in the form of sustained attentiveness required for the virtue and practice of civility.

7. I have adapted these four foci from Haroutunian-Gordon's (2011) account of Plato's philosophy of listening.

REFERENCES

Allport, G. W. 1979. *The Nature of Prejudice*. Basic Books.

American Bar Association. n.d. "Ground Rules for Ensuring a Civil Conversation." Accessed December 6, 2025. https://www.americanbar.org/groups/judicial/american_jury/resources/dialogue_on_the_american_jury/ground_rules/.

Andolina, M. W., and H. G. Conklin. 2021. "Cultivating Empathetic Listening in Democratic Education." *Theory & Research in Social Education* 49 (3): 390–417.

Barber, B. 1984. *Strong Democracy: Participatory Politics for a New Age*. University of California Press.

Barber, B. 1998. *A Passion for Democracy: American Essays*. Princeton University Press.

Barber, B. 2003. *Strong Democracy. Participatory Politics for a New Age*. 20th anniversary ed. University of California.

BBC. 2019. *Question Time*. https://www.youtube.com/watch?v=9p4cv2AqLGw.

Beatty, J. 1999. "Good Listening." *Educational Theory* 49 (1): 281–298.

Boyd, R. 2006. "The Value of Civility." *Urban Studies* 43 (5/6): 863–878.

Boyd, R. 2013. "Adam Smith on Civility and Civil Society." In *The Oxford Handbook of Adam Smith*, edited by C. J. Berry, M. P. Paganell, and C. Smith. Oxford University Press.

Bruneau, E. G., and R. Saxe. 2012. "The Power of Being Heard: The Benefits of 'Perspective-Giving,' in the Context of Intergroup Conflict.'" *Journal of Experimental Social Psychology* 48: 855–866.

Campaign for the Civic Mission of Schools. 2011. "Guardian of Democracy: The Civic Mission of Schools." https://media.carnegie.org/filer_public/ab/dd/abdda62e-6e84-47a4-a043-348d2f2085ae/ccny_grantee_2011_guardian.pdf?_gl=1*baaze8*_gcl_au*OTAxNTA3NTkwLjE3Mzk0Njk1Njk.

Crocco, M. C., A. Halvorsen, P. Jacobsen, and A. Segall. 2017. "Less Arguing, More Listening: Improving Civility in Classrooms." *Phi Delta Kappan* 98 (7): 67–71.

Curzer, H. J. 2012. "An Aristotelian Account of Civility." In *Civility in Politics and Education*, edited by D. S. Mower and W. L. Robison. Routledge.

Dembinska, M., and F. Montambeault. 2015. "Deliberation for Reconciliation in Divided Societies." *Journal of Public Deliberation* 11 (1): 1–35.

Dobson, A. 2012. "Listening: The New Democratic Deficit." *Political Studies* 60: 843–859.

D'Olimpio, L. 2018. *Media and Moral Education: A Philosophy of Critical Engagement.* Routledge.

Duffy, Bobby, Kirstie Hewlett, Julian McCrae, and John Hall. 2019. "Divided Britain? Polarisation and Fragmentation Trends in the UK." King's College London, Policy Institute, September. https://www.kcl.ac.uk/policy-institute/assets/divided-britain.pdf.

Edelman. 2017. "2017 Edelman Trust Barometer: Global Report." https://www.edelman.com/sites/g/files/aatuss191/files/2025-01/2017%20Trust%20Barometer%20Global%20Report_FINAL.pdf.

Edelman. 2023. "2023 Edelman Trust Barometer: Global Report." https://www.edelman.com/sites/g/files/aatuss191/files/2023-03/2023%20Edelman%20Trust%20Barometer%20Global%20Report%20FINAL.pdf.

Edyvane, D. 2017. "The Passion for Civility." *Political Studies Review* 15 (3): 344–354.

Eisenberg, N. 1986. *Altruistic Cognition, Emotion and Behavior.* Erlbaum.

Frankovic, Kathy. 2024. "Polarization Is Getting Worse: Few See Shared Values with Those in the Other Party." YouGov, May 24. https://today.yougov.com/politics/articles/49530-polarization-is-getting-worse-in-us.

Garber, M. 2004. "Compassion." In *Compassion: The Culture and Politics of an Emotion*, edited by L. Berlant. Routledge.

Haroutunian-Gordon, S. 2011. "Plato's Philosophy of Listening." *Educational Theory* 61 (2): 125–139.

Hess, D., and P. McAvoy. 2015. *The Political Classroom: Evidence and Ethics in Democratic Education.* Routledge.

Itzchakov, G., A. N. Kluger, and D. R. Castro. 2017. "I Am Aware of My Inconsistencies but Can Tolerate Them: The Effect of High Quality Listening on Speakers' Attitude Ambivalence." *Personality and Social Psychology Bulletin* 43 (1): 105–120.

Jacobs, L. R., F. L. Cook, and M. X. Delli Carpini. 2009. *Talking Together: Public Deliberation and Political Participation in America.* University of Chicago Press.

Kasriel, E. 2023. "Deep Listening as an Approach to Tackle Polarisation." British Council. https://www.britishcouncil.org/sites/default/files/202309-cultural-relations-collection-2023-deep_listening_as_an_approach_to_tackle_polarisation_edited.pdf.

Kingwell, M. 1994. *A Civil Tongue: Justice, Dialogue, and the Politics of Pluralism.* Pennsylvania State University Press.

Kleinfeld, Rachel. 2023. "Polarization, Democracy, and Political Violence in the United States: What the Research Says." Working Paper. Carnegie Endowment for International Peace, September. https://carnegie-production-assets.s3.amazonaws.com/static/files/Kleinfeld_Polarization_final_3.pdf.

Konstan, D. 2014. "Pity, Compassion and Forgiveness." In *The Politics of Compassion*, edited by M. Ure and M. Frost. Routledge.

Kristjánsson, K. 2014. "Pity: A Mitigated Defence." *Canadian Journal of Philosophy* 44 (3–4): 343–364.

Laden, A. S. 2019. "Two Concepts of Civility." In *A Crisis of Civility? Political Discourse and Its Discontents*, edited by R. G. Boatright, T. J. Shaffer, S. Sobieraj, and D. Goldthwaite Young. Routledge.

Lamberti, P. M. 2018. "Apprentices of Listening." Philosophy Foundation. https://www.philosophy-foundation.org/blog/apprentices-of-listening.

Moser, F. 2024. "Bridging Divides and Overcoming Polarization: The Power of Deliberative Practice." Deliberative Citizenship Initiative, March 14. https://deliberativecitizenship.org/blogposts/bridging-divides-and-overcoming-polarization-the-power-of-deliberative-practice/.

Mount, F. 1973. "The Recovery of Civility." *Encounter* XLI: 31–43.

Muruzábal Lamberti, P. 2018. "Apprentices of Listening." Accessed April 14, 2025. https://www.philosophy-foundation.org/blog/apprentices-of-listening.

National Academy of Education. 2021. "Educating for Civic Discourse and Reasoning." https://naeducation.org/wp-content/uploads/2021/04/NAEd-Educating-for-Civic-Reasoning-and-Discourse.pdf.

National Centre for Social Research. 2024. "British Social Attitudes: Growing Polarisation in Attitudes Towards Immigration." Press Release, June 12. https://natcen.ac.uk/news/british-social-attitudes-growing-polarisation-attitudes-towards-immigration.

Newport, Frank. 2023. "Update: Partisan Gaps Expand Most on Government Power, Climate." Gallup, August 7. https://news.gallup.com/poll/509129/update-partisan-gaps-expand-government-power-climate.aspx.

Oracy Education Commission. 2024. "We Need to Talk: The Report of the Commission on the Future of Oracy Education in England." https://oracyeducationcommission.co.uk/wp-content/uploads/2024/10/Future-of-Oracy-v23-web-13.pdf.

Parker, W. 2010. "Listening to Strangers: Classroom Discussion in Democratic Education." *Teachers College Record* 112 (11): 2815–2832.

Peterson, A. 2011. *Civic Republicanism and Civic Education: The Education of Citizens*. Palgrave.

Peterson, A. 2017. *Compassion and Education: Cultivating Compassionate Children, Schools and Communities*. Palgrave.

Peterson, A. 2019. *Civility and Democratic Education*. Springer.

Pew Research Center. 2023. "Americans' Dismal Views of the Nation's Politics." September 19. https://www.pewresearch.org/politics/2023/09/19/americans-dismal-views-of-the-nations-politics/.

Remen, R. N. 2006. *Kitchen Table Wisdom: Stories That Heal*. Riverhead Books.

Rousseau. 1762/1979. *Emile: Or On Education.* Introduction, Translation, and Notes by Allan Bloom. Basic Books.

Schmoll, K. 2021. "Listening as a Citizenship Practice Post–Arab Spring: Mediated Civic Listening as a Struggle, Duty and Joy in Urban Morocco." *Media, Culture & Society* 43 (1): 84–100.

Shils, E. 1997. *The Virtue of Civility: Selected Essays on Liberalisms, Tradition and Civil Society.* Liberty Fund.

Snow, N. 1991. "Compassion." *American Philosophical Quarterly* 28 (3): 195–205.

Splitter, L. 2011. "Identity, Citizenship and Moral Education." *Educational Philosophy and Theory* 43 (5): 484–505.

Stewart, M. C., and C. L. Arnold. 2018. "Defining Social Listening: Recognizing an Emerging Dimension of Listening." *International Journal of Listening* 32 (2): 85–100.

Stillion Southard, B. F., and Andrew D. Wolvin. 2009. "Jimmy Carter: A Case Study in Listening Leadership." *International Journal of Listening* 23 (2): 141–152.

Sverdlik, S. 2008. "Compassion and Sympathy as Moral Motivation." Occasional Paper 3. SMU Scholar. http://digitalrepository.smu.edu/centers_maguireethics_occasional/3/.

Wahl, R. 2021. "Not Monsters After All: How Political Deliberation Can Build Moral Communities Amidst Deep Difference." *Journal of Deliberative Democracy* 17 (1): 160–168.

Zhou, J., and B. L. Fredrickson. 2023. "Listen to Resonate: Better Listening as a Gateway to Interpersonal Positivity Resonance Through Enhanced Sensory Connection and Perceived Safety." *Current Opinion in Psychology* 53: 1–7.

Zurn, C. F. 2013. "Political Civility: Another Illusionistic Ideal." *Public Affairs Quarterly* 27 (4): 341–368.

Civility, Power, and the Fragility of Democracy

KATHERINE FIERLBECK

INTRODUCTION: THE CONTINGENCY OF DEMOCRACY

In a democratic system, do we need civility at all? We have rigorous procedural requirements (that may of course vary across jurisdictions) as well as legal protections and safeguards (generally in the form of justiciable rights, which again vary across jurisdictions). We have democratic institutions with clearly delineated functions and powers. Why should our behavior matter?

This chapter argues that the "crisis of (in)civility" is not only a serious threat to democracy, but also a logical extension of it. Liberalism, its roots in the bloody battlefields of the seventeenth century, was an attempt to rationalize and de-personalize politics. The concept of "rights," as justiciable entitlement claims supported by a fundamental and compelling justification, while predating the early modern period, began to play an increasingly important political role by the

Katherine Fierlbeck, *Civility, Power, and the Fragility of Democracy* In: *The Virtue of Civility*. Edited by: Andrew Peterson, Oxford University Press. © Oxford University Press 2026. DOI: 10.1093/9780197653791.003.0010 end of the seventeenth century. The right to free speech, originally conceptualized as the "right of conscience," or the ability to worship without fear of persecution, has provided citizens with a protective shield of rights freeing them from a habit of self-censorship that had once been their key protection against arbitrary violence. This kind of freedom of expression became volatile when combined with the institutionalization of universal suffrage, as contempt and disdain could be advantageous weapons for securing popular support. Both the ability to "speak truth to power" and the need to win the widespread support of one's fellow citizens have served as the foundation of a dynamic, adaptable, and stable form of political organization that has both facilitated and tempered the astonishing development of technological capitalism for several centuries. At the same time, however, the institutionalization of secular or "human" rights—along with the focus on a discursive battlefield where political support is obtained through affect—meant that this dynamic and productive form of organization also had, as Tocqueville recognized in the early nineteenth century, the capacity to unleash much darker tendencies as well. In this way the decline of civility is not due to the failure of liberal democracy but is, rather, a natural extension of its logic.

Democracy, in the twentieth century, became the preeminent metric to determine what constituted a "legitimate" form of rule. And as liberal democracy became the gold standard of political legitimacy, measuring the extent to which polities could be considered "democratic" became essential. Typographies and metrics developed, giving a quantitative dimension to the exercise of determining the extent to which states were "acceptable" members of the international community or pariahs which (if they were devoid of desirable natural resources) could be shunned by the wider political community. Complex and sophisticated measurements of the nature and extent of democratic practice have been painstakingly compiled by research consortia like the V-Dem project and the Lexical Index of Electoral

Democracy, which look at indicators such as the extent of suffrage, the way in which elections are run, the ease of political handover following elections, the organization of parties and the accessibility of party membership, the limits on (and behavior of) the executive and legislative bodies, the role of the judiciary, the protection of civil liberties, the engagement of civil society, the role of the media, the level of political and economic equality, and so on.[1] Each of these indicators can be coded to give a fulsome and robust account of the relative democratic nature of any given state.

These measurements, while subject to challenges over the precise application and interpretation, have been invaluable for researchers in seeking to formalize the ability to determine the extent of democracy within and across states. Nonetheless, the quantification of democracy draws attention away from the much messier social or psychological component of democracy as a social value that citizens can choose to prioritize over other political objectives or values (or not). While value surveys do attempt to determine the respective import that citizens place on particular values, they generally do not clearly reflect the distinction between first-order values (those a priori norms and principles that are so important that they must be preserved above all) and second-order ones (the instrumental processes through which all first-order preferences are sorted). Democracy, of course, is a second-order principle; we support it because it provides us with a process that allows the sorting of preferences upon which people might not otherwise agree. But when instrumental principles conflict with first-order ones ("If I support democracy, the majority will impose moral choices that I feel are both wrong and dangerous"), first-order principles, by definition, may be prioritized.[2]

We have codified and quantified modern democracy so much that we have lost sight of the very conditions that were, historically, necessary for it to gain a tenuous foothold in Western societies. Like physical properties such as gravity, democratic institutions now are understood to exist independently of the thoughts, feelings, or expression of those within them. Democracy is reduced to a mechanistic process, a counting of votes independent of affect. This assumption is quite manifest in (but is not limited to) the United States, where electoral campaigns have presented numerous candidates whose seeming incompetence, venality, and contempt for non-supporters is excused because parties, and their supporters, are simply looking for hands to be raised during votes in legislative institutions. Second-order principles—perceptions on the importance of process and protocol—have become reified as *institutions* (with a solidity and constancy) rather than as the ephemeral *values* that they are.

By the beginning of the twenty-first century, the sheer scope and extent of modern democracy encouraged us to suppose that it was a hardy plant that could take root in any terrain, however inhospitable. We have lost sight of the contingency of democracy, and the very specific conditions under which modern democracy was able to gain a foothold in a violent and polarized environment. Early proponents of democracy, like Jean-Jacques Rousseau, who saw collective action within the context of the republican tradition, understood very clearly that bonds of mutual respect and understanding were essential in constructing a robust self-governing polity. *Citizens* would fight to the death in a way that *subjects* might not. At the same time, early defenders of the expansion of liberal rights (especially free speech) made it conditional upon using this liberty to engage in dialogue with their fellow-citizens in order to explain and persuade. Liberalism and democracy, in this way, were a comfortable fit, and the consolidation of the two into "liberal democracy" seemed both natural and unproblematic. Nonetheless, the merging of liberal and democratic ideas was ever a marriage with deep unresolved tensions, and the failure to understand the particular conditions within which each can be expected to function well has only exacerbated these tensions. The following section discusses the role for civility supposed by early proponents of stable self-rule, while the section after that explains how the development of democracy as a liberal phenomenon began to privilege first-order principles over second-order ones. The final section concludes by observing that contemporary rights do precisely the opposite of what Thomas Hobbes, one of the first major "rights" theorists, had wanted them to achieve. Rather than facilitating a "civil" political environment conducive to stable political organization, modern rights-talk precludes the kind of political context early liberal theorists saw as necessary for the exercise of collective self-government.

CONTUMELY AND CONTEMPT: CIVILITY AS A PRECONDITION TO THE ESTABLISHMENT OF DEMOCRATIC ORGANIZATION

We now tend to think of democracy as a rational construct, a set of processes and institutions, independent of sentiment. This would have pleased Thomas Hobbes immensely. Writing in the depths of the English Civil War, Hobbes recognized that first-order principles, a priori normative claims that one simply did or did not accept (religious principles, in his day), simply got in the way of stable political relationships. Compromise on first principles could be quite difficult, if not impossible: we either believed or not; there was no means to arbitrate between opposing beliefs. As conflict based on first-order principles merely provoked people to become more intransigent, he suggested that such first-order principles must be subordinate to second-order ones based firmly on a naturalistic epistemology grounded in our senses. Hobbes realized that voluntary consent, even under conditions of duress, was much more likely if people were willing to recognize each other as equals in some fundamental way. Those treating others with contempt or with an assumption of inferiority would find it difficult easily to secure sufficient trust to enter into a binding agreement.

Yet anyone living in a highly hierarchical society—and especially Hobbes's contemporaries literate enough to read his works—would likely have been quite dubious about the empirical veracity of any claim of thoroughgoing equality between individuals. Gamely, Hobbes ([1651] 1962, 98) countered that we are all equal in key ways: in susceptibility to sudden death, in the hope of a better life, and in the belief that we are all superior to everyone else. Perhaps doubting that this was enough to persuade readers of the need to trust each other—even for the one moment in time when a social contract could be negotiated—he ensconced the acceptance of equality into a principle of natural law. Intriguingly, Hobbes's ninth law of nature does not baldly state that we *are* all equal, merely that we must be willing to *acknowledge* others as our equals. If readers are ready to accept Hobbes's rather sketchy account of why it is that we are fundamentally equal, so be it. ("If nature therefore have made men equal, that equality is to be acknowledged.") For the more skeptical, Hobbes holds that they must go along with the fiction of equality to achieve a greater good: "because men that think themselves equal will not enter into conditions of peace, but upon equal terms, such equality must be admitted" (120).

The civility that Hobbes requires as a precondition to the formation of a social contract may be limited in scope and rendered somewhat grudgingly, but it was essential enough to be posited as part of the rubric of natural law that *simply had to be obeyed* as a condition of human rationality. And, while Hobbes's *Leviathan* is generally notable for its dark, cynical depiction of human conduct, Hobbes's complete list of the natural laws set out a demand for civility that rivals Locke's gentle expectation that people will, in general, tend to treat each other well as a matter of course. For Hobbes, a rational person will, when conditions permit (*in foro externo*), manifest grace and gratitude to others (fourth law of nature); sociability (fifth law of nature); the willingness to accept others' repentance of their bad behavior (sixth law of nature); and a willingness to forgo revenge and retribution, however merited one perceives it may be (seventh law of nature). Just in case the message was not clear enough, Hobbes's eighth law of nature explicitly demands that people avoid "contumely" (abusive and insulting behavior) and that "no man by deed, word, countenance, or gesture, declare hatred or contempt of another" ([1651] 1962, 118–120). Contempt, Hobbes understood, was one of the most destructive disincentives to voluntary collective behavior.

In carefully thinking through the conditions under which people would freely agree to establish a new form of political organization, Hobbes recognized very clearly that a particular kind of attitude and behavior was a requisite condition for the establishment of uncoerced political organization. The understanding that some acknowledgment of equality was essential in persuading agents of the fairness of an applied principle is a thread that runs through much liberal political thought. The formidable jurist H. L. A. Hart, for example, famously argued that, if there are any natural rights, "all men equally have the right to be free" (1955, 175). Restrictions on freedom, in Hart's account, are justified only because there is an equal distribution of restrictions on each member, and so each person recognizes the fairness of this claim.

Hobbes's account was largely an intellectual exercise; the act of consenting was limited to one act—the founding of the commonwealth—and that act can be understood to be more hypothetical than historical (see, e.g., Pitkin 1965). But as the idea of "democratic governance" increasingly became a viable system of political organization in the eighteenth century, the role of civility again became the subject of political debate. The Scottish Enlightenment, in attempting to understand why societies functioned as they did, spent a prodigious amount of time examining the concept of empathy (and its limits). Neither Adam Ferguson, nor Adam Smith, nor David Hume were enthusiastic advocates of widespread universal suffrage. But a continental contemporary—Jean-Jacques Rousseau—was, and he recognized that, to construct a system based on mutual *consent*, there must be an element of mutual *respect*. Empathy was a good place to start: like the Scottish Enlightenment theorists, Rousseau (1964) argued that all of us innately had a sympathetic nature, albeit only to a limited degree. In a startlingly modern twist that still resonates, he further noted that modern society does its best to distort and destroy what little empathy we have. The problem for Rousseau, then, was to construct a system in which contempt was minimized and civility was cultivated. Rather than designing a system around rigid perceptions of human nature, he suggested, one might instead shape human nature in order to achieve the best possible system.

The strategy to achieve this was to shape the mindset of people, both as *individuals* and as *citizens*, to make them instinctively more other-regarding and to capitalize on the innate capacity for empathy with which they are born. Rousseau offers several strategies to this end: emphasize normative virtues, especially via religion (avoiding competing religions and imposing a single state religion if necessary, as this had worked well for the British); encourage social homogeneity (though if this was not possible, maximize heterogeneity to avoid polarization); and limit material inequalities.

Rousseau understood profoundly that the right kind of behavior in a society without burdensome external authority depended very much upon public institutions developing the right kind of thinking—a willingness to respect the common good above individual ends—by whatever means possible. Of course, this discussion regarding the need to inculcate a sense of common purpose above individual right goes back much further, and can be seen in the republican tradition, where city-states distinguished an active class of "citizens" from the passive account of "subjects" given by larger imperial powers. Only by giving individuals a clear sense of ownership in their polity could they depend on them to repel military aggression and other external threats. The Savoyards' unsuccessful attempt to invade the city-state of Geneva in 1602 became celebrated as a political event to underscore to the citizens of Geneva the importance of putting collective well-being above fractious individual demands. This festival was a powerful influence upon Rousseau's thinking of the way in which a democracy could be made to cohere without excessive formal political authority being imposed on the citizenry. Like Hobbes, Rousseau saw the necessity to point out to people that what they had in common—especially non-domination—was far more important than any petty concerns that drove them apart.[3]

Democratic organization for Rousseau, based on republican principles rather than liberal ones, was fundamentally premised on the willingness to forgo individual priorities and preferences in favor of collective ones. Self-interest (as survival) was subsumed into a sense of ownership and responsibility for the well-being of the entire society; civility was not merely a fussy virtue but a sense of mutual recognition that one's material fate rested as much in others' hands as in one's own. But it was, ultimately, not republican democracy that anchored the political successes of eighteenth-century American and post-Chartist Britain; it was a *liberal* democracy grounded in individual rights and freedoms rather than collective citizen engagement.

RIGHTS DISCOURSE AND THE POLITICS OF CIVILITY

Why did the empiricism and rationality of Thomas Hobbes and John Locke, which brought an emphasis on inviolable individual rights, begin to overshadow the earlier republican focus on mutual respect and courtesy? Perhaps, as C. B. Macpherson (1962) suggested, it was because these aspects of liberal thought were so useful in clothing the aspiration of capitalism in a window-dressing of normative discourse. Regardless, the rights-based narrative of democratic liberalism has become the ne plus ultra of democratic organization, particularly because of the assertive role of "human rights" in protecting individual interests and well-being. Indeed, the crisis of civility is not due to the deficiency of the role of "rights" in modern democracy, but to its very success.

The gradual waning of natural law and the growing emphasis on natural rights in the seventeenth century gave people *qua* individuals a claim for recognition and protection absent in republican traditions. Natural law too stipulated a requirement of mutual civility, but this was an indirect obligation owed, ultimately, to God. Mutual respect was based on the recognition that each individual contained a spark of the divine, and, as such, the divine in each person was owed deference. The earliest instantiation of these rights was (in theory, if not in practice) universal and fungible: they were owed to all, and they were owed to all equally. It was this simple assertion of God's unvarying love for His children that provided the normative force for the concept: God did not distinguish between rich and poor, strong and frail; the wealthy or charismatic had no greater claim to His mercy than the marginalized or dispossessed. It was precisely the logic of undiscriminating universality that provided the progressive heft behind liberalism: if men, then why not women? If Protestants, why not Catholics? If Christians, why not Jews (or even atheists)? If white people, why not Black?

One aspect of this universalism was its objective (and often quantifiable) nature. If everyone had equal rights, then these rights could be measured and objectively evaluated. If one person had a right to vote, so did all others, regardless of property ownership, sex, or education. If a male clerk was paid a certain sum for calculating figures, then so too should a female clerk expect the same remuneration for the same labor. If white, English-speaking families could enjoy property ownership in grassy suburban subdivisions, then any other ethnic group should enjoy the same experience without laws or covenants barring them from these residential communities. The logic of universality was a simple and potent force that challenged expectations of privilege and tradition, and the focus on "human rights"—even divorced from its theological antecedents—achieved considerable success in the twentieth century.[4]

But it was nonetheless problematic. Equal treatment, imposed on individuals with vastly different circumstances, could be meaningless (property rights, as early socialists observed, lost much of their attractiveness when bestowed on paupers). Even worse, the demand for equal treatment could reinforce existing inequalities. The protection of free speech for everyone, for example, can privilege the status quo, favoring those with a strong grasp on power to the detriment of those at the margins.[5]

Hobbes's application of natural rights as conditions facilitating the level of mutual trust (via civility and assumptions of equality) conducive to viable collective action has been forgotten. In its place is the idea of rights as bulwarks: secure redoubts from which one can attack perceived injustices. The sharp focus on underlying power relationships (informal, and often invisible) challenges the value of universalism and sharp equality. Rights became deracinated: no longer embedded in the Christian theology that cogently explained (at least to Christians) *why* inviolable rights existed, rights became something that all humans had because of their inherent humanness. To respect a person *qua* their humanity, they were entitled to a certain level of respect. But the problem was that "respect" in and of itself was a subjective concept: one might feel that one is according respect to another, but if the recipient themself does not feel respected, to what extent does respect exist at all?

The subjectivity of rights is a powerful instrument to address concerns of social justice within a contemporary liberal political context, where rights have become a bastion *within* liberal thought from which to effectively attack liberal principles. If you were liberal enough to accept the concept of naturalized rights, then you were also likely receptive to a discussion of the need to resolve historical injustices as a matter of right.[6]

The rights narrative, by the late twentieth century, thus shifted from an articulation of universal claims based on a fairly objective measure of equality (such as votes or wages) to the call for differential rights (the application of which was contingent on the person or group making the claim). Whether a rights-claim was merited began to depend less on empirical accounts of how certain individuals or groups were denied what others had, and more on the subjective perception of those affected by the behavior of others. This subjectivity referenced affect (fear, anxiety, humiliation) rather than material indicators. "Civility" required those experiencing these emotions to absorb them; "incivility"—the refusal to tolerate what was experienced as antagonizing behavior—was to be recognized as a matter of right. These two shifts in rights discourse—to equity and subjectivity—can be understood (as Kymlicka explains) as developing within the liberal paradigm itself. If individuals must be treated equally, then their disparate social positions must be taken into account: some groups are simply valued more highly than others. This privileged the concept of "equity," which entailed treating those in less-valued categories differently in order to acknowledge their equal value. Yet "value" is itself a highly subjective term: even if substantive equality exists, the dismissive or contemptuous attitude of some (especially those in a position of influence) can have a real effect on individuals' own sense of perceived value. Nonetheless, both "equity" and "subjectivity" stand counter to the very principles that had historically facilitated the development of democratic institutions.

Equity

One of the most radical challenges to twentieth-century epistemology has been the charge that enlightenment assumptions of universality, objectivity, and rationalism were themselves contextual. Feminist theorists argued that "objective" standards were largely androcentric constructions that privileged male ways of seeing the world (universal and analytical) over female ones (localized and inferential) (see, e.g., Code 1991; Fricker 2007; Gilligan 1982; Harding 1986; Longino 1990). These ideas were also applied to the dynamics of culture and race. Building on the insight that an equal application of rights simply crystallized existing injustices, the field of rights theory began to endorse the concept of differential rights, in which certain groups (or individuals distinguished by the specific characteristics of a given group) should be recognized as a class of rights-holders who have legitimate claims denied to anyone outside of the group. By the beginning of the new millennium, Kymlicka felt confident in asserting that "[i]n terms of the more general question of whether minority rights are inherently unjust, the debate is over, and the defenders of minority rights have won the day" (2001, 169).

The philosophical grounding for differential rights rests in the privileging of cultural context as an essential requirement for the protection and respect of each individual. A viable culture, in this way, is a necessary context for individual freedom and autonomy. This key feature of the German Romantic tradition—the deep and pervasive influence of one's cultural context on one's sense of selfhood—was given a contemporary relevance by stressing the way in which self-respect depends upon the wider social recognition of the culture that informs one's way of understanding the world: "Since what a person says and does and the plans he or she formulates and revises are partly characterised by his or her cultural identity" argued Tully (1995, 190), "the condition of self-respect is met only in a society in which the cultures of all the members are recognized and affirmed by others, both by those who do and those who do not share those cultures."

The liberal reference to individual self-respect as a justification for differential rights may not persuade all liberals, and especially those who acknowledge the insight of Hobbes's ninth law of nature: that— even if we know that any assumption of fundamental equality between individuals is a dodgy proposition—we nonetheless have to pretend that it is in fact the case, because people who feel that they get less out of a proposed course of action than others will not be eager to ratify it. The focus on equity over equality—that certain people or groups must be granted different kinds of rights in order to compensate for historical injustices—may have a normative appeal, but it is also a tricky argument on which to facilitate collective behavior. For those who see the logic of distinct rights, the principle of differential treatment resonates strongly; for those who do not, there is considerable resistance. The problem is exacerbated when the recognition of a group as collective rights-bearers within a liberal society provides them with the authority to impose internal restrictions against their own members that conflict with the presumption of universal rights seen as protective for all persons. The most common manifestation of this has been the refusal of orthodox religious groups to recognize the rights of women or LBGTQ+ members within their communities, on the grounds that they are superseded by the need to protect the traditional religious mores of the minority group. Will Kymlicka (1996a) and Brian Barry (2013) have discussed in some detail how one might determine whether the ability of minority groups to restrict fundamental individual rights in order to protect religious, language, or other forms of cultural identity is justified, while Charles Taylor and Gérard Bouchard wrote a thoughtful report in 2008, commissioned by the Quebec government, to assist in addressing these conflicts within the sphere of public policy.

Subjectivity

If the move away from "equal rights for all" has led to difficulty in finding a common discursive direction in contemporary liberal democracies, another shift in the way in which we think about rights and rights-claims has further strained the ability (and willingness) of those in democratic societies to converse in measured and respectful ways. The argument here is that civility and incivility are themselves "situational and contextual" (Benson 2011). If respect and self-respect are the relevant determinants of a just society, then respect can only be understood with reference to those experiencing it (or denied a sense of experiencing it). With self-respect grounded in group identity, the metrics of fair and appropriate treatment have moved away from more quantifiable and material measurements (income, education, morbidity and mortality) to perceptions of being respected. The two are, of course, not exclusive. Merely having a formal right does not guarantee its enjoyment.[7] And the failure to attain certain standards of living may itself be caused as much by internal psychological obstacles as by external political ones.

As Stephen Lukes (2005) suggested in his analysis of power, the most pervasive and pernicious form of control may rest in one's ability to get others to internalize certain beliefs about themselves and their interests. The most penetrating description of this dynamic was Frantz Fanon's (1961) explanation of the way in which French colonizers were able to convince their Algerian subjects that the native population was fundamentally incapable of self-rule. Identifying the internalization of oppression and inferiority is the basis of much literature asserting the need to "decolonialize" existing practices. Decolonialization is the practice of challenging the way in which groups of people are described or defined disadvantageously by others. By disputing explicit or implicit characterizations (for example, as weak, or incapable, or violent, or untrustworthy), groups seek to "empower" their members by freeing them from accepting the way in which they are portrayed by others. In this way, power relations are not simply about what some can *do* to others (either preventing them from certain activities, or forcing them into others), but also how they make them *feel*. Any behavior that leads to feelings that entrench existing power relations, such as humiliation, fear, or a sense of inferiority or incompetence, should, on this account, be scrutinized.

These psychological tactics can indeed sometimes be effective against those already marginalized. Nonetheless, a strict policing of words or behaviors that cause feelings of distress can also be quite problematic, as it can be difficult to determine a priori what will cause distress. Social sentiments do shift over time, and anyone paying attention can generally glean a sense of how to avoid the most egregious faux pas. But other dynamics can be much more subtle, and it can be difficult to determine whether one person is more unreasonable for saying certain words, or another person is for taking offense at them. When group identities are the basis for affront, it also assumes that all of those within a group will be similarly distressed by particular words and deeds. But that is frequently not the case (see, e.g., McWhorter 2021); and some tropes are remarkably complex and can lead to a variety of responses. (William B. Black [2018] gives a fascinating example of the role of watermelon in Black culture.) Moreover, proscribed words themselves can be quite acceptable, depending upon who is using them (Coates 2013). Increasingly complex sets of rules can be put into place in order to manage the expectations of civility but, as Rousseau noted, the more intricate the rules, the more likely they were to be broken, leading to even greater offense and resentment. From expectations of consideration, he observes, came the first duties of civility, "and from this any voluntary wrong became an outrage, because along with the harm that resulted from the injury, the offended man saw in it contempt for his person which was often more unbearable than the harm itself" (Rousseau 1964, 149).

The extension of rights to protect individuals from subjective harm also reinforces the peremptory nature of modern rights discourse: one has rights-claims against others because of the way they make one feel. Challenging these subjective responses as unreasonable or disproportionate is itself an act of hostility. Rights now perform precisely the opposite of what Hobbes had wanted them to do: they are given to some but not others, and they inflame acrimony rather than preventing it. But if the attainment of social justice is the very point of liberal democracy, then why should we have any misgivings?

THE TRIUMPH OF RIGHTS OVER DEMOCRACY

The horrors of the Second World War led to an emphatic embrace of the idea of "universal human rights" with the flourishing of bills of rights and charters of rights in liberal societies. The weary and chastened survivors of the Second World War—both victors and vanquished—gave unprecedented support to rights advocates, and within a very short period the world saw the establishment of numerous statements of right in liberal polities, including the UN Declaration of Human Rights (1948), the Council of Europe's Convention on Human Rights and Fundamental Freedoms (1950), and the European Social Charter (1961). But the task was left to philosophers and legal scholars to explain, to a growing secular and pluralistic population, what these rights were based on, if not a thoroughgoing acceptance of Christian doctrine.

At its most basic, as noted above, a right is a justiciable entitlement claim supported by a fundamental and compelling justification. If one has a right, one has a claim that must, at the very least, be heard (and, ideally, be recognized). Desert itself is not an a priori basis for a rights-claim. One may deserve to be treated a certain way without having a right to this treatment; conversely, one may have a right to expect certain treatment despite being a most objectionable and undeserving individual.[8] The principal question underlying modern rights regimes is *why* people have rights at all. Given that societies across time and cultures have enjoyed sophisticated moral regimes without employing the concept of a "right," the modern explanation for why rights are necessary *now* is rather complex.

On the one hand, for example, one could articulate an empirical foundation for human rights: people flourish under some conditions and wither under others; therefore, a case can be made to support those conditions that support human flourishing. People have rights because they preserve those aspects which make us "truly human" and raise us above the level of brute creatures. Feinberg and Narveson, for example, note that rights are "especially sturdy objects to 'stand upon,' a most useful set of moral furniture" (1970, 252). But they are a kind of moral furniture specifically designed to fit a framework based on the respect for human dignity: "To think of oneself as the holder of rights is not to be unduly but properly proud, to have that minimal self-respect that is necessary to be worthy of the love and esteem of others" (ibid.). The "capabilities approach" (e.g., Sen 2005) also uses this line of action: it is based upon "the idea of the citizen as a free and dignified human being, a maker of choices" (Nussbaum 1997, 292). To facilitate the develop of human capacity—to ensure that individuals are able to make the choices that are meaningful to them—certain qualities must be protected.

But this account raises two problems. First, it assumes universality where it may not exist. People flourish under quite diverse conditions. Some respond to a competitive environment; others, to a supportive one. Some may thrive when certain supports are given; others may simply become dependent on them. Some require a sense of connectedness with others; others find solitude more comforting. And so on: beyond very basic conditions (e.g., the absence of starvation or torture) it can become tricky to determine what is meant by universal thriving to the degree required to implement effective public policies. Second, even if we could assume that certain conditions are requisite for "human thriving," why must this need be expressed in the language of human rights? It could just as easily be articulated within the language of obligation (e.g., "We as a society have an obligation to provide adequate housing to all"). This has led some to argue that the function of rights is simply to serve as an intermediary concept—a cognitive shortcut—and that it is just as philosophically coherent (if not more so) to jettison the idea of rights altogether and simply to argue from normative first-order principles.[9]

On the other hand, one could take a much older approach and base inherent human rights on the existence of discoverable "moral truths" that are discernable through the light of the natural faculty of reason given to us by God. Yet this account is problematic in its specificity: the "moral truths" are generally discerned through a theological or ideological filter, making them persuasive to those within the paradigm, and less so to those outside of it. It may be an "observable moral truth" to some that women should be chaste and submissive and that husbands have a right to police their behavior, but, in the absence of religious or cultural homogeneity making sense of these "observable moral truths," there is simply no means to resolve debates over what is or is not a right. (Locke, of course, tried to have things both ways; he used the language of natural reason as given to us by God—which readers of his day would find sensible—while his overarching argument was as naturalistic as that constructed by Hobbes, as the logical conclusions of his argument mattered little whether our reason was God-given or simply inherent in our biology.) This second approach is problematic as it is dependent upon a context of first-order principles (religious or otherwise), and these principles can, as Hobbes understood, be extremely divisive. Conflicts about first-order principles, like the religious doctrines of the seventeenth century, cannot be easily resolved. First-order principles are even less likely to be resolved when they are articulated as a matter of *right*: the claim being made is so fundamental and obvious that one should not even be required to make a case for one's claim. One *simply has a right*, and failure to acknowledge this is a moral injustice. On this view, addressing injustice requires whatever action is required, and arguably even violent or arbitrary actions, simply because the impugned state of affairs is *morally wrong*.

Yet a pluralist society can survive as a self-governing one only if there is a recognition, however begrudging, of the need to protect second-order principles. And the second-order principles that democratic processes are based on are not grounded in particularistic identities. We respect our fellow democratic citizens not because of their unique characteristics but because—as Hobbes argued—they are all alike in their capacity to make our political life miserable if we do not come to some sort of mutually agreeable working relationship. Whoever they are, and whatever shapes meaning in their lives, we respect them as citizens because we *must*. We cannot survive otherwise. This is not an uplifting political vision, but its logic is clearly comprehensible to everyone: one surrenders the *summmum bonum* to avoid the *summum malum*.

This does not mean that we can or should ignore the experiences and conditions of others, or the observation that universal rights may not be valued uniformly across populations. But it does require us to give reasons for our objections, and to listen to those who make them. "Civil" discourse does not mean that an interlocutor will like what is being said. The speeches of Martin Luther King, for example, despite burning with outrage, nonetheless were designed to communicate to a wide audience using language "that would invite audiences to understand the common humanity of blacks and whites and the meaning of making real the promises of democracy" (Hall Jamieson 1993, 333). Civility does mean that one must treat one's interlocutors as moral agents who possess the capacity to make well-informed decisions (even if, like Hobbes, one thinks they are often unlikely to do so).

The consolidation of liberalism and democracy was achieved with John Stuart Mill's argument that a self-governing society, *pace* Rousseau, required rights of free speech. For it was only by engaging with one's peers on matters of fundamental importance that a society could best adapt nimbly and flexibly to both external and internal pressures. Liberal rights reinforced the instrumental function of democracy; democracy itself was silent on the direction in which a society would move. But Mill had a very specific account of "free speech" in mind. It was not simply saying what one liked whenever one wanted, but rather being accountable for what one said, and being present to explain and defend one's words.[10] Thus he would not consider honking air horns on a commercial truck as a message of protest to be a form of free speech, nor would unlimited corporate spending on elections, or anonymous social media trolling, be considered legitimate forms of free speech. For modern liberals such as John Rawls (1996), free speech was similarly grounded in a moral duty of civility to reason publicly and to make the effort to determine whether requested accommodations in policymaking should be granted. Free speech without civility is dangerous; it can effectively muster political support to a cause, but only at the risk of incurring collateral damage.

The loss of the capacity for efficient self-rule—democracy—is one possible form of collateral damage. Mill may have done us a disservice. His argument that liberalism and democracy were mutually reinforcing has dulled our ability to recognize that the relationship between liberalism and democracy also contains inherently fundamental tensions, and that too much emphasis on rights discourse could undermine democratic processes. It is difficult to whip anyone into a frenzy over prosaic, instrumental second-order principles like fair conduct or civil behavior, but they are essential for the functioning of democratic systems. This is the reason that the British (and the Canadian) House of Commons have strict prohibitions on calling members' honorability into disrepute; similarly, Thomas Jefferson in 1896 codified norms of civility for the House of Representatives.

Like democracy itself, heterogeneous, pluralist societies present a challenge when they create groups who feel passionately about the championing of first-order principles. Pushing too hard for these first-order principles places a dangerous strain on second-order ones. Those who believe that the sacrifice of these second-order principles is an acceptable price for their first-order ones should nonetheless think hard about how well non-democratic societies are able to contain the centralization of power over time regardless of first principles. Power is a constant in human society, and left-wing authoritarianism is no more palatable than right-wing authoritarianism. As Hobbes noted, we are by nature provided with magnifying glasses that make the grievances in front of us the only matters of immediate concern, but we fail to use binoculars to take stock of the pitfalls that lie in front of us in our myopic pursuit of our singular interests.[11] An emblematic acceptance of all citizens as fundamentally equal in the first instance, and a willingness to listen to accounts of why this may not be entirely sufficient, may not be profoundly palatable to many, but it may be a sufficient compromise to maintain democratic institutions, however wobbly they may seem.

CONCLUSION

The task of protecting democracy is at least partly the task of bringing civility back to the forefront of public discourse. The project of democracy has, at least in theory, been the creation of an inclusive social group, where everyone could expect acceptance "as a member of the social community" (Honneth 2021, 135). But the application of the idea of *rights* to groups intent on preserving some aspect of common identity, no less than the resistance against this exercise, has exacerbated the ever-present frictions of democratic contest to a point of tribalism and civil breakdown, where people see the fundamental human difference as that between "our kind"—those who can expect the norms of civility—and everyone else (see Neiman 2023). The language of civility denotes the recognition of inclusivity: that we are all members, regardless of our differences. As Hobbes understood, contempt is the poison that precludes the ability of any social group to function effectively. True goodwill and solicitousness may be beyond the capacity of many people much of the time. But civility—the recognition that there is a minimal standard of propriety and respect that everyone can expect as a member of the community—is within the capacity of most of us, most of the time. It may not be enough to save democracy, but it is a start.

NOTES

1. For V-Dem, see Varieties of Democracy (n.d.); for the Lexical Index of Electoral Democracy, see Skaaning (2021).
2. See Christian Rostboll's helpful account of second-order political thinking (2021, 561).
3. "As soon as public service ceases to be the chief business of the citizens, and they would rather serve with their money than with their persons, the State is not far from its fall. . . . By reason of idleness and money, they end by having soldiers to enslave their country and representatives to sell it" (Rousseau 2004, ch. 15).
4. One example of this was T. H. Marshall's (1950) optimistic view of the fluid expansion of citizenship rights from civil to political rights, and thence to social rights.
5. This was a key theme addressed by Wolff et al. (1965).
6. Will Kymlicka's (1996b) *Multicultural Citizenship*, for example, poses a challenge to liberal rights theory within the context of liberal principles themselves; a clear shift from critiques of rights situated outside of liberal theories (e.g., using Marxist or postmodern frameworks).

7. On inquiring why African Americans did not vote in Pennsylvania despite having the right to do so, Alexis de Tocqueville was informed, in 1830, that "the truth is, that they are not disinclined to vote, but they are afraid of being maltreated; in this country the law is sometimes unable to maintain its authority without the support of the majority. But in this case the majority entertains very strong prejudices against the Blacks" (1835, ch. 15).

8. For example, you may have to deal with rude people on a daily basis and feel that you really *deserve* better, but unless you can come up with a fundamental and compelling reason why your interlocutors be compelled to desist, you have no recourse beyond a plea for common decency. The social context is very important here: if this rude behavior is ascribed to your gender, race, or sexual orientation, you may in some jurisdictions be able to argue that your *right* not to face derogatory behavior because of your gender, race, or sexual orientation has been compromised. If the rude behavior addresses your weight, age, or idiosyncratic characteristics (such as, say, a propensity for malapropisms), then you may be much less able to articulate your displeasure within the context of rights-claims.

9. As Robert Young argues, "there does not seem to be any greater moral dignity in expressing the claim in the language of rights than in the language of what (objectively) it would be *right* morally to do" (1978, 69).

10. "The steady habit of correcting and completing his own opinion by collating it with those of others, so far from causing doubt and hesitation in carrying it into practice, is the only stable foundation for a just reliance on it: for, being cognisant of all that can, at least obviously, be said against him, and having taken up his position against all gainsayers—knowing that he has sought for objections and difficulties, instead of avoiding them, and has shut out no light which can be thrown upon the subject from any quarter—he has a right to think his judgment better than that of any person, or any multitude, who have not gone through a similar process" (Mill [1859] 2001, 22).

11. Hobbes ([1651] 1962, 141): "For all men are by nature provided of notable multiplying glasses, (that is their Passions and Self-love,) through which, every little payment appeareth a great grievance; but are destitute of those prospective glasses, (namely Morall and Civill Science,) to see a farre off the miseries that hang over them, and cannot without such payments be avoided."

REFERENCES

Barry, Brian. 2013. *Culture and Equality: An Egalitarian Critique of Multiculturalism.* Polity Press.

Benson, Thomas W. 2011. "The Rhetoric of Civility: Power, Authenticity, and Democracy." *Journal of Contemporary Rhetoric* 1 (1): 22–30.

Black, William B. 2018. "How Watermelons Became Black: Emancipation and the Origins of a Racist Trope." *Journal of the Civil War Era* 8 (1): 64–86.

Coates, Ta-Nehisi. 2013. "In Defense of a Loaded Word." *New York Times*, November 23. https://www.nytimes.com/2013/11/24/opinion/sunday/coates-in-defense-of-a-loaded-word.html.

Code, Lorraine. 1991. *What Can She Know?* Cornell University Press.

Fanon, Frantz. 1961. *The Wretched of the Earth.* Penguin.

Feinberg, Joel, and Jan Narveson. 1970. "The Nature and Value of Rights." *Journal of Value Inquiry* 4: 243–260.

Fricker, Miranda. 2007. *Epistemic Injustice.* Oxford University Press.

Gilligan, Carol. 1982. *In a Different Voice.* Harvard University Press.

Hall Jamieson, Kathleen. 1993. "Discourse and the Democratic Ideal." *Proceedings of the American Philosophical Society* 137 (3): 32–338.

Harding, Sandra. 1986. *The Science Question in Feminism.* Cornell University Press.

Hart, H. L. A. 1955. "Are There Any Natural Rights?" *Philosophical Review* 64: 175.

Hobbes, Thomas. (1651) 1962. *Leviathan.* Collier Macmillan.

Honneth, Axel. 2021. *Recognition: A Chapter in the History of European Ideas.* Cambridge University Press.

Kymlicka, Will. 1996a. "The Good, the Bad, and the Intolerable: Minority Group Rights." *Dissent* 43 (3): 22–30.

Kymlicka, Will. 1996b. *Multicultural Citizenship.* Clarendon Press.

Kymlicka, Will. 2001. "The New Debate over Minority Rights." In *Canadian Political Philosophy: Contemporary Reflections,* edited by Ronald Beiner and Wayne Norman. Oxford University Press.

Longino, Helen. 1990. *Science as Social Knowledge.* Princeton University Press.

Lukes, Steven. 2005. *Power: A Radical View.* Palgrave Macmillan.

Macpherson, C. B. 1962. *The Political Theory of Possessive Individualism.* Oxford University Press.

Marshall, T. H. 1950. *Citizenship and Social Class: And Other Essays.* Cambridge University Press.

McWhorter, John. 2021. *Woke Racism: How a New Religion Has Betrayed Black America.* Portfolio Penguin.

Mill, J. S. (1859) 2001. *On Liberty.* Batoche Books.

Neiman, Susan. 2023. *Left Is Not Woke.* Polity Press.

Nussbaum, Martha. 1997. "Capabilities and Human Rights." *Fordham Law Review* 66 (2): 273–300.

Pitkin, Hanna. 1965. "Obligation and Consent—I." *American Political Science Review* 59 (4): 990–999.

Rawls, John. 1996. *Political Liberalism.* Columbia University Press.

Rostboll, Christian. 2021. "Second-Order Political Thinking: Compromise Versus Populism." *Political Studies* 69 (3): 559–576.

Rousseau, Jean-Jacques. 1964. *The First and Second Discourses*. Edited by Roger Masters. St. Martin's Press.

Rousseau, Jean-Jacques. 2004. *Social Contract*. Penguin.

Sen, Amartya. 2005. "Human Rights and Capabilities." *Journal of Human Development* 6 (2): 151–166.

Skaaning, Svend-Erik. 2021. "Lexical Index of Electoral Democracy (LIED) Dataset v6.0." Harvard Dataverse. https://dataverse.harvard.edu/dataset.xhtml?persistentId=doi:10.7910/DVN/WPKNIT.

Taylor, Charles, and Gérard Bourchard. 2008. "Building the Future: A Time for Reconciliation" (Fonder l'avenir: le temps de la conciliation). BAnQ Digital. https://numerique.banq.qc.ca/patrimoine/details/52327/66277.

Tocqueville, Alexis. 1835. *Democracy in America*. Vol. 1. Saunders and Otley. https://www.gutenberg.org/files/815/815-h/815-h.htm.

Tully, James. 1995. *Strange Multiplicity: Constitutionalism in an Age of Diversity*. Cambridge University Press.

Varieties of Democracy. n.d. "The V-Dem Dataset." https://www.v-dem.net/data/the-v-dem-dataset/country-date-v-dem-v12/.

Wolff, Robert Paul, Barrington Moore, and Herbert Marcuse. 1965. *A Critique of Pure Tolerance*. Beacon Press.

Young, Robert. 1978. "Dispensing with Moral Rights." *Political Theory* 6 (1): 63–74.

INDEX

For the benefit of digital users, indexed terms that span two pages (e.g., 52–53) may, on occasion, appear on only one of those pages.